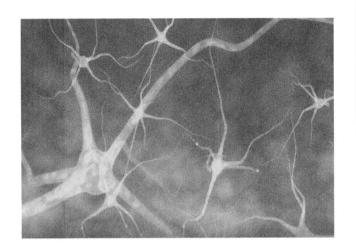

YOU ARE WHAT YOU THINK

Applying a Christian Worldview to All of Life

SERIES #1

SUBJECTS 1-6

CHRISTIAN WORLDVIEW TEXTBOOK

This course has been developed for the purpose of equipping the next generations of Christians to successfully overcome the increasingly godless ideas that are attacking our faith and our society. We believe that God can and will do great things through those who put their trust in Him.

Greater Than I Ministries
by Roger Wheelock and B.J. Wheelock

Edited by Brenda Palmer

Envisioning a Great Awakening through Christian Education

Greater Than I Ministries, Inc.

A 501 (c)(3) non-profit corporation

GTImin.com

P.O. Box 6133, McKinney, TX 75071

(562) 458-8758

Cover Photo Credits:

By: iDesign
Can Stock Photo csp31750757

Dedication

These works are dedicated, above all, to the glory of God. HE is our Teacher, our Light, and the Inspiration for anything we do that is good.

Secondly, we dedicate this work to all who have come to saving faith in Jesus Christ, as well as those who may participate in these studies, but have not yet come to full faith in Him as the Author and Finisher of life.

We trust that these studies will cause all to think deeply on the ideas and issues discussed; and in the end you will have found greater understanding and clarity regarding what you believe and why you believe it.

As always and forever, a special thank you to my faithful wife, Elaine, who has had to endure the many hours I've spent in my office alone as this book and other GTI resources have been developed. Without you none of these tools would have ever come to be. I love you!

I'd also like to express my gratitude for many of those who have encouraged me and this ministry over the last several years:

To our children, Breck, Tressa, and Brennen, for your collaboration in so many ways. Each of you has contributed in supporting this work through your time, your efforts, your inspirations as we talked through ideas, and your financial assistance. My prayer is that your children and grandchildren will benefit as a result of these efforts.

To John Santana for your faith in this ministry and your trustworthy support from the very start of the ministry.

To Christopher and Tallulah Perky, for your faith in our ministry from the very beginning, without which it may never have begun!

To Roger and Diana Herren, who have proved to be trusted and dear friends to Elaine and me these last few years and who have brought great encouragement and help to me – giving me hope and keeping the vision alive.

To Rick Needham for your mentorship and enthusiastic support of this ministry at a time when I really need it!

To Pastor Ray Loo for trusting us with the pulpit to present and film these classes at Calvary Chapel, Santa Fe Springs in 2012. It was your faith in us that helped prompt the start of this ministry and we are forever grateful.

A special thank you to Brenda Palmer for the many hours she spent editing both volumes of these textbooks and for her excellent contributions in the process!

To John and Anja Carley for your invaluable encouragement, support, and inspiration as we've all engaged in the good fight!

To Roger Herring, for your steadfast support and encouragement to this ministry!

Acknowledgements

Our ministry would like to express our immense gratitude to the following parachurch ministries and conservative news outlets that have inspired and challenged us throughout our 35-year journey in the Faith. It was the exposure to their bold and enlightening resources from the early years of our Christian walk that brought light and understanding to our worldview and gave us added strength to persevere through these many years of social and religious upheaval.

In particular, we wish to acknowledge the following organizations[*]

Dr. James Dobson and Focus on the Family Ministry

Family Research Council (FRC.org)

American Family Association (AFA.net)

David Barton and Wallbuilders Ministry (Wallbuilders.com)

Josh McDowell Ministry (Josh.org)

Barna Research Group (www.barna.com)

Summit Ministries (Summit.org)

The Trinity Foundation (trinityfoundation.org)

The Heritage Foundation (heritage.org)

Hillsdale College (Info available at Imprimus@Hillsdale.edu)

Alliance Defending Freedom (adflegal.org)

Illustra Media (Creation science videos - illustramedia.com)

Genesis Science Network (genesissciencenetwork.com)

Cold Case Christianity (coldcasechristianity.com)

Townhall.com – News from a conservative perspective

AmericanThinker.com – News from a conservative perspective

[*]Please note that our acknowledgements do not imply an express endorsement of every position or statement made by these ministries. The reader is responsible to consider all positions through the lens of the Bible

TABLE of CONTENTS – Series #1

Subject Six: The Christian Worldview of Science 207

Subject One: What Is a Worldview & Why Does It Matter?

Lesson 1 – Intro to the Series

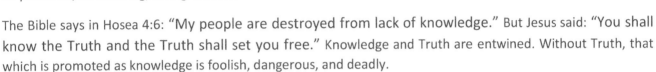

We live in an increasingly chaotic world. It is chaotic because Truth and Knowledge -- which come from God alone -- are being suppressed by those who refuse to acknowledge and submit to the all-powerful, all-knowing, loving Creator.

The Bible says in Hosea 4:6: "My people are destroyed from lack of knowledge." But Jesus said: "You shall know the Truth and the Truth shall set you free." Knowledge and Truth are entwined. Without Truth, that which is promoted as knowledge is foolish, dangerous, and deadly.

This series is designed to educate and inspire you with the Truth of God in those areas of your life that you have concerns and questions.

We are basing this series on the scripture **2 Cor. 10:4-5** which states:

> *"The weapons we fight with are not the weapons of the world. On the contrary, they have divine power to demolish strongholds. We demolish arguments and every pretension (or idea) that sets itself up against the knowledge of God, and we take captive every thought to make it obedient to Christ".*

In other words, we are born into a battleground. But we don't fight in a war involving weapons such as tanks or guns or knives. Our battle is over *ideas*. BAD ideas cause wars, arguments, poverty, slavery and death. But it is the GOOD ideas that come from the Creator of all Life Himself – the timeless truths contained in the Bible – that promise success and joy for everyone who will embrace them. These truths have a great historical track record. They can be observed and verified in reality.

God's ideas need to be spotlighted and translated into the context of our everyday lives – into today's world - so that we can recognize and tell the difference between the bad ideas and the good ones and *not get caught up following the crowd over a cliff.*

Christianity Under Attack

It seems as if everything we have believed about Christianity is being attacked today. And those of us sitting in church are crying out for answers that will help us make sense of life and rise above the confusion. The good news is that our God does not want His children to live in confusion or fear; thus, He has provided the answers that can bring clarity to our lives in His personal diary to us, the Bible.

To some who read this, there most assuredly may be doubts regarding the above statement, and this is understandable. *We live in a battlefield of ideas and it is difficult to know which ideas are true and trustworthy and which are not*. The purpose of this series is to confront those ideas head-on as we compare and contrast God's *IDEAS* against those of the opposing worldviews of today.

In each of the 12 categories of life that we investigate, you will find:

1. A summary of what the God of the Bible promises as blessings to those who follow His precepts, as well as the curses that must come to those who choose to live by another worldview.
2. A summary of the various opposing worldviews that permeate our world.
3. Side-by-side comparisons of the real-life results that flow out of each worldview.

As we do so, we will reveal the main points of difference between each. We will weigh each of these worldviews using history, logic, and reality-based statistical examples of the results or consequences of following each worldview. We encourage everyone to not blindly trust our interpretations, but to examine for yourselves if the conclusions we are drawing from the evidences are true. *This course is designed to develop critical thinking.*

A Key Principle in this series is that

Laws are Necessary for life.

This is a fact that cannot be ignored without consequences. Furthermore, we will demonstrate that the physical laws *enforce* the moral laws presented in the Bible. This leads to the logical conclusion that there are *universal moral laws (of right and wrong)*, as well as universal physical laws; and the moral laws are *even more consequential* when disregarded and disobeyed. Therefore, whatever worldview one chooses to embrace must take into consideration the fixed laws that govern life. To ignore the power and consequence of the universal physical and moral laws is to live in a fantasy world outside of reality, and unpleasant consequences promise to follow.

Our claim is that the Bible contains the Eternal Moral Laws that, when obeyed, lead to a *successful life*.

Pause and Consider

Without Laws There Would Be NO Life.

Without law there is chaos. Simply consider for a moment the results if all traffic signals stopped working at rush hour!

The Power of Laws

Science has revealed over 20 physical laws (forces) that govern the universe, and all are finely tuned to allow for life. If just one of those Laws was to go out of tune by even the tiniest fraction, all the other laws would collapse. The result would be *no life!*

Lesson 1 Study Questions

A. In the introduction, we spoke about the battle of ideas. Name at least 3 ideas that are being fought in the culture around you and how those ideas might affect your life.

1. _____

_____

2. _____

_____

3. _____

_____

B. It was stated that there are both physical and spiritual (moral) laws that govern the universe, and that it is unwise to blatantly disregard or disobey universal laws.

1. Would you jump off a 20-story building just for the kicks? _____ Why not? _____

_____

2. What physical law would come into play in this situation? _____

3. Name 2 traffic laws and the consequences that might come if you disobeyed those laws

1)_____

_____

2)_____

_____

The physical laws *enforce* the moral laws presented in the Bible.

C. The Ten Commandments (**READ Exodus 20:1- 17**) represent the fundamental moral code presented by the God of the Bible. When any one of those ten moral laws are rejected or ignored, there will be consequences in the physical world. For example, when a society rejects the principle that adultery is always morally wrong, both the society and the individual people within that society – from adults to the youngest children - will suffer.

List 3 other examples of the physical consequences that might result from rejecting any of the remaining Ten Commandments.

1. _____

2. _____

3. _____

Lesson 2 - Ideas Have Consequences

In this chapter, you will clearly see that all worldviews (and the cultures that are framed by those worldviews) are *not the same*. Worldviews are composed of ideas; and ideas, when embraced, lead to moral choices that will have consequences, either positive or negative.

We will begin by displaying the biblical blueprint for **a successful worldview**, followed by examples of what happens when that blueprint is lived out in society and a nation. We will then define the ideas that make up the basic worldview found in America today, along with the results that have proceeded from those ideas.

Over the last 5 decades, Christianity has taken a beating in the western world. Our faith and our God have been accused of being the source of all the world's problems. This lie has been repeated for so long without opposition in our state education system and in the media that most people simply accept it to be true. After working through this chapter, we are confident that you will view Christianity's influence over our world in a much different light than that which the world has painted it to be.

 As the saying goes, we can choose our own opinions, but we can't choose our own facts. Living in a fantasy world cannot be sustained. Sooner or later the illusion will be exposed and only the consequences will remain. It is much wiser to choose carefully those ideas we will build our life upon -- and live in -- *reality*.

YOUR worldview matters!

Our foundational scripture is Hosea 4:6

"My people perish from lack of knowledge".

Now, this Scripture isn't referring to the knowledge of how to perform quadratic equations, or how to take apart an engine and put it back together again. No, it's speaking of the *intimate knowledge* of the principles and precepts contained in the **supernatural book** that we call the Bible, that give us answers for how to live a righteous and a blessed life, if we simply would apply these principles into our everyday lives.

Let's begin by taking a look at an example in the Bible to illustrate what we mean. In Deuteronomy chapter four, we see that the Israelites had been given detailed instructions for their lives earlier from God through Moses, but the people forgot those instructions, and didn't obey them. This resulted in the majority perishing in the desert. The Bible has often been defined by the acronym B-I-B-L-E, or *Basic Instructions Before Leaving Earth* because it is a virtual living diary from a loving Father to His children that lays out in written form all the instructions that we need to live a successful and fulfilling life on this planet, preparing us for the everlasting life to come. And if you have ever tried to assemble a Lego machine or bake brownies, you know how important it is to follow the instructions! All you need is to miss one part of the instructions and the project will be a failure. Forgetting or skipping a key command from the instruction manual can have drastic results, and those results are far more impacting when the manual (the Bible) deals with our very lives. Therefore, we'll read from the Manual to gather some fundamental principles that God sets as priorities for the Israelites prior to their entrance into the new land God promised to them.

The Word of God is Relevant to Every Generation.

Keep in mind that we are always to look for personal applications to our lives from the scriptures we study. As we read through the passages below, we can draw three different (yet similar) applications from these portions of scripture. The first is the *contextual application*. Moses is giving the law to the people of Israel for the second time, because the first time, the people didn't obey God's words. As a result, the vast majority of that generation perished in the desert. So now, Moses is giving the law once again to the next generation, just before they enter the Promised Land. Notice as we read this passage that **promises and warnings** are given to the people, **so that they can prosper** in this new land.

> ## Pause and Consider
>
> ### *The Bible is a SUPERNATURAL Book*
>
> **What do we mean by this statement? The Bible is a collection of 66 books authored by 40 men, written in 3 distinctly different languages from 3 continents over a 1500 year time-span. Yet, the message is miraculously identical from beginning to end. At is as if one Editor oversaw what each man wrote.**

The second application is a *historical application*. Imagine that you're a Pilgrim on the Mayflower, and your pastor reads this section to you, just as you're about to go ashore in this new world of America. You and those with you are going to have a chance for the first time in all of history to be ruled -- not under the thumb of a king or a tyrant -- but by the very Word of God. You're going to be self-governing, as you sign the covenant to live under the authority and the commands of the Bible. And as the pastor reads this section to you, again you hear those same promises and warnings.

The third application is *today's application*. God's Word is alive and active and, therefore, is always applicable to our lives. These promises and warnings apply to us *today*, just as they did to the Jews and the Pilgrims in the past. They're given to each one of us individually, and we're each accountable to God, based upon how we respond. Let's **READ Deuteronomy 4:1-3** now, beginning at verse 1.

> *"Now, O Israel, listen to the statutes and the judgments which I teach you to observe, that you may live, and go in and possess the land which the Lord, the God of your fathers is giving you. You shall not add to the word which I command you, nor take from it, but keep the commandments of the Lord your God which I command you. Your eyes have seen what the Lord did at Baal Peor, for the Lord your God has destroyed from among you all the men who followed Baal of Peor."*

Now, what happened at Baal of Peor? **(Look up and read: Numbers 25:1-11)** Many of those Israelites got caught up in the culture of the nations around them. So much so that you couldn't see the difference between the way they lived, and the way the unbelievers lived around them, so God destroyed them. But notice the very next verse (**READ Deuteronomy 4:4**).

"But you who held fast to the Lord your God are alive today, every one of you."

God didn't lose anyone who remained faithful to Him. This reveals a principle that we're going to be seeing over and over again as we go through this series. The principle is this. *You just focus on your responsibility as a Christian. Seek first His kingdom.* (**Look up and READ Matthew 6:25-34**) *Obey His Word.* (**Look up and READ Ecclesiastes 12:13**) *No matter what's going on in your life, no matter how bad things seem to look around you in your life, whether the culture appears to be morally sinking all around us, and it looks like everything is coming against the church and the family, trust this: You, just you, focus on what God calls you to do, and He promises that He will see you through.*

The Scripture continues in verse 5 (**Deuteronomy 4:5-9**). It says,

"Surely, I have taught you statutes and judgments, just as the LORD my God commanded me, that you should act according to them in the land which you go to possess. Therefore, be careful to observe them; for this is your wisdom and your understanding in the sight of the peoples who will hear all these statutes, and say, 'Surely this great nation is a wise and understanding people. For what great nation is there that has God so near to it, as the Lord our God is to us, for whatever reason we may call upon Him? And what great nation is there that has such statutes and righteous judgments as are in all this law which I set before you this day? Only take heed to yourself, and diligently keep yourself, lest you forget the things that your eyes have seen, and lest they depart from your heart all of the days of your life. And teach them to your children and your grandchildren, especially concerning the day that you stood before the Lord your God in Horeb, when the Lord said to me, "Gather the people to Me, and I will let them hear My words, "that they may learn to fear Me all the days that they may live [thrive] on the earth, and that they may teach their children."

The Fear of the Lord

Let's pause here for a moment, because this concept of **fearing God** will again come up repeatedly in this series, it's very important that we define our terms. In this context, fear does not mean simply showing reverence or honor to God, of course it does. But it is actually a *fear* -- a fear of the consequences that must come whenever we disobey or disregard His Word. The Bible says that the *fear of the Lord is the beginning of wisdom*. Think of it like *fire*. We all appreciate, we even revere and honor fire, because when we use it respectfully it gives us heat on a cold night and cooks our food. But we don't put our hand over a flame and hold it there, because we know that the physical laws that God put into place will cause our hands to be burned.

> ## Pause and Consider
>
> ### Key Principle: Seek First His Kingdom
>
> **"Make knowing the Creator God your #1 priority. Put nothing and no one else first. If you do so, He promises success in all you do."**
>
> **Although this is the Christian Worldview, it doesn't mean everyone will believe it. The point of this study is to give you sufficient information to come to your own decision.**

Physical laws, moral laws. God placed all the physical laws in the universe, to govern it and to establish order, and to keep us safe. If there are no laws, what is there? As stated earlier, without laws there will be chaos. So, because He cares for us, God placed moral laws over us for this same purpose, to keep order. And the *moral laws* are *more powerful* and more lasting that the physical laws. "Heaven and earth will pass away", Scripture says, "but my

---

Key Scripture: Proverbs 9:10 - *"The FEAR of the LORD is the Beginning of WISDOM"*

---

words by no means will pass away". So, it is wise for us to *fear* disobeying God's moral laws.

For believers in Christ, the fear of the Lord takes on an even more relational meaning. As we "fear" hurting or grieving our closest loved ones, we deeply desire the same for our Lord and Savior. We do not want to grieve Him—on the contrary, we want to please Him because we love Him.

What can we learn from this passage?

1. It's important that we know God's laws and His principles for life.
2. It's important that we obey those laws and principles.
3. It's important that we remember our past. The word *remember* is one of the most often emphasized words in the whole book of Deuteronomy.
4. It's important that we teach the next generations. It is our responsibility to pass on the knowledge of God's Word, His principles and precepts for life. We've been placed here like runners in a relay race, and we're responsible not only to run the race, but to successfully pass on the baton without dropping it.

You've probably heard the saying: "those who don't know their history are condemned to repeat it", and it sure seems like we're following that pattern in our country today, doesn't it? For instance, we read in the book of Judges that though Israel was blessed by God, they became complacent and forgot God. Then they fell into slavery, eventually repented, and God lifted them up. Throughout the book, the cycle seemed to repeat over and over again. All of this occurred repetitively because they forgot the history of God's **supernatural works** in establishing their nation, and the responsibilities that they each had to obey God's simple commands.

One of the greatest problems of the church today seems to be that we've lost the knowledge of Christianity's proud heritage, while the world has been busy rewriting history. As a result, we don't know what to believe. Again, "My people perish from lack of knowledge" (Hosea 4:6). In the next section we will begin opening the pages of history to examine the importance of knowing the past.

Lesson 2 Study Questions

A. Read Hosea, chapter 4.

1. List 4 similarities between Israel in Hosea's time and America today.

    1)_____

    2)_____

    3)_____

    4)_____

2. In verse 6, what does God say the nation is lacking? _____What have they rejected

    and/or ignored? _____

B. Read Deuteronomy 4:1-18

1. List 4 <u>blessings</u> you can find that God promised for Israel if they would simply hear (listen to and

    obey) His words?

    1)_____

    2)_____

    3)_____

    4)_____

2. Name at least 6 commands that God says either to do or *not* to do.

    1)_____

    2)_____

    3)_____

    4)_____

    5)_____

    6)_____

3. Application Question: How might your commitment to obey the commands listed above affect your life today as well as in the future?

_____

_____

_____

_____

Lesson 3 - History Matters!

The book "How Christianity Changed the World"[1], by Alvin Schmidt, details the areas of our society that we simply take for granted which, if Christ had never been born, we would not be enjoying today. Here are a few examples.

1. **The Sanctity of Human Life.** Christianity is the only religion or worldview in history to hold this idea as one of its main tenets. Christianity alone considers every life to be sacred. Before Christ, human life was of little value in every culture throughout the world. If a woman gave birth to too many baby girls, for example, they'd simply put that infant out on the street, and let the elements or the creatures take that baby's life, or they would take the baby down to the river and drown it.

And consider this. For over 800 years in the Roman Empire (800 years -- that's a long time!), gladiator games were the favorite entertainment of the people. They would come from miles around to watch the sport of one person fighting with another until death, or they would watch a beast ripping a man, a woman, or a child limb from limb. The more blood, the louder the screams, the better.

And think about how, as we read through our Bibles, we quickly pass over statements like *the Pharisees plotted to kill him*. The religious leaders were plotting to kill Jesus! Violence was a normal part of life because   all human life was *not* considered to be sacred. But Christianity turned that around.

2. **Sexual Morality** – The belief that one man and one woman should covenant to be married for life, till death do them part. That idea, that concept never existed before Christ, in any society, ever. Multiple wives for men was always the norm. The man could divorce his wife for almost any reason, but the woman could almost never divorce her husband. Women were virtual slaves. It was Christianity that established the idea of the sanctity of marriage.

3. **Women's Freedom and Dignity**.   The sanctity of marriage led to this revolutionary concept. Even in Old Testament Israel, women were often considered lower than dogs. But Christianity freed and elevated women, giving them rights equal to those of men. Try going to a non-Christian country today and see what kind of rights women have.

4. **Charity and Compassion.** Caring for the poor was never a consideration before Christ, because there were only two classes of people in most cultures up until then, upper and lower, the rich and the poor. The lower classes weren't worthy of compassion. Their purpose, as far as the upper class was concerned, was to serve them. If they weren't fit, let them simply starve.

5. **Hospitals and health care**. Hospitals as we know them never existed before Christ. They were developed by Christians as those Christians followed Jesus' teachings when he said, "I was naked and you clothed me, I was sick and you visited me, I was in prison and you came to me... Assuredly I say to you, inasmuch as you did it to one of the least of these my brethren, you did it to me"(Matthew 25:36,40). Because of that, Christians have ever since looked at taking care of the sick as a way of showing our love for God. Before Christianity began developing hospitals to serve everyone, healthcare was available only to the rich and the royalty.

---

[1] How Christianity Changed the World, Alvin J. Schmidt, 2009, Zondervan

6. Education: Universal and for all classes and for both sexes.

Education was given only to the upper classes, and was never made available especially for women, until Christianity. Universal education for both men and women of all classes actually began in America.

7. Hard work and economic freedom will create wealth. This idea is

a completely unique concept to Christianity. It doesn't exist, it won't work in humanism, atheism, Islam, Hinduism, or Buddhism. Before Christ, the nobility considered work to be undignified. It was only meant for the poor, and most often, the poor worked for virtually no pay. Christianity elevated hard work. The Bible repeatedly teaches that if you don't work, you don't eat, and the Bible speaks highly and often about the virtue of hard work and diligence. You look in Genesis, for example, and you see that God worked six days, and at the end of each day, He said, *this is good*. He was proud of what he did. And we're made in His image. He wants us to enjoy the same fruits of our labors. It's part of why we're here.

Regarding economic freedom, this is a Christian concept alone. It was never established in any nation until America. And once it was unleashed, it brought uncanny blessings to the entire world. But the idea of allowing all people to own private property, and to manage their money freely - without the control of a king or a country or a tyrant - came only from Christianity.

8. The development of science. If it wasn't for men and women

looking to discover God in creation, it's impossible to imagine how little we would have that we enjoy today. These Christian scientists believed that God was a God of order, and they went about to look for the actual laws of the universe. They believed that God wanted them to discover more about him by studying His creation.

9. The principle of liberty and justice for all. This concept, based

upon the belief that all men are created equal, does not exist in any worldview or religion in all of history except in Christianity. Where do you think the Founders got the idea that all men are created equal? It came from Galatians 3:28 and other passages, where the Apostle Paul introduces this revolutionary concept.

10. Art, architecture, music, and literature. Where would the world be without the amazing creations by artists and architects and musicians and authors who were inspired by the life and teachings of Christ? Compare the amazing detail and the excellence involved in the paintings of people like Michelangelo and others, to the supposed artwork being displayed in some of the most famous museums in the world today. If you ever get a chance to walk through some of the cathedrals in Europe that were built in the late Middle Ages, you'll be amazed at the astounding beauty, the brilliance, and the complexity of the designs, all of which were meant to cause the worshiper to look upward in awe toward the heavens.

In music, if it wasn't for Christianity, most likely we wouldn't be enjoying the beautiful symphony orchestras that we've been blessed by over the last 600 years. Why? Because before a Christian monk developed the musical staff in 1100 A.D., music couldn't even be written down. And if it couldn't be memorized, then it couldn't be passed on to the next generation. And the concept of multiple musicians playing separate parts on different instruments at the same time would be impossible. But the Christians wanted to praise God together as a unified body. Thus, with the development of the musical staff, for the first time, men and women could join together in great symphonies and choirs, singing and joining together in complicated harmonies with multiple melodies, all for the glory of God. The works of Christians like Bach, Beethoven, Handel, among many others, still astound and uplift audiences around the world.

Then, just imagine what a loss it would be without the beautiful and inspiring literary works of Christians over the last several centuries. Works such as C.S. Lewis' *The Lion, the Witch and the Wardrobe,* John Bunyan's *Pilgrim's Progress*, Charles Dicken's *A Christmas Carol,* and, of course, the *Holy Bible* have moved, aroused, and educated generations among all races and nations.

11. Slavery was abolished twice in the Western world by Christians over the past 1,000 years.

When the Roman emperor Constantine embraced Christianity in the fourth century, slavery began to be looked down upon. And by the 14th century, it had been virtually eradicated from all of Western Europe, as a result of the effect of Christianity upon the Roman Empire. But when Britain, Spain, Italy, and Portugal began developing the West Indies and the Americas in the 1500s, the slave trade came back with a vengeance. But notice this. Contrary to what is taught in most American universities and even high schools today, America received only 7% of all the slaves taken between 1500 and 1800. But America still became so entrenched in slavery because of its effect on the economy in the South, that many professing Christians, including many pastors, found ways to justify it, although the New Testament never promotes it. As a result, Christians fought and died again, in the bloodiest war in all of America's history, to again eradicate slavery. Yet slavery still exists in many non-Christian nations in the world today.

The Musical Monk: Guido of Arezzo and Development of the Musical Staff

Guido of Arezzo was a monk who lived during the Middle Ages (10th century, AD), and may be considered as one of the most influential figures in the history of modern music. During the Middle Ages, the monastery was one of the most important European institutions. The worship of God was of paramount importance in the life of a medieval monk, and one of the ways this worship was rendered was through the chanting of sacred music. Guido of Arezzo sought to rectify the problem that plagued these chants: there was no way to record the music on a manuscript to ensure the melodies could be passed along to others or to succeeding generations with accuracy. The result was Guido's creation of the musical staff that we use today. It is thanks to Guido that we have the 'do-re-mi' today.
(https://www.ancient-origins.net/history)

So you see, Christians have been continually raising the standards of life for everyone around the world ever since Christ. We enjoy so much of what we have today because Christians who came before us dedicated themselves to being Salt and Light in a decaying, dark and dangerous world.

Not Random Spectators in History

In light of all this, it's imperative that we see ourselves as part of a relay team, again. Not as simple inhabitants of our small corner of the world, here for our own short time of pleasure and amusement, dis-attached from all the generations of Christians who fought and died to give us what we have today. No, we should see ourselves as chosen, special individuals, whom God has uniquely designed and placed in our city, in our state, and our nation, and at exactly this moment in His grand timeline in history, for a purpose – For a Time Such as This (Esther 4:14).

We have a job to do, each one of us. We are the keepers of the greatest treasure of all time: The Truth, the only Truth. The Truth that can set anyone and everyone free who will embrace this Truth. Scripture says: "to whom much is given, much is required". And we are required to seek God's Truth, to *know* it, to *live* it, and to *speak* it in every area of our lives.

And though this may seem overwhelming, it is important to remember that our part is simply to take small, consistent steps towards Him and He will take giant steps toward us. Philippians 1:6 says,

"He who began a good work in you will be faithful to complete it."

Just by continuing in this course, God will bless you for doing your part in seeking Him. He will equip you.

Lesson 3 Study Questions

The Effects of Christianity Though History

A. Name what you consider the 7 most important changes Christianity has been responsible for, and what

difference it might make in your life today if each principle had never been established.

1._____

_____

2._____

_____

3._____

_____

4._____

_____

5._____

_____

6._____

_____

7._____

_____

B. What does this say to you about the value of Christianity compared to other faiths?

_____

_____

C. Why do you think the Bible has been so influential for the good?

_____

_____

_____

Lesson 4 - History Matters! (Pt 2)

Part 2: The 5,000 Year Leap

NOTE: We use America only as a case study showing the blessings that come when a nation—or family—establish the God of the Bible as King. Later we will see what happens when God is rejected by that nation or family.

Now, to give you a God's-eye view, if you will, of our place in His grand timeline of history, consider this.

For 1,000 years, the most reliable copies of the Bible were hidden away in secluded monasteries, virtually unreachable and unread. And the few copies that were accessible were available only in Latin, a language that most of the common people couldn't even understand, much less read. The only knowledge that the people had of the Bible, at that time, came from what the priests told them that it said.

Most people lived in poverty and educational ignorance, while the ruling class lived in outlandish luxury. Freedom was, and had always been, unknown to the average person. But then, in the year 1440 A.D., Johannes Gutenberg printed the first book from his new printing press, and that book was the Holy Bible. And the Reformation, a revolution, began. For the first time in history, the common man could now hold and read his own copy of the Bible, and the people began to teach themselves to read by using the Bible. Within just 100 years, it is said that the common peasants became more knowledgeable than their lords. These new believers took God at His word. They believed it was possible to govern themselves by the Word of God alone, without a king. But they needed a place to put their ideas into practice.

But God had kept America hidden from the civilized world for 5,000 years...for just that moment in time.

(The following is an excerpt from the book *The 5,000 Year Leap* [2], by S. Cleon Skousen.

> When the Pilgrims landed in America, not much had changed in the last 5,000 years. From the beginning of recorded history most things had been done the same way, using the same methods and tools.

> The settlers of Plymouth had come in a boat, powered by sails, no larger or more comfortable than those of the ancient Phoenicians. They navigated by the stars. Their tools still consisted of the wooden axe, shovel, and hoe, which were not much more improved from those of ancient Egypt or Babylon. They planted and harvested their grain by the same primitive methods, using a wooden plow pulled by oxen. They wore clothes made of thread spun on a wheel and woven by hand. They thought alcohol was a staple food. Their medicines were noxious concoctions based on superstition rather than science. Their transportation was by cart and oxen or horse. Their communication was by hand-written letter delivered by mule, horseback, or boat. It took months –even years - for a reply. Most of them died young. The average life span was only 40 years! But these pioneers believed that this new freedom was worth dying for, and in time, the American colonies miraculously broke free from one of the mightiest empires ever and established a government that -- for the 1st time in human history -- was based upon the Judeo-Christian principles of the Bible.

---

[2] *The 5,000 Year Leap*, by S. Cleon Skousen , National Center for Constitutional Studies (2007)

Dr. Skousen continues,

Soon two centuries had passed. By 1976, the "great experiment" of American biblical morality, individual freedom and responsibility and personal independence, coupled with biblically-based free-enterprise economic principles had produced radical results. Within merely 200 years from its founding, America gave the world the wonderful new power resources of harnessed electricity, the internal combustion engine, jet propulsion, exotic space vehicles, and nuclear energy. Communications were revolutionized, first by the telegraph, then the telephone, followed by radio and television, then the computer, the Internet, and now we even have the I-Phone. The whole earth was explored from pole to pole -- to the very depths of the sea. Americans walked on the moon!

The average life span was doubled. The quality of life was dramatically enhanced in every way -- In our homes, our food, in textiles, communications and transportation. We developed central heating and cooling, surgical miracles, medical cures for age-old diseases, entertainment at the touch of a switch, and instant world news. Affordable and amazingly fast world travel was made possible and accessible to virtually all. Literacy skyrocketed as education and libraries full of millions of books were made available to everyone -- not just the privileged class.

Of course, all of this did not happen just in America, but it did flow primarily from the transforming, revolutionizing concepts of individual rights and freedoms guaranteed to its people by the governing documents of the United States. *In 200 years, the human race had made a 5,000-year leap in progress.*

Pause and Consider

Key Principle: All Rights Come from God Alone

Think about the idea that is communicated here: If God is the giver of rights based upon His perfect laws, and those laws are made for our benefit, then those rights are eternal - - they NEVER change. But if Man is the giver of rights, he can change them whenever he chooses, and can decide who lives and who doesn't.

What was it about America that brought about such radical change to the world?

The answer: Freedom. biblically-based freedom. Freedom for the individual. Freedom of worship. Freedom of speech. Freedom to pursue one's dreams. Freedom to pursue the career of your choice. Freedom to create. Freedom to carve a life for yourself and those you love without the ruling powers of the day holding you down by their tyrannical governments.

What brought about this freedom?

The single most unique and exceptional concept in the history of governments as stated simply in the Declaration of Independence: "All men have been endowed by their Creator with certain unalienable rights, namely: Life, Liberty, and the Pursuit of happiness."

This principle—that rights come from God and not from man—never existed in the founding documents of any nation throughout the entire history of man, and to this day it is unique to the United States of America alone! That statement is HUGE! America was built upon a Declaration of

Independence, a Constitution, and a Bill of Rights that were all constructed solidly upon this foundational Judeo-Christian principle -- that **rights come from God ALONE** and He has made man to be free to live and pursue his dreams in accordance with His (God's) unchangeable laws.

America was supported at its very foundation by Christians who put into practice the principles of the Word of God in every aspect of life.

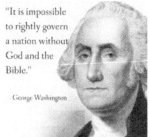

"It is impossible to rightly govern a nation without God and the Bible."

- George Washington

They led the country in education, establishing universities that quickly became the envy of the world. Their work ethic established them as the most industrious, creative, persevering people perhaps in all history.

It was their wide ranging knowledge of history, law, politics, science, economics, and so on, that made them leaders in this new nation and in the world.

The Founders viewed the world – and every part of life –through the lens of the Bible.

When we read the Old Testament history of Israel, we see that when they honored God, God gave them freedom which led to their prosperity. But then, when they forgot that God's blessings come with responsibilities, they became complacent -- and **complacency always leads to slavery**, or the *LOSS* of freedom.

For several generations now, we in America have not been taught the true history of this unique and blessed nation; thus, we have forgotten what a miracle God did in its creation. The result is that we and our children cannot see that, like Queen Esther of old, we have been set in this nation at exactly *this* moment in history for a purpose – "for a time such as this" (Esther 4:14).

The blessings of God come with responsibilities, and among our chief responsibilities is to educate ourselves and the next generation

We repeat, Scripture says: "My people perish from lack of knowledge". In Deuteronomy 4:9, God states:

> *"Only be careful and watch yourselves closely so that you do not forget the things your eyes have seen or let them fade from your heart as long as you live. Teach them to your children and to their children after them."*

To reinforce these principles, consider the following quotes from a few of the Christian Founding Fathers of America:

"No people will tamely surrender their Liberties, nor can any be easily subdued, when knowledge is diffused and virtue is preserved. On the Contrary, when People are universally ignorant, and debauched in their Manners, they will sink under their own weight without the Aid of foreign Invaders." - Samuel Adams

"A general dissolution of the principles and manners will more surely overthrow the liberties of America than the whole force of the common enemy.... When the people are virtuous, they cannot be subdued; but once they lose their virtue, they will be ready to surrender their liberties to the first external or internal invader.... If virtue and knowledge are diffused among the people, they will never be enslaved. This will be their great security." - Samuel Adams

"Our Constitution was made only for a moral and religious people. It is wholly inadequate to the government of any other." - John Adams

Pause and Consider

Key Principle: Complacency Always Leads to Slavery

When a free people become complacent and neglect their responsibilities to take part in the society around them, others will. And history shows that those "others" often want absolute control at all costs, ...and that cost is **our freedom.**

Lesson 4 Study Questions

A key element of holiness is a grateful heart, which is exercised by our daily appreciation of God's grace in giving us what we don't deserve. Thus, one of the main purposes of this lesson is to help all to understand the big picture of where God has placed us in History, and to cause our hearts to burn with thankfulness.

A. The average lifespan in the 1600's was less than 40 years (some estimates say closer to 30). What difference would that make in your spiritual journey if this was true today?

_____

_____

B. Up until the Reformation, freedom for all was never a consideration. Tyranny always ruled. How different would our lives be today if we were born in China, Russia, Cuba, or Venezuela?

_____

_____

C. Have you ever thought about the radical advances that America brought to the world in such a short time?

What impression did this segment make upon your view of Christianity's role in America's prosperity?

_____

_____

D. How does this put in perspective the importance of knowing history?

_____

_____

E. Did the information in this section change your belief about America's early history? In what way?

_____

_____

F. List as many reasons as you can for why America prospered so greatly and so quickly compared to all other nations in history.

_____

_____

_____

G. The word "freedom" was emphasized greatly in this section. Thomas Jefferson defined Freedom as *the ability to make choices*. List 4 of the freedoms mentioned in this day's study or that come to your mind. How important is each freedom to you, your family or friends?
    1. Freedom: _____ Importance: _____

_____

2. Freedom: _____   Importance: _____

_____

3. Freedom: _____   Importance: _____

_____

4. Freedom: _____   Importance: _____

_____

H. How or why might those freedoms lead to prosperity in a Christian nation, but not in an atheistic nation?

_____

_____

I. In your own words, explain and comment upon the Key Principle: *Complacency always leads to slavery*

_____

_____

_____

Lesson 5 - Why Worldview Matters!

There are two main conclusions we can draw from the _5,000 Year Leap_ account.

1. America is no accident – it was created by the miraculous design of God. We are part of God's Story – His-Story – History - Jesus is the "Playwright", "Producer" and "Director" of His-Story. We are the cast. We have parts to play and lines to deliver. **God did not stop the story with the completion of the Bible**. In our next class we'll see some amazing examples of how God worked miracles in America very similar to the miracles of Israel of old.
2. America is the only nation in history to be founded and grounded upon the principles of the Bible. The worldview of early America was clearly biblical.

The RESULT was the 5,000 year leap – the miraculous leap in innovation and sociological progress that occurred in the short 200 years immediately following America's founding as a nation. American Christianity blessed the world by bringing the light of God into all disciplines: Law, Science, Philosophy, Economics, Ethics, Education, and so on.

What Changed?

Alexis de Tocqueville (1865) was a French Philosopher and writer who was amazed by the success of America and studied it to find out the reasons for its greatness. He said: "There is no country in the whole world, in which the Christian religion retains a greater influence over the souls of men than in America." [3] But this is no longer true.

The following is a quote from Dr. Kenyn Cureton of the Family Research Council (FRC.org), a Christian parachurch ministry that is active in leading Christians to be engaged in the battle over the ideas that are attacking our culture. He says:

"The Culture War has been raging for at least 50 years in America. It is a war against our nation's Christian heritage.

Pause and Consider

"Whether or not you are engaging the enemy, he is engaging you!"
1 Peter 5:8 says: *"Be alert and of sober mind. Your enemy the devil prowls around like a roaring lion looking for someone to devour."*

• It is a war against the biblical accounts of our origins as created human beings.
• It is a war against our biblical convictions about unborn human life as being sacred and precious.
• It is a war against our biblical beliefs about human sexuality being only for a man and woman in a marriage relationship
• It is a war against our biblical values of faith and family. It is a war against our freedom of religious expression.

We are at war! Whether or not you are engaging the enemy, he is engaging you!"

---

[3] Democracy In America, Chapter XVII; Published 1835

"Why join the battle", he asks? "It is a foundational biblical truth that God expects His people to join Him on His mission to redeem and transform our lost world. The problem is that many Christians today want to limit that mission to *the saving of the soul*, while excluding the concept of *changing the culture*. This narrow understanding of God's mission finds its expression in a kind of Christian dualism. A schizophrenia, if you will. It is a misconception of reality that on one hand regards church-related activities such as worship, fellowship, discipleship, ministry, and evangelism as spiritually significant and worthy of effort, but on the other hand regards everything else outside this 'sacred' realm as 'secular' and therefore having no real spiritual significance.

Consequently, engaging the culture in the arenas of government, education, entertainment, the arts, media, science, etc. is deemed unimportant and even a distraction. However, Christian Americans influenced the world greatly in the past because the Christians diligently sought after God, then fought for, debated, and convinced the world of their Worldview."[4]

But today, if the American Church doesn't become more aggressive, we will be known just like the Church of Laodicea: *Lukewarm.* Ronald Reagan said: "History may well judge that those who had the most to lose did the least to prevent it from happening." Let that not be said of us!

"My people perish from lack of knowledge." – Hosea 4:6

Let's look at some sobering statistics...

 At the time of the signing of the Constitution of the U.S., less than 50% of all adult males in Western Europe were literate, while adult male literacy in the American colonies exceeded 90%.[5] Americans were the most educated society the world had ever seen! But, by 2010, it was estimated that nearly 50% of Americans are now functionally illiterate. What does that mean? It means that in order to function in this complex society we live in today, it's more important than ever to be able to *read* and *think* clearly. Yet almost half of all Americans are not able to do so.

The result of our poor educational system is that...[6]

- 20% of High School Grads can't read their own diplomas
- 85 percent of all juveniles in the juvenile court system are functionally illiterate.
- More than 60 percent of all prison inmates are functionally illiterate.
- One child in 4 grows up not knowing how to read.
- 3 out of 4 food stamp recipients perform in the lowest 2 literacy levels
- 90% of welfare recipients are high school dropouts
- 16 to 19 year old girls at the poverty level and below, who possess below average reading skills, are 6 times more likely to have out-of-wedlock children than their reading counterparts.

---

[4] Dr. Kenyn Cureton, quote taken from the FRC (Family Research Council) Culture Impact Team Resource Manual, p.41
[5] https://www.history.org/foundation/journal/winter11/literacy.cfm
[6] 2005 National Adult Literacy Survey (NALS), National Assessment of Adult Literacy (NAAL); 2011, Digest of Education Statistics 2010, Table 393; https://www.creditdonkey.com/illiteracy-in-america.html

In the same survey, literacy was measured in levels, 1-5. With "1" being the lowest level, "5" the highest. It was found that 43% of adults who have Level 1 literacy skills live in poverty compared to only 4% of those at Level 5 skills live in poverty... and yet many today are blaming the rich for the problems in our nation, instead of looking at the problem being education – or the lack of it.

So, you can see there are serious consequences that affect us all when we don't consider education – especially a moral education – to be one of the most valuable assets in our lives. That's why, as Christians, it's so important for us to learn now how to think like Christ in every area. The world depends upon us!

How did we fall so far?

By the late 1800's, individuals like you who make up the Church – the Body of Christ -- allowed the State to take over the education system. And now, as one pastor said: "If we send our children to Caesar to be educated, we shouldn't be surprised when they come back as Romans".

The good news is that we live in the Information and Communication Age, and although the mainstream media and the government-controlled education system is biased against Christianity, we have the ability today -- like never before in History -- to educate ourselves. At the press of a simple keyboard stroke on the Internet, we can access true and accurate information and news that the modern mainstream media – the NBC's, ABC's, CBS and CNN's of the world won't tell us about. And we can become more knowledgeable than even a liberal university professor on virtually any key issue if we look at the world through the lens of a biblical worldview – with God at the center.

Another reason we've fallen so far so fast is that we've lost the knowledge of how to apply our Bible to the culture around us. Francis Shaeffer said: "the basic problem with Christians in the last 100 years, in regard to society and government, is that they have seen things in bits and pieces instead of totals."

Christians today generally are not taught the importance of thinking in biblical categories. In other words, how to apply a certain teaching to a current issue in life ...whether it deals with how to get through a bad economy or what position Christians should hold regarding a health care debate. The point is we need to know what the Bible says on the various issues that affect our lives. But most Christians don't understand the great importance of consulting the Bible over every issue we find ourselves involved in.

As a result, the Christian community is having little influence in the larger society.

The 2nd reason that we need to develop a biblical worldview is this: We are losing our Christian youth to alien worldviews that dominate popular culture and the college campus. Studies have concluded that over 70% of all professing Christian teens abandon their faith by their 2nd year in college.[7] That's a frightening statistic, and one we cannot ignore!

Pause and Consider

Many Christians today "see things in bits and pieces instead of totals."

It's like trying to put together a jigsaw puzzle without the box cover to show you what you were aiming at.

Christianity isn't effective if we only practice our faith in limited areas of our life.

---

[7] Thom Rainer and Sam. S. Rainer III, Essential Church (Nashville: B&H Publishing, 2008); Dyck, Drew (2010-10-01). Generation Ex-Christian: Why Young Adults Are Leaving the Faith; Southern Baptist Council on Family Life Report, 2002; Josh McDowell, David H. Bellis, Green Key Books (2006); Assemblies of God Study, Dayton A. Kingsriter (2007)

Dr. David Noebel of Summit Ministries says: *"Our generation has lost the art of thinking deeply about why we believe what we believe. We are not accustomed to considering seriously life's most foundational questions."*

And honestly, don't people generally put more thought and effort into research for buying a car or a cell phone than they do about their eternal destiny, or the consequences of their beliefs or actions?"

This leads us to the question: What's YOUR worldview? To know the answer, we must first define the term ***Worldview***.

Lesson 5 Study Questions

1. Do you agree with the statement "It is a foundational biblical truth that God expects us to join Him on His mission to redeem and transform our lost world?". Why or why not?

   _____

   _____

2. What do you think the terms mean when Jesus says we are the "salt of the earth; the light of the world"?

   _____

   _____

3. Do you think the section on "the culture wars" was in line with what you are seeing today in society? How does this information help to clarify the reasons for the chaos in the world today?

   _____

   _____

4. Name at least 4 areas of life where Christianity is being attacked today.

   1)_____ 2)_____

   3)_____ 4)_____

5. Read **Matthew 5:13-16** along with **Ezekiel 3:17-21**. What promises and warnings do you find in these passages?

   _____

   _____

   _____

   1. According to the Matthew passage above, what are God's people commanded to be and do?

   _____

   _____

6. From those scriptures, why do you think Christianity is having so little influence in the culture today?

   _____

   _____

7. Do you think God will hold Christians at least partially responsible for the moral collapse of our nation?

    _____ Why? _____

8. Read 2 Chronicles 7:14. Where is there hope for us?

    _____

    _____

Lesson 6 - What's YOUR worldview?

According to two prominent Christian apologists of our time, NORMAN GEISLER and WILLIAM WAIKINS, a worldview is "a way of viewing or interpreting all of reality. It is an interpretive framework -- or lens -- through which one makes sense of the information of life and the world."

In other words: a worldview is the composite of your most basic and fundamental beliefs -- those beliefs you hold to so deeply that you would bet your life on them.

Dr. Cureton says:

"A worldview is the Big Picture -- the basic set of presuppositions, beliefs, convictions through which you look at and make sense of the world. Think of it like a pair of tinted sunglasses that color how the world looks to you. For example, if you look at the value of human life through glasses tinted with the belief that we are the unique creation of a loving God, you will arrive at one view of abortion. However, if your glasses are tinted with the belief that man simply evolved as a result of chance and we're therefore no different than the animals, you will arrive at a completely different view of abortion. Your worldview matters!"[8]

But unfortunately, very few people who claim to be Christians actually have a biblical world view. In fact, according to surveys taken by a prominent research organization - the Barna Group - only 4% of Americans have a biblical worldview.[9]

In one survey they conducted, people were asked the following questions to define a biblical worldview:

A. Do you believe that absolute moral truths exist?
B. Do you believe that such truth is defined by the Bible?
C. Do you believe in the following six specific religious views:
    1. Jesus Christ lived a sinless life
    2. God is the all-powerful and all-knowing Creator of the universe and He stills rules it today
    3. Salvation is a gift from God and cannot be earned
    4. Satan is real
    5. All Christians have a responsibility to share their faith in Christ with others.
    6. The Bible is accurate in all of its teachings.

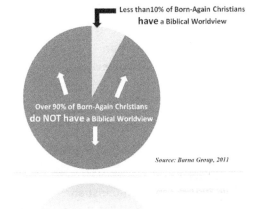

Less than10% of Born-Again Christians **have** a Biblical Worldview

Over 90% of Born-Again Christians do **NOT** have a Biblical Worldview

Source: Barna Group, 2011

If you strongly agree with every statement, you are – frankly – part of the minority because the survey concluded that only 9% of Born-again Christians passed that test. That means that more than 9 out every 10 Born-again Christians don't have a biblical worldview! Is there any wonder why America is falling and failing in so many areas

Your worldview matters because YOUR BELIEFS directly and dramatically impact YOUR BEHAVIOR

---

[8] Dr. Kenyn Cureton, quote taken from the FRC (Family Research Council) Culture Impact Team Resource Manual, p.41-42

[9] "Changes in Worldview Among Christians over the Past 13 Years" - The Barna Group (2009) and "A Biblical Worldview Has a Radical Effect on a Person's Life," Barna Research Online, 12-1-03 posting. The site contained this notation: "The data described above are from telephone interviews with a nationwide random sample of 2033 adults conducted during September through November 2003. The maximum margin of sampling error associated with the aggregate sample is ±2.2 percentage points at the 95% confidence level." See also George Barna's book, "Think Like Jesus" (Nashville: Thomas Nelson, 2003).

in life today? The danger is that so many of us Christians may say we believe these things, but when it comes down to it, are we really living them out in every area of our lives?

Belief and Behavior

According to Barna's research, adults with a biblical worldview possessed radically different views on morality and demonstrated vastly different lifestyle choices.[10]

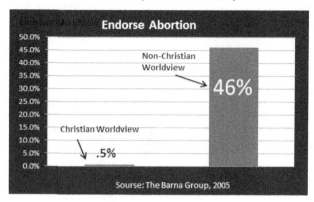

.5% of Christians WITH a biblical worldview endorse abortion

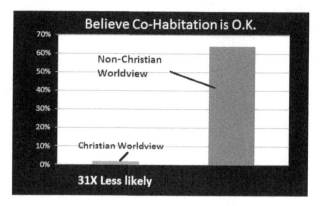

Christians WITH a biblical worldview 31X less likely to agree to cohabitate

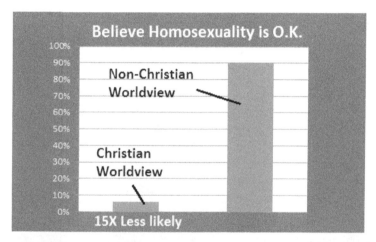

Christians WITH a biblical worldview 15X less likely to endorse homosexuality

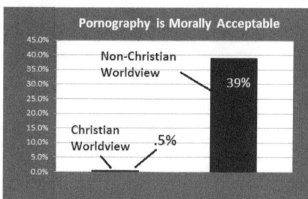

.5% of Christians WITH a biblical worldview endorse pornography

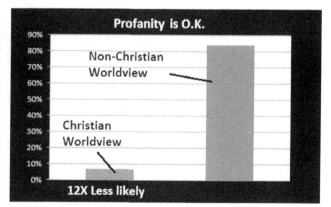

Christians WITH a biblical worldview are 12X less likely to endorse profanity

---

[10] IBID

Each of these behaviors violates a Physical law and/or a Moral law, and as stated earlier, when we violate these laws there are always consequences. As we continue through this series, those consequences will be revealed in each behavioral area. Again, the purpose is to inform and warn the reader so that he or she may be best equipped to make wise choices.

Session Summary

1. The cause for the decline in America can be summarized in the scripture "My people perish from lack of knowledge." If we want to reverse this decline, we need to seek to know the God of the Bible and understand His laws which guarantee success when we follow them.

2. The laws of God promise blessings when we obey, but they also require consequences when we don't. Thus, knowing God's laws, principles and precepts and being able to apply them in all the areas of our life is *vital*. That's why we study the Christian worldview.

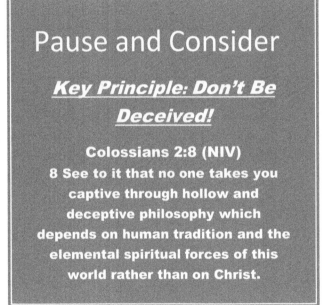

3. Because we've forgotten the proud history of the church, the world has been busy re-writing it. Therefore, it is vital that we go back and learn our history, so we can stand proud and stand up as Christians.

4. God calls us all to be Salt and Light. That's part of our responsibility to obey. Therefore, engaging the culture in the areas of government, education, entertainment, in the arts, in the media, in Science, etc., is vital in order to prevent the world from falling into utter depravity and chaos. And judging from the statistics that we just viewed, it certainly appears that there seems to be a great shortage of Salt and Light in the world today.

5. Last of all, for years the church had considered a well-rounded education to be an absolute priority for the people, but that idea has faded over the last 150 years as the religion of Humanism has taken Christianity's place in America. By once again placing a high priority upon studying and putting into practice a biblical worldview, we can become equipped as never before to understand the times that we're living in and to thrive in the midst of these times -- regardless of what's going on around us all!

Lesson 6 Study Questions

1. How would you define a worldview?

   _____

   _____

2. Do you think there is any difference between a worldview and a religion? If so, what?

   _____

   _____

3. Point out a few news issues being talked about on today's news broadcasts or newspapers that have at least 2 different sides that one might take on them.

   _____

   _____

4. What is a Worldview?

   The Barna survey asked these questions: "Do you believe.. 1.) Absolute moral truth exists? 2.) Those truths are defined in the Bible? 3.) Do you believe in ALL these 6 religious views: 1- Jesus Christ lived a sinless life 2- God is the all-powerful and all-knowing Creator of the universe and He stills rules it today 3- Salvation is a gift from God and cannot be earned 4- Satan is real 5- A Christian has a responsibility to share their faith in Christ with other people 6-The Bible is perfect in all of its teachings"

   1) Do you believe in every statement? _____ State which, if any, you are unsure of: _____

      _____

      _____

      (If you have doubts, we ask that you keep an open mind as you continue through these classes)

   2) What can we expect the result will be if Christians are not unified in what they believe?

      _____

      _____

   3) How do our core beliefs about what is true and what is not affect our behavior? Give 3 examples

      1- _____

      2- _____

      3- _____

   4) Read 2 Corinthians 10:4-5 and Colossians 2:8. In light of what was presented in this chapter, what do you think these verses mean in today's world?

_____

_____

_____

5. Interpreting Colossians 2:8 in today's world:
    1) What do you think it means to be taken captive, and can you give some examples?

    _____

    _____

    2) What does "hollow and deceptive philosophy" mean to you?

    _____

    _____

    3) What does it mean to depend on Christ rather than on human tradition and the principles of the world? Read John 15:1-17 and Prov. 3:5-6 to help you answer.

    _____

    _____

Recommended reading:

"The 5,000 Year Leap - the 28 Great Ideas That Changed the World", by W. Cleon Skousen; published by the National Center for Constitutional Studies, 2006 (NOTE: Although Mr. Skousen professes Mormonism as his religion, this book expresses truth without espousing Mormon doctrine. The writers of this textbook do not endorse Mormon theology because it veers far from many of the fundamental beliefs of Christianity, but Christians should never discount truth simply because a non-believer states it)

"How Christianity Changed the World", copyright 2004 by Alvin J. Schmidt; Published by Zondervan

You Are What You Think   Subject One: What Is a Worldview & Why Does It Matter? Lesson 6 Study Questions

34

Subject Two: The Christian Worldview of History

Lesson 1 – The Importance of History

History is either of extreme value, or it is of no value at all.

We live in an era where history is often re-written for the purpose of achieving a personal or political agenda. Today's modern ideology states that *the only thing we learn from history is that nothing can be learned from history*. Those who hold to this viewpoint might simply say that history is random and unguided – just like evolution.

The Christian worldview is quite the opposite. The Bible views all history through the eyes of God. All history, therefore, is HIS-story. Our God is the AUTHOR of all history. He has a plan and He is working it... through us!

With this in mind, the foundation for our worldview of history is the Bible. Thus, we will begin by considering the proposition that the Bible is a **SUPERNATURAL** source of truth and knowledge; and as such, it is absolutely reliable as our basis for true history. As we investigate this principle, we will compare the reliability of the Bible alongside the most highly revered secular writings in all of history. How does the Bible stand up? ...We'll see.

Next, we will consider the proposition that God is still as INVOLVED in the lives of His people today as He was in the times of the writing of the Bible.

Our purpose in this class is to awaken Christians to the reality that our lives are playing an active part in God's plan *whether we acknowledge it or not*; and on that Final Day when we meet Him face-to-face, we will be rewarded or reprimanded accordingly for our participation in His plan.

- Is our knowledge of history valuable and even vital? Yes!
- Can our knowledge of history protect us from repeating the same mistakes of generations past? Absolutely!
- Will that knowledge lead us to wiser choices for our future? You can count on it!

The Value of Remembering

We begin by stating that if you're going to build your worldview view upon something, that something had better be solid. We need to have utter confidence that our foundational belief system is standing on solid ground – not moving and shifting like sand – but solid – solid as a rock. And Christianity sinks or stands upon the Words in the Bible. Can we count on the Bible to be accurate and true? That is a question we must investigate.

Let's begin by asking a question. Can you remember the name of a person you attended elementary school with that you haven't seen since? If you thought for just a minute, you could probably remember several names – and even recall their faces in your mind. The point is this, our memories are incredible. It is astounding to consider all the information they contain. Our memories hold virtually our entire life story. And if we lost our memory - if we had a radical sort of amnesia - it would be almost as if we never lived. We'd be like newborn babies. Our memories are so important.

The Bible can be likened to the beginning of God's memory passed on to us. You could say it is our Father's diary that he left to us so that we would know how to live successful lives (See Psalm 1:3, Joshua 1:8) and everything that has gone on in history since the completion of the Bible is still a continuation of God's memory. History is a record of everything that God has done in His workings with people. Therefore, as children of God, for us to forget any portion of God's history is like forgetting a portion of Him. If the Christians don't remember the true history of God and what He's done through the ages, who will?

The Outline for This Segment

First, the Bible is supernatural in its origin. If you go to a college or university today the professors are most likely going to teach from the *naturalist* worldview. They were raised under the Darwinian theory of evolution and believe that there's nothing else except what you can taste, touch, see, hear, and smell. But Christianity goes beyond that. We firmly believe in the supernatural. The word *supernatural* simply *means above and beyond the natural*. What we will show you in this class is that the Bible is supernatural in its origin. It has come to us from a source above and beyond this world.

Second, the Bible is supernatural in its transmission. *How did it get to us?* It is often repeated that said that the Bible has been translated so many times over so many years it can't be trusted. We'll be destroying that objection through this study!

Third, the Bible is supernatural in its message. We'll reveal that the *Message* – specifically confirmed by the <u>fulfilled prophecies</u> of the Bible – provides uncanny testimony that supports the proposition that it is of *supernatural* origin.

I. The Bible is Supernatural in its Origin (Pt 1)

(**READ Second Timothy 3:16**). This is one of the most fundamental scriptures in the entire Bible. It is fundamental because of what the Bible says about itself. And It says "ALL Scripture" - not part, not some - but *all* scripture is given by inspiration of God... that means the words came directly from God Himself - from outside of our dimensions of time and space.

> ## Pause and Consider
>
> <u>**Key Principle: ALL Scripture is God-Breathed (2 Timothy 3:16-17)**</u>
>
> "**All Scripture is given by inspiration of God (God-breathed) and is profitable for doctrine, for reproof, for correction, for instruction in righteousness, that the man of God may be complete, thoroughly equipped for every good work.**"

- And it is profitable for doctrine. That is, for the beliefs and ideas that we hold to.
- For reproof - which is like slapping us on the hand when we get out of line.

- For **correction** – or, in other words - for correcting our path. When we are going the wrong way, the Bible can turn us around.
- And for **instruction in righteousness**. In other words, for showing us how to walk rightly. If we walk rightly God promises to always be there to hold us up. It's when we get off that path of walking rightly -- that's when we get hurt.

2 Peter 1:16-21 states,

16 For we did not follow cunningly devised fables when we made known to you the power and coming of our Lord Jesus Christ but were eyewitnesses of His majesty. ...18 And we heard this voice which came from heaven when we were with Him on the holy mountain....

Here we find that Peter, James, and John - who were all present on the mount of transfiguration with Jesus, Moses and Elijah (Matthew 17:1-13) - actually heard the voice of God. It's important to know that in a court of law, eyewitness testimony is among the most powerful and convincing testimonies that can be provided. Peter, James and John all heard God's voice speaking to Jesus, calling Jesus His Son. As stated above, if you have an eye witness to an event, you have a very strong claim to the truth. But look what Peter says after that...

"But we have the <u>**more sure**</u> *word of prophecy*, which you do well to heed as a light that shines in a dark place, ..."* (*Note: "Prophecy" in this case refers to all supernatural communications made directly from God to those who collectively penned the Old and New Testaments. In other words, the entire Bible is "the more sure word of prophecy")

Peter is saying that our Bibles are more trustworthy than even the eyewitness testimony of the three apostles who witnessed Jesus' transfiguration and heard God's voice! Peter continues in vs. 21...

...for prophecy never came by the will of man, but holy men of God spoke as they were moved by the Holy Spirit.

He's saying that no words of the Bible came from any source other than from God Himself. In other words, the writers didn't just dream up some idea of what they thought God was saying and then paraphrase it in their own way. No - it is word for word *exactly* what God meant. What we have, Peter claims, is the perfect, inerrant Word of God.

Therefore, if we decide to ignore or reject *any portion* of scripture we might as well throw it all out. If we can't trust the Bible for what it says about itself, we can't trust it at all! Which, by the way, has been the state of most mainline denominations in America since the early 1900s. Once they rejected the principle that the Bible is perfect and inerrant, changing the message became fair game. No wonder American Christianity is suffering from disunity today -- most churches aren't following the words in the Bible as if they are the perfect, holy words of God Himself.

Lesson 1 Study Questions

1. It was stated that the Bible is the beginning of God's memory passed on to us. What does this mean to you? _____

2. But God did not stop His work with us upon the completion of the Bible. H _ _ _ _ _ is the continuation of God's workings with mankind through the ages. This should be important to us because, as it has been said, "those who don't know history are condemned to r _ _ _ _ it. To illustrate this...
   Give an example of the consequences you might suffer if you forgot a lesson you learned earlier.
   _____

3. A large portion of the role of parents is to pass on to their children the wisdom of how to avoid making the same mistakes they made. What would happen to the child if even one of the parents lost their memory entirely?
   _____

4. Read Romans 15:4 and 1 Cor. 10:11. Why, then, is it important that we have a reasonable knowledge of history – especially in regard to God's monumental interventions of the past? _____
   _____

5. We have defined "history" as "His-Story". In your own words, what does this mean?
   _____

   _____

6. What might be the results if the media, government or educational system of a nation taught a false version of significant historical events? And can you think of any examples?
   _____

   _____

7. Name at least two current social or political "battlegrounds" that might benefit if everyone had a better understanding of the true historical background of the ideas in conflict? (ex: Israel vs Palestine).
   1)_____

   2)_____

8. We have stated that the Bible is S _ _ _ _ _ _ _ _ _ _ in its Origin. What does that mean to you and why is that important? _____
   _____

   _____

Lesson 2- Supernatural in Origin, Pt.2

One of the great objections that throws so many people is this:

"I can't rely on the Bible to give me absolute truth because it was written by too many authors over too long a time span – and has been edited so much that it is impossible to know what the original message or intent was." People say that God can't control the circumstances necessary to pass along His words perfectly through the ages. Have you heard or thought this yourself? This objection has kept many from embracing – or even considering – the Christian worldview. But the answer to that argument is a very simple:

If you can get past the first verse of the Bible, everything else is a piece of cake.

What's the 1st verse?

Now, if God created the entire universe, would it be difficult for Him to part the Red Sea or raise a man from the

"In the beginning, God created the Heavens and the Earth" (Genesis 1:1)

dead or allow a man to survive in the belly of the whale for three days? Obviously, if He created all of this, then it would be a simple thing for Him to ensure that His word is passed along perfectly throughout the generations. In our upcoming class on science we will prove that there must be an intelligent designer. The evidence for a creator is so strong scientifically, a person would have to be a fool to not believe that there is a Designer.

But again, people say, "you can't trust the Bible because it's been translated so many times".

In other words, it's as if *God has been foiled by the Telephone Game*.

The Telephone Game

Maybe you have played this game in one form or another …

Everybody gets in a circle. One person tells a short story into the ear of another, and then that person repeats the story - as best as he or she remembers - into the ear of the next person. This continues until the last person in the circle relates it to everyone as he or she was told. Inevitably, the story becomes mutated to the point that it's laughably different from the original tale. The point is that even a true story will inevitably be transformed into a tall tale after it has been passed along year after year.

So. Let's apply that illustration to the Bible.

Imagine questioning 40 different people on their beliefs about God.

• We ask them what God is like. What does He like? What doesn't He like? What does He say is good and what does He say is bad? What does He say is right and what does He say is wrong?

• We make sure that these people come from widely different social and economic backgrounds, ranging from the richest of the rich to the poorest of the poor. And then, ask people from nearly every walk of life... we'll ask kings and peasants, statesmen and fishermen, poets and physicians.

• Then, let's divide these people into three separate continents --- we'll ask people from Asia and Africa and Europe about their god.

• Next, we divide our contestants into those who speak in three different languages – Hebrew, Greek, and Aramaic.

• We'll have them describe their God in different literary forms such as poetry or history, or civil and criminal law, in ethics, in parables, in biographies, prophecies and personal correspondence.

• Lastly - so that we don't make it really easy - let's interview these people over a period of 1500 years.[11]

That describes how the Bible came to us.

It's a collection of 66 books, written by over 40 authors, over the span of 1500 years, with all the variations stated above. One would certainly expect the book to be disjointed, and nonsensical; and the god they described would be a strange combination of all kinds of ideas. But amazingly, astoundingly, miraculously, the Bible presents the same cohesive, coherent message from front to back: the same concept of sin, the same concept of grace, the same balance between mercy and judgment. It reveals God as being a God of compassion, but who will not wink at sin. God is presented in exactly the same way from the beginning of Genesis to the end of Revelation. The lessons, the truths, and the principles remain consistent from first to last.

Pause and Consider

Explain THIS!

The Bible was written by over 40 authors from every walk of life over a period of 40 generations. For example, Moses was a political leader, trained in the universities of Egypt; Peter was a fisherman; Amos, a herdsman; Joshua, a military general; Nehemiah, a cupbearer; Daniel, a prime minister; Luke, a doctor; Solomon, a king; Matthew, a tax collector; Paul, a rabbi.
It was written in different places: Moses in the wilderness; Jeremiah in a dungeon; Daniel on a hillside and in a palace; Paul inside prison walls; Luke while traveling; John on the isle of Patmos.
Yet, the entire message is miraculously consistent!

---

[11] McDowell, Josh. *Evidence that Demands a Verdict, eBook: Historical Evidences for the Christian Faith* (pp. 16-17). Thomas Nelson. Kindle Edition.

Through all this, its message is miraculously consistent. Its subject matter includes hundreds of controversial subjects which would create opposing opinions when mentioned or discussed. But these biblical authors spoke on hundreds of controversial subjects with harmony and continuity from Genesis to Revelation. There is one unfolding story:

"God's redemption of man."

How could this be? The most plausible answer is -- *The Bible is Supernatural in its origin*.

Some Divine Intelligence outside of time must have personally revealed to each of the authors His character in order for them all to be in such perfect agreement. What other logical explanation could there be?

Lesson 2 Study Questions

1. Read Isaiah 46:10, Daniel 2:21. What does God say about His role in history? _____

   _____

2. Read 2 Timothy 3:16; 2 Peter 1:16-21; Jeremiah 1:2-3; Ezekiel 1:3. From these scriptures, how would you

   explain in your own language whose words make up the Bible? _____

   _____

3. Read Romans 1:18, 21-22, 28, 32. Why do you think so many denominations have veered from this
   absolute truth, and how has that hurt Christianity?

   _____

   _____

4. Why do you think God gave to us – and preserved for us – the Bible? _____

   _____

5. It was stated that the Bible consists of 6__ books by 4__ authors written in __ languages, on __ continents

   over a period of _____ years, and yet its message never changes. How can that be explained, especially

   when compared to any other book? What words would you use to describe this?

   _____

   _____

6. Why is it important for all Christians to be aware of the overwhelming evidence of the *reliability* of Bible

   translations – especially compared to all other famous classical literature?

   _____

   _____

   _____

Lesson 3 - Supernatural in Transmission

II. The Bible is Supernatural in Its Transmission

There is no book in all of history that can hold a candle to the reliability and accuracy of the translations of the Bible. Someone may ask, "how do we know that it hasn't been translated wrong or tampered with?" The answer is that the Bible - compared against ALL other ancient writings - has more manuscript evidence to support its accurate transmission than any 10 pieces of classical literature combined![12]

If you were to inquire at a modern university, you would find that nearly all professors highly revere and honor the works of men such as Plato, Caesar, Homer, or Herodotus. Well, let's compare the evidence for the trustworthiness of their writings in relation to the Bible.

Compare and Contrast: The Classic Literary Works of History vs. the Bible

The Works of Caesar were written between 100 & 44 BC... the earliest copy we have in existence is from 980 AD. That means the time span between its first writing and the earliest copy is 1000 years. And we only have 10 manuscripts in existence.

The Works of Plato. Plato is very highly revered among college professors. Why? Because he was a socialist. And socialism is cool on college campuses today. Plato wrote between 427 and 347 BC. The earliest copy we have in existence was written in 980 AD. That means there is a twelve-hundred-year time span between its writing and the first copies that we have. And we only have seven copies.

The Works of Herodotus. The famous Greek historian Herodotus, considered the Father of History, wrote between 480 and 425 BC. The first copy of his works is dated 980 A.D., which means there is a 1300 year time span between its first writing & the first copy. We only have eight manuscript copies in existence.

The Works of Tacitus. Tacitus wrote these works in 100 A.D. The 1st copy is 1100 A.D. Thus, the time span between the original and first copy is 1,000 years. We have only 20 copies.

Homer's Iliad. The most treasured of all ancient literary works was written in 900 BC. The earliest copy we have is from 400 BC. Compared to the others, that is quite impressive because that's a time span of only 500

NO BOOK IN ALL OF HISTORY COMPARES TO THE BIBLE

The Bible has been read by more people and published in more languages than any other book. There have been more copies produced of its entirety and more portions and selections than any other book in history. Some will argue that in a designated month or year more of a certain book was sold. However, overall there is absolutely no book that reaches or even begins to compare to the circulation of the Scriptures.

John Warwick Montgomery says that "to be skeptical of the resultant text of the New Testament books is to allow all of classical antiquity to slip into obscurity, for no documents of the ancient period are as well attested bibliographically as the New Testament."

---

[12] IBID, p-42

years. And we even have 643 manuscripts! That makes the Iliad stand out far above the all the other ancient manuscripts...Until we compare it to the New Testament.

The Number and Accuracy of NEW Testament Manuscripts [13]

- Written between 40 and 100 A.D., the earliest copy we have is from **125 A.D**. That means the time span between the original writing and the first copy is only **25 to 50** years. And we have 24,000 manuscripts!

- There is no book in all of history that compares to the Bible. People have said that there is more evidence that Jesus Christ lived and walked as the Bible describes than that Abraham Lincoln ever lived. With so many early manuscript copies to compare to today's New Testament translations, it's been easily proven that the New Testament we hold in our hands today is over 98% accurate in comparison to the original texts of 2000 years ago. YES. We can depend on it to be accurate!

Sir Frederic Kenyon (one of the great authorities in the field of New Testament textual criticism) wrote: "No fundamental doctrine of the Christian faith rests on a disputed reading.... It cannot be too strongly asserted that in substance the text of the Bible is certain: Especially is this the case with the New Testament. The number of manuscripts of the New Testament, of early translations from it, and of quotations from it in the oldest writers of the Church, is so large that it is practically certain that the true reading of every doubtful passage is preserved in some one or other of these ancient authorities. This can be said of no other ancient book in the world".[14]

Philip Schaff 'in *Comparison to the Greek Testament and the English Version* concluded that only 400 of

the 150,000 variant readings caused doubt about the textual meaning, and only 50 of these were of great significance. Not one of the variations, Schaff says, altered "an article of faith or a precept of duty which is not abundantly sustained by other and undoubted passages, or by the whole tenor of Scripture teaching."[15]

Millar Burrows of Yale says: "Another result of comparing New Testament Greek with the language of the papyri is an increase of confidence in the accurate transmission of the text of the New Testament itself." 17/52 Burrows also says that the texts "have been transmitted with remarkable fidelity, so that there need be no doubt whatever regarding the teaching conveyed by them." I believe one can logically conclude from the perspective of literary evidence that the New Testament's reliability is far greater than any other record of antiquity. [16]

---

[13] Hort, Fenton John Anthony and Brooke Foss Westcott. The New Testament, p-2
[14] McDowell, Josh. Evidence that Demands a Verdict, eBook: Historical Evidences for the Christian Faith (p. 45). Thomas Nelson. Kindle Edition.
[15] Schaff, Philip. Companion to the Greek Testament and the English Version. Rev. ed. New York: Harper Brothers, 1883., p-177
[16] Burrows, Millar. What Mean These Stones? New York: Meridian Books, 1956. P-2

The Accuracy of the OLD Testament [17]

> The Dead Sea Scrolls, which were discovered in 1947, have proved to be among the most monumentally-historic treasures in all of archaeology. Included within these invaluable scrolls was an ancient copy of the book of Isaiah. The scroll, dating from approximately 100 B.C., was found to be *identical to the modern Hebrew Bible in over 95% of the text.*
>
> The remaining 5% consisted chiefly of obvious slips of the pen or variations in spelling.

Flavius Josephus, the Jewish historian, writes: "We have given practical proof of our reverence for our own Scriptures. For, although such long ages have now passed, no one has ventured either to add, or to remove, or to alter a syllable; and it is an instinct with every Jew, from the day of his birth, to regard them as the decrees of God, to abide by them, and, if need be, cheerfully to die

Dead Sea scrolls Portion

for them. Time and again ere now the sight has been witnessed of prisoners enduring tortures and death in every form in the theatres, rather than utter a single word against the laws and the allied documents." [18]

How accurate is the book that you hold? It has been translated more accurately than any other book in all of history – far and above.

Pause and Consider
The Bible is Unique in Its Survival Throughout History

There is no book in all history that has been so loved, yet so hated by its enemies. Sidney Collett in *All About the Bible* says, "Voltaire, the noted French infidel who died in 1778, said that in one hundred years from his time Christianity would be swept from existence and passed into history. But what has happened? Voltaire has passed into history, while the circulation of the Bible continues to increase in almost all parts of the world, carrying blessing wherever it goes. For example, the English Cathedral in Zanzibar is built on the site of the Old Slave Market, and the Communion Table stands on the very spot where the whipping-post once stood! The world abounds with such instances.... As one has truly said, 'We might as well put our shoulder to the burning wheel of the sun, and try to stop it on its flaming course, as attempt to stop the circulation of the Bible.'" [19] Concerning the boast of Voltaire on the extinction of Christianity and the Bible in 100 years, Geisler and Nix point out that "only fifty years after his death the Geneva Bible Society used his press and house to produce stacks of Bibles." [20]

1st Peter says: "The grass withers and the flower falls away, but the word of the Lord endures forever". The Bible is **Supernatural in its Transmission.** Some hand outside of Man had to play a part in this, for these translations to have been passed down to us so accurately.

The conclusion is the Word of God is a Sure Foundation. You can depend upon it.

---

[17] Archer, Gleason, A Survey of the Old Testament. Chicago: Moody Press, 1964.
[18] Josephus, Flavius. "Flavius Josephus Against Apion." Josephus, Complete Works. Translated by William Whiston, Grand Rapids: Kregel Publications, 1960. P-179, 180
[19] Collett, Sidney. All About the Bible. Old Tappan: Revell, n.d.
[20] Geisler, Norman L. and William E. Nix. A General Introduction to the Bible. Chicago: Moody Press, p-123-4

Lesson 3 Study Questions

1. Read: Matthew 5:18, Matthew 24:35, Psalm 119:89, Isaiah 55:11. What does God say about the enduring power of the words in the Bible? _____

   _____

   _____

2. The Bible, compared with other ancient writings, has more manuscript evidence than any _____ pieces of classical literature combined. There are over _____,000 manuscripts of various portions of Scripture in existence. How does this compare with Homer's Iliad? _____

   _____

3. In light of the facts as presented in the last question, read **John 3:19**. According to this scripture, why do the majority of "knowledgeable college professors" reject the Bible as more reliable than other ancient works?

   _____

   _____

4. Both the New Testament has been proven to be over _____% accurate, and the Old Testament has been proven to be over _____% accurate in words and _____, in their translations over 1900 - 2,200 years. No other ancient book comes close to that degree of accuracy. Why are these important facts for Christians to be aware of?

   _____

   _____

5. Knowing this, does the phrase "supernatural in its transmission" seem appropriate? _____

   State this principle in your own words: _____

   _____

6. The Dead Sea Scrolls, discovered in 1947, contain many Old Testament manuscripts dating from 100 B.C. One of the scrolls – the book of Isaiah – proved to be identical to the contemporary Hebrew Bible in over _____% of the text.
   a. Why would the Jews take such care to make such perfect copies?

   _____

   _____

   b. What might that say to us today about our attitude toward Scripture? _____

   _____

Lesson 4 – Supernatural in Message

III. The Bible is Supernatural in its **Message**

We have divided this section into 3 parts. The first is: "God is the *Author* of all History".

The Second is: God is *Above* all History. Third: God is *Involved* in all History.

1. God is the *Author* of all History

The word "Remember" is prominent in Deuteronomy, appearing over 15 times; thus, Deuteronomy has been appropriately called the "Book of Remembrance". Why? Because God's people had forgotten His Words the 1st time He proclaimed them to Israel; therefore, God is reminding them a 2nd time …Don't Forget my Word or my Works!!!

In Psalms, the word Remember appears 31 times. And it is repeated many, many times throughout the remainder of the Bible simply because God has a memory and He wants us to remember the things that are important to Him.

Some examples:

"I will remember My covenant which is between Me and you and every living creature of all flesh; the waters shall never again become a flood to destroy all flesh. The rainbow shall be in the cloud, and I will look on it to remember the everlasting covenant between God and every living creature of all flesh that is on the earth." And God said to Noah, "This is the sign of the covenant which I have established between Me and all flesh that is on the earth." (Gen 9:15-17)

Speaking of the rainbow, God made a promise that he'll never bring a worldwide flood to us again. Aren't we glad He remembers His promises?

They (speaking of His people) did not **remember** *His power: The day when He redeemed them from the enemy (Ps 78:42)*

In Jude 6-7, it reads:

In a similar way, Sodom and Gomorrah and the surrounding towns gave themselves up to sexual immorality and perversion. <u>They serve as an example</u> of those who suffer the punishment of eternal fire. (God wants us to remember such examples from His-story and learn from them)

God's Memory is very important. Therefore, history is very important.

Eighteenth-century historian Charles Rollin wrote:

> "Nothing gives history a greater superiority to many branches of literature, than to see in a manner imprinted, in almost every page of it, the precious footsteps and shining proofs of the great truth...that God disposes of all events as supreme Lord and Sovereign; that He alone determines the fate of kings and the duration of empires and that He transfers the government of kingdoms from one nation to another because of the unrighteous dealings and wickedness committed therein."

God is timeless – His domain is not bound by days, months and years. He would not be God if He was limited by the dimension of time. The Bible records hundreds of prophecies that are always fulfilled to the letter (we will

Remember the former things of old: for I am God, and there is none else; I am God, and there is none like me, declaring the end from the beginning, and from ancient times the things that are not yet done, saying, "My counsel shall stand, and I will do all my pleasure"

review a couple of them in the next section). Therefore, He declares in Isaiah 46:9-10:

What He says will happen ... Happens!

> There are **2 Key Principles** which have been all but lost or forgotten among many within today's Christian circles:
>
> 1. God is **Omnipresent**: He is everywhere at all times. He is present in our day-to-day lives.
>
> 2. God is **Omniscient**. He knows everything about every individual and has created us unique and exactly as we are, and for a specific purpose.

When we view both these principles in the same light, we see that God is active in all of history and has made each of us as who allow ourselves to fall in line with God's plan to live a marvelously purposeful life. History is filled with examples of ordinary people of God who did extraordinary things for Him. We are all placed here *"for a time such as this"* (Esther 4:14)

Ephesians 2:9 says: "For we are His workmanship, created in Christ Jesus for good works, which God prepared beforehand that we should walk in them."

This means that every person who submits to the Lordship of Christ has been created to fulfill his or her appointed mission while in this life. That mission God has already predestined that we will do. In other words, God has already written the script of history and is actively working in and alongside each of us every moment to help us accomplish His purpose for us.

2 Chronicles 16:9 -

For the *eyes* of the Lord *run to and fro* throughout **the whole earth,** to show Himself STRONG on behalf of those *whose heart* is LOYAL to Him

God is the Author of all history!

Lesson 4 Study Questions

1. Why do you think the emphasis on *remembering* or *not-forgetting* is so prominent in the books of Deuteronomy and Psalms? _____

    _____

2. In light of the last question, why should the study of history be important to Christians, and how might it benefit us? _____

    _____

3. Considering the word Omnipresence, look up each of the scriptures below and paraphrase them according to how they relate to YOU and your life.

    a. Psalm 139:7-12 _____

    _____

    b. Jeremiah 23:23-24 _____

    _____

    c. Proverbs 15:3 _____

    _____

    d. Colossians 1:17 _____

    _____

    e. Acts 17:27 _____

    _____

4. Considering the word Omniscience, look up each of the scriptures below and paraphrase them according to how they relate to YOU and your life.

    a. Matthew 10:30 _____

    _____

    b. Psalm 147:4 _____

    _____

    c. Psalm 139:1-3 _____

    _____

    d. 1 Chronicles 28:9 _____

    _____

    _____

Lesson 5 – Supernatural in Message, Part 2

Part 1. God is *Above* all History - The Prophecy of Babylon

It has been said that God's view of history may be likened to a man looking down from a hot-air balloon at the Rose Parade. While the spectators see the parade as each float and marching band passes by, the one in the balloon sees it all at once from above. He can see the end and the beginning, and everything in between in one glance. That describes, in a sense, how God views time; and because He is above - or outside of – time, God can speak accurately of events before they occur in time. As such, the eternal God reveals this by way of fulfilled prophecy in Scripture.

The Bible records many, many examples that prove God's supernatural predictions. There are over 1,800 prophecies of some nature in the Bible that accurately predicted an event that took place long after the time the author wrote the Scripture. We are going to touch mainly upon two such prophecies in this section: The Prophecy of Babylon and the Prophecy of Tyre. If you want to do a little research on your own, we would highly recommend Josh McDowell's book *Evidence that Demands a Verdict* (we will be including several quotes from this valuable resource throughout this subject). We believe this book should be in every Christian's household. It is filled with answers to the questions that we get all the time as Christians, and it helps us to become equipped with those answers.

Isaiah 48 says…

"I have declared the former things from the beginning; They went forth from My mouth, and I caused them to hear it. Suddenly I did them, and they came to pass. Because I knew that you were obstinate. Even from the beginning I have declared it to you; Before it came to pass I proclaimed it to you,.." (Isaiah 48:3-5 NKJV)

God tells us the end from the beginning. He does that partly because He wants to show the doubting Thomas's of the world that He is whom He says He is. He also often does so for the purpose of warning His audience of the impending doom awaiting those that ignore His principles.

EXHIBIT A: The Prophecy Against Babylon

In 690 BC the city of Babylon was 196 square miles. That means it was nearly the size of the city of Chicago.

To give you an idea, the picture below is just downtown Chicago. That's not even a quarter of Chicago and Babylon was much bigger than this.

The City of Babylon
as imagined from historical descriptions

- It was surrounded by a 30-ft moat ...which must have been quite a deterrent for anyone thinking they might be able to jump over the wall and conquer it!
- It had double walls around the entire city
- The outer wall was 30 Stories High ...how high is 30-stories? About this high:
- This wall was 87 Ft. Wide –That's the equivalent of an 11-lane freeway 300 feet in the air!
- It had 100 gates of solid brass
- There were 250 watchtowers 100 ft. higher than walls[23]

This city was built so that no one could ever conquer it. In 690 B.C. it was at the height of activity, it was the center of the world at that time. Between 701 and 680 B.C. Isaiah wrote this prophecy and it was fulfilled 150 years later, point-by-point.

We'll begin in Isaiah 45:1, where it says:

"Thus saith the Lord to his anointed to Cyrus." Who was Cyrus? Cyrus the Great, King of Persia, *who wouldn't be born until a hundred years later!* It continues: "Cyrus - Who's right hand I have held. To subdue nations before him and loose the armor of Kings (in other words to take down kingdoms and become king himself). "To open before him the double doors (notice that term 'the double doors') so that the **gates** (plural) will not be shut." In verse 3, it goes on: "I will give you the treasures of darkness and hidden riches of secret places, that you may know that I, the Lord, Who call you by your name, Am the God of Israel."

Is. 13:19 says: "Babylon, the jewel of kingdoms, the glory of the Babylonians' pride, will be overthrown by God like Sodom and Gomorrah." (NIV)

---

[23] McDowell, Josh. Evidence that Demands a Verdict: Historical Evidences for the Christian Faith (pp. 303-309). Thomas Nelson, 1979

Isaiah 13:20-21 adds: "It will never be inhabited, nor will it be settled from generation to generation; nor will the Arabian pitch tents there, nor will the shepherds make their sheepfolds there. But wild beasts of the desert will lie there. And their houses will be full of owls; ostriches will dwell there and wild goats will caper there." (NKJV)

(now, remember this line…) *"The hyenas will howl in their citadels and jackals in their pleasant palaces*. Her time is near to come, and her days will not be prolonged." (Isaiah 13:22 NKJV)

Isaiah 14:23 continues: "I will turn her (Babylon) into a place for owls and into swampland; I will sweep her with the broom of destruction," declares the Lord Almighty.

So, to recap, Prophecy states:

> - The man responsible for conquering Babylon would be named Cyrus
> - God would open the gates of Babylon for Cyrus and his army.
> - Babylon – a city the size of Chicago and a world power at two different times in history - would be completely wiped out…never again to be inhabited.
> - It would be reduced to swampland.
> - Hyenas and Jackals will howl. Only Desert creatures will inhabit it
> - The city would rarely even be visited for ever after

A Radical Prophecy for That Day

Now, this would be like someone standing in front of all the press and saying: "San Francisco is going to be completely wiped out very soon. As a matter of fact, it's going to become a swampland! No one will ever live there again – even though it has one of the greatest natural harbors in the world. And I'll tell you the name of the king – a man who has not even been born yet - who will conquer it.

Now, if someone did that, he'd be called crazy. But that's, in effect, what Isaiah prophesied.

What Actually Happened?

5. We know from historical records[24] that Babylon's water source, the Euphrates, flowed in channels below the walls, through **double gates**, and on through the city. Despite Babylon's seemingly impregnable defenses, Cyrus diverted the flow of the Euphrates River into a large lake basin and marched his army through the dry riverbed, under the wall, and into the city. Once inside, **soldiers opened the gates** for the rest of the army. Secular history confirms that when Cyrus conquered Babylon in 539 BC, it never again rose to power as an empire.

---

[24] Ibid

Thus, as Isaiah prophesied 2700 years ago, the Babylonian Empire never recovered from Cyrus' victory. For many centuries, Bible critics believed the story to be a fable until archaeologists excavated the Babylonian site in the early 1800s. Some parts of the city could not even be dug up because they were buried deep under a water

table that had risen over the years. Babylon had become a swampland. Could this just be a coincidence?

The Eerie Testimony of History

Many centuries later, an archaeologist by the name of Edward Chiera, was excavating a city by the name of Kish, an ancient city 8 miles from Babylon. He was a Christian theologian who became so captivated by the Biblical accounts of the Old testament, that he devoted his life to finding the cities mentioned in the bible. While excavating Kish, He wrote to his wife this letter.[25]

He said: "This evening I made my usual pilgrimage to the mound covering the ancient temple tower …… from the top the eye sweeps over an enormous distance on the boundless, flat plain. The ruins of Babylon are nearer. All around the tower small heaps of dirt represent all that remains of Kish, one of the oldest cities of Mesopotamia. Even the Euphrates has abandoned this land by changing its course.

"It is a dead city! I have visited Pompeii and Ostia, and I have taken walks along the empty corridors of the Palatine. But those cities are not dead -- they are only temporarily abandoned. The hum of life is still heard, and life blooms all around. Here only is real death. Not a column or an arch still stands to demonstrate the permanency of human work. Everything has crumbled into dust. The very temple tower, the most imposing of all these ancient constructions, has entirely lost its original shape. We see nothing but a mound of earth - all that remains of the millions of its bricks. On the very top are some traces of walls. But these are shapeless. Time and neglect have completed their work.

"Under my feet are some holes which have been burrowed by foxes and jackals. At night they descend stealthily from their haunts in their difficult search for food and appear silhouetted against the sky. This evening they appear to sense my presence and stay in hiding, perhaps wondering at this stranger who has come to disturb their peace. The mound is covered with white bones which represent the accumulated evidence of their hunts.

"Nothing breaks the deathly silence. A jackal is now sending forth his howl, half-cry and half-threat…

"But a certain fascination holds me here. I should like to find a reason for all this desolation. Why should a flourishing city, the seat of an empire, have completely disappeared? Is it the fulfillment of a prophetic curse that

---

[25] Chiera, Edward. *They Wrote on Clay: The Babylonian Tablets Speak Today.* Chicago: University of Chicago Press, 1938.

changed a superb temple into a den of jackals? Did the actions of the people who lived here have anything to do with this, or is it the fatal destiny of mankind that all its civilizations must crumble when they reach their peak?"

Pause and Consider

How About US?

Does this make you think of our society today? Have we reached our peak? Are we about to crumble? Is there anything we can do? We hope you'll find that as we continue through this series, there is a lot we can do! But it must start first in our own homes.

Lesson 5 Study Questions

1. Why did God record prophecies in the Bible and what does this matter to us?

   _____

   _____

   _____

   _____

2. Name 6 statements from the prophesy of Babylon that were fulfilled in the historical accounts that

   followed.

   1)_____

   2)_____

   3)_____

   4)_____

   5)_____

   6)_____

3. How does this support the statement that the Bible is *supernatural* in its *message?*

   _____

   _____

   _____

4. What was your impression from the account of archaeologist Edward Chiera about the devastation he witnessed of the remains of the city of Babylon?

   _____

   _____

   _____

5. READ Deuteronomy 18:20-22 along with Matthew 7:15,16. How can we know if a prophecy is from God and is reliable or not, and what does this say about the trustworthiness of the prophet?

   _____

   _____

   _____

   _____

Lesson 6 – Supernatural in Message, Part 3
Part 2. God is *Above* all History - The Prophecy of Tyre

The prophecy of Tyre in the book of Ezekiel is one of the most definitive proofs of the supernatural origin and message of the Bible, due to the massive historical and archaeological evidence supporting it.

The ancient city of Tyre was a Phoenician port city located on the southern coast of modern-day Lebanon. This city and its people are mentioned in numerous places in the Bible, and much of what we know about the city and its history is a result of those biblical refences that pointed latter-day archaeologists to the exact locations and events described in Scripture.

Between 970-930 B.C., Hiram, the King of Tyre, was a friend of King Solomon, and even provided the cedar for Solomon's temple. However, 400 years later, the city had become the virtual capital of the idolatrous and pagan Canaanite culture, and they were dragging Israel down with them. Thus, God - through the Prophet Ezekiel – promises the eradication of this most famous seaport of ancient times.

READ Ez. 26:1-14. Notice the six specific predictions made in this text:

> 1. King Nebuchadnezzar of Babylon would destroy the mainland city of Tyre (26:7-8).
> 2. Many nations would rise up against Tyre. These nations would come like waves of the sea, one after another (26:3- 4).
> 3. Tyre will be made like a flat rock (26:4, 14).
> 4. Fisherman will dry their nets there (26:5, 14).
> 5. The ruins of the city would be cast into the sea (26:12).
> 6. Tyre would never be rebuilt (26:14).

Let's look at the actual history of Tyre from this point. Notice that the prophecy is fulfilled in stages and by various nations and enemies over a period of roughly 1800 years.[26]

The first fulfillment occurred just a few years after Ezekiel penned this prophecy, when King Nebuchadnezzar of Babylon laid siege against the city beginning in 585 B.C. But by the time he finally broke down the gates, he found that the people of Tyre had moved all their possessions by ship to an island a half mile offshore. Even though Nebuchadnezzar had destroyed the mainland city - fulfilling Ezek. 26:8 - the new city offshore continued to flourish for nearly 250 years.

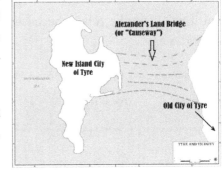

But, the prophecy of Ezekiel 26:12 says that their enemies will also "break down your walls and demolish your fine houses and throw your stones,

---

[26] McDowell, Josh. *Evidence that Demands a Verdict: Historical Evidences for the Christian Faith* (pp. 274-281). Thomas Nelson, 1979

timber and rubble into the sea"; and this portion remained unfulfilled until 332 B.C. when Alexander the Great performed a virtual military miracle to overcome the city.

Writing about 400 years after this event, a Greek historian by the name of Arrian, detailed this feat in his writings titled "The Campaigns of Alexander".[27]

His description of the fortification of the island of Tyre resembles that of Alcatraz, because the city sat offshore like a rock with walls that came down to the edge of the water and seemed impenetrable. But Alexander devised a brilliant plan to build a land bridge - or "causeway" - to the island by having his soldiers throw the ruins from the original city that Nebuchadnezzar had destroyed into the water - leveling the new causeway as they went - so that they could march across it and directly assault Tyre at its walls.

However, the people within the city and the Tyrian navy on the sea constantly attacked Alexander's men as they worked on the causeway. So Alexander, realizing that he needed ships of his own to help defend his soldiers, returned to the cities he had conquered and demanded their assistance. Thus, the prophecy that God "will cause many nations to come up against you, as the sea causes its waves to come up" (Ezek. 26:3), was fulfilled in even greater detail.

Alexander succeeded in his plan. It took him just seven months to conquer Tyre. In the end, 8,000 people were slain and thirty thousand were sold into slavery.

Amazingly, the causeway he built can still be seen to this day!

Historian Philip Myers said, "Alexander the Great reduced Tyre to ruins. The city recovered partly from this blow, but never regained its prominence in the world. The larger part of the site is now as bare as the top of a rock—a place where the "fishermen spread their nets to dry" (Ez. 26:14)

In time, the island city was again repopulated, only to be levelled again in 1281 A.D. by the Muslims. However, Ezekiel had prophesied that the powerful mainland city would never be rebuilt—and it never has been. There have been many cities throughout history that have been destroyed and rebuilt, but not Tyre even though it is in a perfect location for the commerce of a large, sprawling, powerful city, and has several natural springs that could supply a huge population with water.

But it will never be rebuilt because The Lord proclaimed over 25 centuries ago,

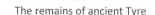

"You shall be built no more!" (Ezek. 26:14).

The remains of ancient Tyre

[27] The Campaigns of Alexander, by Arrian (translated and Edited by Betty Radice and A. De Selincourt), Penguin Books, 2003

The conclusion:

God is ABOVE of all History. Because He governs over all time, what he says will happen, **happens.** And just as assuredly, we can trust that every word in the Bible is trustworthy.

Lesson 6 Study Questions

In the space below, paraphrase (minimum 120 words) the account of the prophecy against the city of Tyre (Ezekiel 26). Include in your essay the following:

1) Why did God condemn Tyre? (READ Ezekiel 28:1-10)

2) Describe each phase of the "waves" of destruction that came upon the city and how many years it took for the entire prophecy to be fulfilled

3) Your conclusions after studying this prophecy and how it supports the proposition that the Bible is *Supernatural in its Message.*

_____

_____

_____

_____

_____

_____

_____

_____

_____

_____

_____

_____

_____

_____

Lesson 7 – God is Involved in all History
Was God Involved in the Founding of America?

Up until this point in our examination of the subject of history, we've concentrated on substantiating our claim that the Bible is supernatural in its origin, transmission, and message. We'll now spend our remaining time revealing how God did not stop writing history with the completion of the Bible. He is continuing the Story even today – and we are involved!

Remember, the central point in this chapter is that – from the perspective of a Christian worldview - *all of history is His-story*. Not only did God write the story, but He is involved intimately in the process of the entire "production". God doesn't do everything on His own, making all things happen by Himself. He employs us in the process. That's what we mean when we say that God uses *means*. We are the *means* through which God accomplishes His purposes. This perspective should make history come alive to us as we recognize that He not only *can* but *will* work in and through us to do extraordinary things when we put our trust in Him.

With that as our introduction, let's look at how the Author of His-story worked through His people in the founding of America, which in itself is considered to be a miracle by many. Keep in mind that the emphasis is not to be on America, but on how God can work in and through all His people everywhere when we put Him first in our lives, trusting Him to lead us and fight our battles ahead of us.

Divine Providence at Work in Early America

Though America is not specifically mentioned in the Bible, are there examples in history of His active work in our country that reveal powerful and miraculous interventions on behalf of His people similar to those we see toward Israel in the Bible?

The answer, as you'll see from the following examples, is absolutely!

The point is that God is involved in our lives. HE is our Strength, our Provider, our Comfort, our Guiding Light, and so much more. These descriptive words are not simply random combinations of letters on a page, they define a portion of who He is and what He does. He moves within us and among us.

The Founding Fathers called this working of God "Divine Providence". Now, think about that word. It's root comes from the word *provide*.

We see a clear example of this reference to God in the Declaration of Independence, when it says: "…with a firm reliance on the protection of *Divine Providence*, we mutually pledge to each other our lives, our fortunes and our sacred honor." They were willing to bet their lives on this God of the Bible!

> ## Pause and Consider
>
> **Key Principle: The God of the Bible is Intimately Involved the Lives of His People**
>
> **Psalm 145:18-20a states:**
>
> *"The Lord is near to all who call upon Him, To all who call upon Him in truth.*
>
> *He will fulfill the desire of those who fear Him; He also will hear their cry and save them.*

A quote from one of the pages of the diary of George Washington says: "By the miraculous care of Providence that protected me beyond all human expectations, I had four bullets through my coat, and two horses shot under me, and yet escaped unhurt."[28]

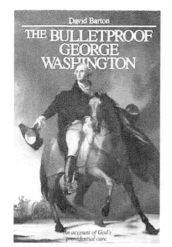

The following is an excerpt from David Barton's book titled "The Bulletproof George Washington" which gives the full story of the battle described below and it should be noted that this is a historically verified account which had been a part of American history textbooks until the early 1900's. It tells the story of what happened during the French and Indian War at **The Battle of Monongahela**.[29]

Washington was only a 23 year-old colonel at the time of the battle. Fifteen years after the battle, the chieftain of the Indians Washington had fought, personally sought him out and gave this account to Washington of what had happened during the battle: He said: *"I am chief and ruler over my tribes and I have traveled a long and weary path that I might see the young warrior of the great battle. It was on the day when the white man's blood mixed with the streams of our forest that I first beheld this chief [Washington]...I called to my young men and said... Quick, let your aim be certain, and he dies. Our rifles were leveled. Rifles which, but for him, knew not how to miss. 'Twas all in vain, though, a power mightier far than we, shielded him.*

I am come to pay homage to the man who is the particular favorite of Heaven, and who can never die in battle. The Great Spirit protects this man, guides his destinies. A people yet unborn will hail him as the founder of a mighty empire."

At this battle, Washington had 2 horses shot out from under him and 4 musket balls pass through his coat. He wrote this, he said: "Death, was leveling my companions on every side of me, but by the all-powerful dispensations of Providence (of God), I have been protected.

As we see from this example, God was intimately involved in America's early history.

And an even greater example follows.

New England Stood Still and Saw the Salvation of the Lord!

In the book *"The American Covenant, the Untold Story"*, by Marshall Foster and Mary-Elaine Swanson, the authors relate this amazing account: [30]

In 1746, in retaliation for the American colonist's participation in the capture of the town of Louisburg in Nova Scotia, the French sent ½ of their Navy to America under the command of the Duc d'Anville' to "lay waste the whole seacoast from Nova Scotia to Georgia".[31] In other words, to wipe out the American Colonies.

---

[28] July 18 1755, The Writings of George Washington, vol 1, page 752
[29] The Bulletproof George Washington", available at Wallbuilders.com
[30] "The American Covenant, the Untold Story", Marshall Foster and Mary-Elaine Swanson (The Mayflower Institute, 1983) p-39-42
[31] George M. Wrong, The Conquest of New France (New Haven: University Press, 1918), pp. 82-91

Even when rumors reached the colonists, they were not initially worried because they understood the British fleet – which owned the seas at that time - would prevent the French Armada from leaving the shores of France. However, unknown to the colonists, the French eluded the British navy and slipped out to sea.

The Reverend Thomas Prince, pastor of the South Church of Boston, later preached a Sermon on God's miraculous delivery of the colonies. He wrote: "While we knew nothing of danger, God beheld it, and was working Salvation for us. And when we had no one to help in America, He even prevented our Friends in Europe from coming to our aid; so that we might see that our Salvation was His Work, and His work alone, and that the Glory belongs entirely to Him."[32]

Having eluded the British, though, the proud French fleet "of about 70 ships" put to sea on June 20, 1746. As the vessels crossed the Atlantic, heading for Halifax, they were delayed at first in a prolonged calm and

Old South Church,

then encountered storms in which several ships were disabled by lightning. Pestilence broke out; then the entire fleet was scattered to the four winds by tremendous storms. By this means, "they were...so dispersed in the midst of the Ocean that by Aug. 26, they counted only 53 Ships of the original 70...."[33] On Sept. 2, they encountered another violent storm and lost several more vessels.

When the Duc d'Anville's ship finally reached Halifax he fully expected to rendezvous with other French ships sent from the West Indies to meet him. The West Indies Squadron had indeed been there, but discouraged by the long delay of d'Anville's fleet, they had given up and left!

During all this, what had the New England colonists been doing? Another New England pastor, Rev. Jonathan French, writes that as soon as the French vessels were sighted off the coast, the people were ``filled with dread. The streets filled with men, marching for the defense of the

sea ports. And the distresses of women and children, trembling for the event, made deep impressions upon the minds of those who remember these scenes. But never did the religion, for which the country was settled, appear more important, nor prayer more prevalent, than on this occasion. A prayer-hearing God, stretched forth the

Key Principle

God is Our Deliverer

As the Israelites were fleeing from the slavery of Egypt and the army of Pharaoh, Exodus 14:10 states: "As Pharaoh approached, the Israelites looked up, and there were the Egyptians, marching after them. They were terrified and cried out to the Lord."

Then, in verse 13-14, Moses answers them, saying: "Do not be afraid. Stand firm and you will see the deliverance the Lord will bring you today. The Egyptians you see today you will never see again. The Lord will fight for you; you need only to be still."

---

[32] Mr. Prince's Thanksgiving Sermon on the Salvation of God in 1746 (Boston: D. Henchman, 1746) p-27

[33] IBID, P-27

arm of His power; and destroyed that mighty Armada, in a manner almost as extraordinary as the drowning of Pharaoh and his host in the Red Sea."[34]

What happened was this: Shortly after his arrival at Halifax, the Duc d'Anville was so appalled at the loss of the major part of his fleet and "finding his few Ships so shattered, so many men dead, so many sickly, and no more of his Fleet had come in; he sunk into deep discouragement, and Sept. 15 died; but in such a condition, it was generally thought he poisoned himself, and thus, was buried without Ceremony."[35] More ships finally limped into port, but many of the men on board were ill and their food supplies were fast running out. The commander who took d'Anville's place committed suicide only days after their arrival by falling on his own sword. The third in command ordered the men ashore to recruit French and Indians who lived ashore, so that they could proceed on their planned attack on Annapolis. But before they could leave Halifax, up to 3,000 more men died of a pestilence.

Finally, the fleet's new commander, La Jonquiere, set sail on October 13, 1746 intending to attack Annapolis. He was probably unaware of the fact that on October 6, the New England colonies had set aside October 16 as a day of Fasting and Prayer for their deliverance.

Rev. French describes the events that followed: He says: "On this great emergency and day of darkness and doubtful expectation, the 16th of October was observed as a day of FASTING AND PRAYER throughout the Province. And, wonderful to relate, that very night God sent upon them a more dreadful storm than either of the former ones and completed their destruction. Some capsized, some floundered, and a remnant only of this miserable fleet returned to France to carry the news; thus, he said: NEW ENGLAND STOOD STILL, AND SAW THE SALVATION OF GOD."[36] (See Exodus 14:13)

In just 4 months, God destroyed nearly half the French navy without the Americans lifting a finger.

They were simply united in prayer.

A wonderful story, isn't it? Isn't it sad it is not in our history books any longer. And there are many inspiring examples like this can be uncovered with just a little investigation. Even up to World War II we have chilling examples of how God worked supernaturally for the sake of America; and how He used the U.S. and its allies to rescue the world!

----

[34] IBID, p-28

[35] Reverend Jonathon French, Thanksgiving Sermon, Nov. 29, 1798 quoted in Hall, Christian History of the American Revolution, p-51

[36] IBID

Lesson 7 Study Questions

1. Had you ever heard the account of George Washington at the Battle of Monongahela? _____ What was

   your impression? _____

   _____

2. This account was available in textbooks in America's schools until the late 1800's. Why do you think it is not

   included any longer? _____

3. From the segment "New England Stood Still and Watched the Salvation of God", what observations or

   comments do you have? _____

   _____

4. List 4 few similarities between this account and the biblical account of the Israelites fleeing Egypt in Exodus
   14:10-14
   1) _____

   2) _____

   3) _____

   4) _____

5. If God can deliver nations as He has Israel and America, can He deliver you through trials? _____ Read
   Jeremiah 32:27, 1 Peter 4:12-13, Deuteronomy 31:6, Proverbs 3:5-6, Isaiah 41:10, John 14:26-27, Matthew
   6:25-27.
   From these Scriptures, what advice does the Bible give us for navigating through our trials?

   _____

   _____

   _____

   _____

6. Based upon the scriptures listed above, how does the God of Christianity respond when His children are in
   trouble?

   _____

   _____

   _____

   _____

7.   Read Psalm 2. Compare the statements of God in this Psalm to the account of the French Armada and its

foiled attempt to wipe-out the American colonies. Name 4 similarities.

1)_____

2)_____

3)_____

4)_____

_____

Lesson 8 - God is Involved in all History, Part 2

What does this mean to us today?

It means History is important to God. It is a record of what He has done as He accomplishes the Grand Plan that He began before the Garden and He's still working and putting into play today. And until He drops the curtain, the plot is still being developed. And we have parts to play – influencing the world around us for the glory of God.

But unfortunately, history is being aggressively re-written by the enemies of God!

Edward Gibbons, who is considered to be a "renowned" historian wrote: "History is merely the recounting of the crimes of the [evolving] human species". He says: "We learn from history that we have nothing to learn from history."

This, unfortunately, reflects a common philosophy of history that many hold today. It's called the "Who Cares" philosophy.

Edward Gibbons

Marshall Foster, author of *The American Covenant, the Untold Story*, writes:

"Many Christians have subconsciously adopted this 'who cares' view of history. They de-emphasize their importance (as Christians) in a God-ordained historical chain of Christianity and see themselves simply as individuals God has plucked out of an evil world who are now just awaiting heaven. Their sense of responsibility for the past and their hope and planning for the building of the future are lost in the 'now generation' where they are called to focus on 'self-improvement'. Their greatest emphasis is worshipping God in their own life, (now, there's nothing wrong with that – we're all supposed to be worshippers of God in our own lives) but what about the 2nd Great Commandment - *Love your neighbor as yourselves?* Isn't that how we prove our love for God? By loving those that often seem unlovable?

This "Who Cares" View of history is really no different than Deism.

What's Deism?

Deism is the belief that the universe was created by a "god", but that this god left man alone from that point on. In short, they say that God does NOT intervene in the affairs of man.

Today's schools often point to Ben Franklin as a Deist, which he was for most of his life ---until the Revolutionary War. Then, like for many of us, it took a crisis to bring Him to that point when he finally recognized that God does intervene on our behalf when our cause is righteous, and we cry out for His help!

Benjamin Franklin and the Continental Congress

The following is a quote from Benjamin Franklin when he was near the end of his life, shortly after the colonists had won their fight for independence from Great Britain. He is addressing the 55 members of the Continental Congress who had been given the task of writing a new Constitution to unite the 13 colonies. Here is the context.

The year is 1787. The delegates had reached a stalemate and were about to give up in this attempt to come up with a constitution. Some had already departed for their home state when the elder statesman of all at age 81, Ben Franklin, stood and spoke these words:

 "The small progress we have made after 4 or five weeks of close attendance & continual reasonings with each other - (without coming to any major agreements) - is a melancholy proof of the imperfection of the Human Understanding.

We indeed seem to feel our own want (need) of political wisdom, since we have been running about in search of it. We have gone back to ancient history for models of Government, and examined the different forms of those Republics ... And we have viewed Modern States all round Europe, but find none of their Constitutions suitable to our circumstances.[37]

In this situation of this Assembly, groping as it were in the dark to find political truth, and scarce able to distinguish it when presented to us, ...how has it happened, Sir, that we have not hitherto once thought of humbly applying to the Father of Lights to illuminate our understandings?

In the beginning of the Contest with G. Britain, when we were sensible of danger, we had daily prayer in this room for the Divine protection. Our prayers, Sir, were heard and they were graciously answered. [...does that sound like a Deist?]

All of us who were engaged in the struggle must have observed frequent instances of a Superintending Providence in our favor (miracles by the hand of God). To that kind Providence we owe this happy opportunity of consulting in peace on the means of establishing our future national felicity (our happiness) And have we now forgotten that powerful Friend? or do we imagine that we no longer need His assistance?"

"I have lived, Sir, a long time and the longer I live, the more convincing proofs I see of this truth -- that God governs in the affairs of men. And if a sparrow cannot fall to the ground without His notice, is it probable that an empire can rise without His aid? We have been assured, Sir, in the Sacred Writings (in

---

[37] https://wallbuilders.com/franklins-appeal-prayer-constitutional-convention/

the Bible) that "except the Lord build they labor in vain that build it." I firmly believe this; [now THAT is a Christian worldview!] He continues: "and I also believe that without His concurring aid we shall succeed in this political building no better than the Builders of Babel".[38]

Franklin then made a motion that a pastor be appointed and salaried to begin every session of Congress with prayer. Soon afterward, according to New Jersey delegate Jonathon Dayton, the congress adjourned for 3 days and went as a group from church to church hearing one sermon after another - addressing the very situations they had been arguing over!

When they returned, Dayton stated that "every unfriendly feeling had been expelled and a spirit of conciliation had been cultivated." Within a few short weeks, our Constitution, now known as the greatest governing document in history, was completed. Why? Because this ex-Deist urged everyone to pray to the God of the Bible.

There are No Accidents in History

America was no accident! God kept it hidden from civilized man for 5,000 years, and then created a "perfect storm" of people and circumstances that brought the Pilgrims and Puritans to America and established a new nation – under God - based upon the principles taken from the Bible.

To reiterate, we are here at this moment in time, not as accidental appearances upon the scene of history; but as chosen, unique, instruments of God's providential hand, called to accomplish very specific tasks which will prepare the next generation of the "chosen and called" for their task. We're a link in the chain, and our responsibility is to grab that chain, learn of its Maker, know how to apply His principles in our lives, and pass that knowledge on to the next generation. We must not let it be forgotten. It is a great, high-calling!

In summary:

> 1. We hold the supernatural all-powerful WORD of God in our hands. It is reliable, true, and trustworthy. You can bet your life on it!
>
> 2. God is still working His plan. He judges nations and He blesses nations according to their obedience to His laws
>
> 3. The biblical worldview sees history as a vast series of meaningful events which God orchestrates for His glory and purpose. The Bible records verifiable history that shows God is in control of all things and that He cares for His people. This is our hope-filled reality.

---

[38] Max Farrand, The Records of the Federal Convention of 1787 (New Haven: Yale University Press, 1911), Vol. I, pp. 450-452, from James Madison's Notes on the Convention for June 28, 1787.Chapter ENDNOTES

Lesson 8 Study Questions

1. From the historical accounts of Washington and the Battle of Monongahela, the French Armada's attempt to destroy the colonies, and Ben Franklin's speech at the Constitutional Convention, state 3 principles dealing with God's involvement in America's history?

   1)_____

   2)_____

   3)_____

2. Go online and read the Declaration of Independence. (http://www.ushistory.org/declaration/document/) and answer the following:
   1. How many times is "God" – or names representing God – referenced? Give those names.

   _____

   _____

3. List the main reason (stated in the 2nd paragraph) why the American Colonies believed they had a natural

   right to break away from the rule of the King of England. _____

   _____

4. According to the Signers of the Declaration, what basic God-given rights was the King violating, and how important is each?

   1) L_ _ _ . See Leviticus 24:17, Psalm 139:13-16, John 10:10.

   This right is fundamental because _____

   _____

   2) L _ _ _ _ _ _ . See Luke 4:18, 1 Tim. 1:10 (references kidnappers/men stealers/slave-traders). This right

   is fundamental because _____

   _____

   3) The Pursuit of H_____. See Psalm 16:11, Psalm 37:4, Psalm 73:25–26, Matthew 13:44, John

   15:11.

   This right is fundamental because _____

   _____

   Scriptures for additional study: See Isaiah 33:22; Ezra 7:24; Deuteronomy 17:6; Exodus 18:21.

Recommended Books:

- "Evidence That Demands a Verdict" by Josh Mcdowell
- "The Light and the Glory" by Peter Marshall
- "The American Covenant" by Marshall Foster (out of print, but used copies can be found on Amazon.com)
- "Our Godly Heritage", by David Barton (Wallbuilders.com)

Subject Three: The Christian Worldview of Theology

Lesson 1 – Who Cares About Theology?

Why Does Our Theology Matter?

Many people today, when reading the title of this chapter, might think: *Who cares about theology? It sounds boring. How can studying theology help me?* With this in mind, let's address that question from the start.

When a non-Christian wants to know something about Christianity, he most likely will decide on one or more churches to check out to satisfy his curiosity. Most people will choose one of the large and (possibly) well-attended churches in their neighborhood.

Why was Gutenberg's printing press so revolutionary?

First, prior to Gutenberg's press there were very few complete Bibles available anywhere, and most of the Bibles in Europe were chained to the pulpits in the Roman Catholic churches. Second, most common people couldn't read at all. And third, the vast majority of all Bibles available were only in Latin, a language that most European commoners could not even understand. So, once this new type of printing press was made available across Europe, thousands of Bibles, tracts, and portions of the Bible began to be dispersed among the common people in the language of their own tongue and at a price they could afford. The people then began learning to read, and within just a hundred years it was said that the common peasants knew the Bible better than their own lords. This caused entire congregations to be raised up with a burning desire to live under the rule of Scripture, not under kings or tyrants. Miraculously at the same time, God opened up the New World so these newly literate Christians could virtually begin a new civilization. They went on to established America, based on the principles of the Bible. Civilization experienced a leap in progress as we've never seen in all of history. We called that the 5,000 year leap. All of this came about because the Bible provides the most clear and defined theology of any faith the world has ever known.

For example, consider one such young man – we'll call him Justin – who was curious about Christianity and chose to visit a large church that he passed by every day on his way to work. It was the oldest and largest church in the city. Having been established in the mid-1800s, it looked impressive and was a landmark in the community. As he was walking around, he was fascinated by one of the many stained-glass windows in the sanctuary. Etched into the glass was a representation of the famous Gutenberg printing press which had spawned the printing of thousands of Bibles at prices even a common peasant could afford. This one invention is considered to be a monumental event that literally changed the world. And, as we learned in our earlier classes, this is what brought about a revolution in the thinking of the common people of the world. And here we see this church, established over 150 years ago, commemorating the Gutenberg printing press for this very reason.

As Justin continued to peruse the church, a bulletin board grabbed his attention. It featured an image of Che Guevara. To a lot of young people today, Che Guevara seems to be a pretty cool guy. We see many wearing t-shirts, hoodies, hats, and jackets proudly bearing his image. After all, Che Guevara was a revolutionary, and everybody wants to be revolutionary when they're young. But who was this man? Here is a quote from him:

"Hatred as an element of struggle, unbending hatred for the enemy, which pushes a human being beyond his natural limitations, making him into an effective, violent, selective, and cold-blooded killing machine. This is what our soldiers must become."

Che Guevara was cold-blooded. He was a murderer of thousands of people. Justin asked himself – as should we – *"What's he doing on a bulletin board in church?"* He was featured on this bulletin board because the youth of the church were promoting socialism – a very dangerous and deadly political worldview (which we will address a bit later).

As Justin continued walking through the church, he stumbled upon yet another bulletin board that he didn't expect. Decorated with a large rainbow in the background, it read: "Celebrate family and friends and love and life and equality and respect and pride and joy. Celebrate Gay pride!" This proclamation was being boldly announced in what used to be one of the most fundamentally sound churches in America in the middle of the 1800's.

That is what happens when we don't define our worldview. When we don't really know what we believe. Therefore, it is vital that we know our theology, … our fundamental beliefs about the God we claim to worship. We must be certain of what we believe about this most important topic of life. And that is, *who is God, and what does he require of us*? Because if we get that wrong, it will bring disastrous results to our lives.

Defining THEOLOGY

Theology is a composite of two Greek words: "Theos" which means "God", and "logia" (from the word *logos* from which we get our word *logic*), meaning "word, discourse, reasoning", or simply, "the study of". Thus, theology is *the study of God*. Why do we study theology? Because it's the only way that we can answer the following three questions:

1. *Why am I here?* Does my life have a purpose? Statistics reveal that more than half of all people surveyed say that they don't know their purpose in life, and further studies confirm that living life without a purpose is not healthy – neither physically or mentally. As Christians, it is important that we know what our purpose is. If we don't study the Word of our Creator, then we'll never know why He created us. In other words, if we don't study theology, we'll never know why we're here.

2. *What does God require of me?* Romans 1:18-21 and 28-32 clearly states that God has placed the knowledge of Himself – that He is the righteous judge of mankind – in every human heart, so we are without excuse if we ignore Him and go our own way. Every man, as an image-bearer, is born with knowledge of God's moral law (Romans 2:14-15); thus, God requires every man to keep His moral law.

3. *What does God provide for me?* In other words, what does this God that you offer me promise for me if I commit to following Him? Or, to put it crassly: *what's in it for me?*

> ### Pause and Consider
>
> **Which do we follow, our heart or our minds? Do Christians "check our brains in" at the church door?**
>
> Proverbs 23:7 states: "For as [a man] thinks in his heart, so is he." Many today confuse the heart with the mind; but over 90% of the times the Bible mentions the heart, it is referring to the innermost being of man (the soul) which encompasses, first of all, the thoughts and beliefs of his mind followed by his morality and emotions. The verse above clearly states that our intellectual thoughts provide the steering mechanism for our entire soul. This implies that we are not to be controlled by our emotions.

Answers—According to the Christian Worldview

The Bible provides answers to these critically important questions.

First, *we are here to worship Him*. We were created to worship God. Not just with our voice, when we attend church on Sunday or a mid-week service, but in every way, in all of life. The Westminster Confession states that our purpose is *to glorify God and enjoy Him forever*. This requires that we learn of Him.

Secondly, *what does God require?* Very simply, God requires our obedience. Once we come to Him and receive His mercy and grace, then we must take a step in His direction, learning and putting into practice His commands.

Lastly, *what does God provide?* He provides *forgiveness*. There have been many, many surveys asking average people, *what is the thing that eats at you the most?* The most frequent response is, "I feel ashamed. I feel I need forgiveness". Everybody needs forgiveness for all we do that is wrong. Because God came as a man and laid down His life as a ransom and substitute for us, we can be forgiven of all our sins – past, present, and future. Even as we continue to make mistakes, hurt others, or fail in our attempts to do right, we can become clean and forgiven as we daily come before God and confess these sins to Him (1 John 1:9). In addition, He becomes our Provider – promising to supply our daily needs. In Matthew 6:25-33, He promises that as He provides for the birds, so much more will He provide for us. And that brings us peace, love, and hope. We receive salvation and are promised eternal life in His loving kingdom. Christianity is the only worldview that knows such a God as this.

Don't be Deceived

Because the true knowledge of God is vital to life, we can expect Satan to do his best to deceive. As we pursue theology, it is important that we remember our key verse: 2 Corinthians 10:4-5: "The weapons of our warfare are not carnal" (worldly) but they are mighty in God for pulling down strongholds." A stronghold can be as simple as a **bad idea.** Believing bad ideas and lies can chain you down and deprive you of your freedom. Verse five continues: "Casting down (demolishing) arguments and every high thing that exalts itself against the knowledge of God and bringing every thought into captivity to the obedience of Christ." We demolish bad ideas. That's what we are called to do.

Beware lest anyone cheat you through philosophy and empty deceit, according to the tradition of men, according to the basic principles of the world, and not according to Christ.   *Colossians 2:8 (NKJV)*

As we suggest a few bad ideas that we are to battle in today's culture, remember that bad ideas have penalties attached to them. God set laws in the universe to create order. Without physical laws, life would not exist. Therefore, laws are for our benefit and protection. If we disobey physical laws, there will always be consequences. For the same reason, there are moral laws in place for our protection and to allow for life. And just like the physical laws, if we break a moral law, there will be - there *must* be - consequences. Therefore, every one of the following bad (morally unlawful) ideas has a consequence. (Note: We will expand upon these penalties as we continue through this course)

Some Bad Ideas Promoted in Our Culture
- *Abortion is a right* - Abortion is a bad idea. Obviously, in an abortion the child pays the ultimate price. But the mother will suffer, as well (we'll cover this subject more in the Sociology chapter).
- *Evolution is a scientific fact.* That's a really bad idea that has led to terrible consequences.
- *Same-sex marriage is a right.* Another terribly bad idea that is killing our society today.

- *Men and women are the same.* Many people in western culture have bought into this thought.
- *He who dies with the most toys wins.* This lie, materialism, has captured the lives of many Christians.
- *It takes a village to raise a child.* Hillary Clinton wrote a book with this title. But frankly, it's a bad idea that has resulted in countless broken families.
- *All religions lead to God,* or... *all religions are the same.* All religions are not the same. In this chapter we will demolish that bad idea.
- *Man is essentially good.* Another bad idea that leads to catastrophe, which we will address later.

Interestingly, all these ideas have their roots in theology - or more correctly - false theology. True knowledge of the true God is of utmost importance to every person. Once we know the Truth, we must love it and share it in love. Or rather, we must love Him and share our love of Him. That is the point of theology. And because there is such a huge need for Truth in our world, we need to know how to speak it in all kinds of different ways; to open up our vocabulary so that we may engage the people of the world in a gentle, yet thought-provoking way. Our goal for this entire biblical worldview series is to assist you in that process.

Lesson 1 Study Questions

1. Define "Theology"

    _____

2. Name some of the "gods" that people idolize in today's culture, and what lifestyles these "gods" often lead them into.

    1) _____

    _____

    2) _____

    _____

    3) _____

    _____

    4) _____

    _____

3. Name at least 4 IDEAS that are being hotly debated in our culture today, along with the possible results if those ideas were to be adopted by *everyone* – including those in your family.

    1) _____

    _____

    _____

    2) _____

    _____

    _____

    3) _____

    _____

    _____

    4) _____

    _____

    _____

4. The "gods" we set up in our lives will directly influence our behavior and determine our future. That is why we say that the most important topic of life is: "Who is _ _ _ , and what does He r _ _ _ _ _ _ of us."

5. Everyone, at some time or other, wonders about God. When they take the time to think deeply about this, they ask at least 3 basic questions. Name those questions and the biblical response to each.

   1) W __ __ am I here?   The biblical response: _____

   2) What does God r__ __ __ __ __ __ of me?   The biblical response: _____

   3) What does God p __ __ __ __ __ __ for me? The biblical response: _____

   NOTES:

   _____

   _____

   _____

   _____

   _____

   _____

Lesson 2 – Arguments for Belief, Part 1

The Basic Questions Everyone Has About God

> **The Outline for this Chapter**
>
> A. How can we know there *is* a God?
> B. How can we *know* God?
> C. What is God like? What are His characteristics?
> D. How does the Christian God compare to all other gods?

A. **How do we know there is a God?**

Before we begin to address this subject, let us begin by stressing this point*:*

Christians should not get caught up in attempting to prove the existence of God to anyone!

Why? Because never in all of Scripture do we find any attempt to *prove* that God exists. God does not need to prove to any man that He exists because He has written that knowledge onto every man's heart (Romans 1:18-20); thus, no one has an excuse for denying that God exists.

Nevertheless, we still have a responsibility to intelligently defend our Christian worldview and to cast down arguments and every high thing (e.g., naturalism, atheism) that exalts itself against the knowledge of God. To that end, evidences and logical argumentation can be very useful for defending our worldview, and for refuting opposing worldviews, such as Naturalism.

In a moment we'll look at three compelling arguments in support of the biblical worldview of science. But consider that quite often we hear that science stands in opposition to the Bible. But we have forgotten that the sciences were actually developed out of biblical theology. Let's take a look at a few statements from several of the most prominent names in the history of modern science.

Pause and Consider

Can the Existence of God be Proven?

The book of Genesis famously begins by stating, "In the beginning God." The Bible simply assumes the existence of God, it never argues for His existence, nor does it imply that we should attempt to do so. The Bible tells us that God has made Himself known to every man (Romans 1:18-20); thus, why argue something that every man already knows? Moreover, no amount of evidence or logical argumentation will ever convince the fool who says in his heart, "There is no God." Jesus said, "If they do not hear Moses and the prophets, neither will they be persuaded though one rise from the dead." Even if the fool witnessed a dead person rise from the grave, he would not be convinced by such evidence!

The unbeliever doesn't have an information problem, he has a moral problem. Thus, the conscience is the greatest "proof" of God's existence, as it points man back to the knowledge of a universal lawgiver (i.e., God) who will judge all men according to the moral law that He has written upon the heart of man (Romans 2:14-16).

Testimonies from Scientists

We are given life on this Earth to learn our purpose and our place in the Master Creator's universe, and this involves investigation and observation of the world He created for us in order that we might know Him better. The sciences were initially developed with this motive in mind as evidenced by the following quotations…

"There are two books laid before us to study, to prevent our falling into error: first, the volume of the Scriptures, which reveal the will of God; then the volume of the Creatures, which express His power."
   -Francis Bacon, Father of the Scientific Method

"Atheism is so senseless. When I look at the solar system, I see the earth at the right distance from the sun to receive the proper amounts of heat and light. This did not happen by chance."
   - Isaac Newton, Physics, Mathematics

"O God, I am thinking Thy thoughts after Thee."
   -Johannes Kepler, Astronomy

"The more I study nature, the more I stand amazed at the work of the Creator."
   -Louis Pasteur, Medicine

Johannes Kepler

"Finite man cannot begin to comprehend an omnipresent, omniscient, omnipotent, and infinite God … I find it best to accept God through faith, as an intelligent will, perfect in goodness and wisdom, revealing Himself through His creation."
   -Werner Von Braun, Rocket Science

"It is His work, and He alone carried me thus far through all my trials and enabled me to triumph over the obstacles, physical and moral, which opposed me. 'Not unto us, not unto us, by to Thy name, O Lord, be all the praise.'"
   -Samuel Morse, Inventor

Robert Boyle

"When with bold telescopes I survey the old and newly discovered stars and planets when with excellent microscopes I discern the inimitable subtility of nature's curious workmanship; and when, in a word, by the help of anatomical knives, and the light of chemical furnaces, I study the book of nature I find myself oftentimes reduced to exclaim with the Psalmist, 'How manifold are Thy works, O Lord! In wisdom hast Thou made them all!'"
   -Robert Boyle, Chemistry

Evidences for God in our universe
<u>Three Arguments in Support of the Biblical Worldview</u>

1. The Cosmological Argument (or the argument from the cosmos):

Everything has a beginning, therefore there must be a Beginner.

In the early 1900s, Albert Einstein developed his theory of relativity which led to the conclusion (the Big Bang) that the universe must have had a beginning at a singular moment in time. This created a problem for Einstein because it didn't fit into his worldview. This new cosmological theory revealed the necessity for a beginning and the presence of a superior reasoning power. So, he spent months trying to disprove his own theory, but to no avail.[39] Another scientist of Einstein's day, Nobel prizewinner Arthur Compton, said, "For myself, faith begins with the realization that a Supreme Intelligence brought the universe into being and created man. It is not difficult for me to have this faith, for it is incontrovertible that where there is a plan there is intelligence. An orderly, unfolding universe testifies to the truth of the most majestic statement ever uttered, '*In the beginning, God'*."

Arthur Compton

The question is, what caused the universe to come into existence? The Big Bang theory that is predominant in modern science states that all time, matter, and energy came into being at a finite time in the past. The obvious implication is that none of these factors were present beforehand. This points to a reality beyond the physical realm, and that reality requires certain characteristics: 1) It must be eternal (not bound by time constraints); 2) It must be immaterial (not bound by material constraints); 3) It must be omnipotent, or supernaturally powerful (not bound by energy constraints). Therefore, even the Big Bang theory points to a Christian view of cosmology – an eternal, immaterial, omnipotent reality. However, the Christian worldview doesn't stop there. This eternal, immaterial, omnipotent reality is also *personal* (more will be said about this when we discuss the teleological argument below). Thus, the real question is not *what* caused the universe to come into existence; rather, *Who* caused the universe to come into existence? Answer: The initial *cause* of the universe was God. He is the Beginner.

DNA – The information for life.
Information requires an

The Crux of the Argument – Where Did Life Come From?

Every theory, scientific or philosophical, has a starting point that cannot be proven (if it could be proven, then it would not be the starting point). This starting point is called an *axiom*. An axiom, by definition cannot be proven, but it must be *defensible*.

All evolutionary theory is grounded upon the fundamental **axiom** (first principle) that *all of life came from non-life*. However, there is absolutely no evidence in all the universe of life coming from non-life. The mere thought seems absurd to the unbiased mind. The Christian worldview is grounded upon the fundamental axiom that *all life comes from life*… "In the beginning God…". We find billions of supporting evidences for our axiom occurring every day. Since no human was present at

---

[39] Douglas, A. Vihert, "Forty Minutes with Einstein," in Journal of the Royal Astronomical Society of Canada. (1956), p.100

the beginning to confirm either axiom, we must ask, *which worldview requires <u>blind</u> faith, and which is supported by reasonable faith that is grounded in reality?*

Lesson 2 Study Questions

1. We have stated that Christians should not get caught up in arguments trying to prove the existence of God. Give 2 reasons why not, as stated in this day's study.

    1) _____

        _____

    2) _____

        _____

2. In your own words, give a brief summary of the Cosmological Argument

    _____

    _____

    _____

    _____

3. Define *axiom*, and why is this principle important when discussing biblical creation with an evolutionist?

    _____

    _____

    _____

    _____

4. Explain the difference between the axioms of the biblical creation model versus the evolutionary model.

    _____

    _____

    _____

    _____

Lesson 3 – Arguments for Belief, Part 2

Three Arguments in Support of the Biblical Worldview (continued)

2. **The Teleological Argument.**

Every design requires a designer.

Furthermore, every design is created with a specific **purpose** in the designer's mind. In fact, the word "teleological" comes from the Greek word "telos", which means *the aim, the purpose*. Thus, the teleological argument is not only meant to draw our attention to the abundant design we see in the universe, but more importantly, to explain the meaning and significance of the universe and of mankind. The teleological argument is intended to answer questions such as: Why was the universe created -- for what purpose? What is the significance of man? What was he designed for?

It seems that everywhere we look in the natural world – whether at stars or planets, trees or human beings – we find abounding evidence of design, especially in the last 100 years with the development of high-powered telescopes and microscopes.

Evidence of Design: The Fine-Tuning of the Universe, Solar System, and Earth

The Finely Tuned Parameters of the *Universe*

Barrow & Tipler, in their book, <u>The Anthropic Cosmological Principle</u>,[40] admit that "there exist a number of unlikely coincidences between numbers of enormous magnitude that... appear essential to the existence of carbon-based observers in the Universe." The author's list includes 16 "wildly unlikely combinations" that are "coincidentally-perfect" in their relationship between the subatomic particles upon which our universe is built. Here are a few:

- There is the same number of electrons as protons to a standard deviation of one in ten to the thirty-seventh power, that is, 1 in 10,000,000,000,000,000,000,000,000,000,000,000,000 (37 zeros).
- The 1-to-1 electron to proton ratio throughout the universe yields our electrically neutral universe
- All fundamental particles of the same kind are *identical* (protons, electrons, photons, etc.)
- The electron and the massively greater proton have exactly equivalent opposite charges
- The electron to proton mass ratio (1 to 1,836) is *perfect* for forming molecules.

The Finely Tuned Parameters of the *Solar System*

The authors continue by presenting another 15 equally highly unlikely "coincidences" that allow for the existence of our solar system.

- Our Sun is positioned just far enough from the Milky Way's center in a galactic *Goldilocks zone* (not too hot, not too cold!) to allow for the low radiation required for life
- Earth's orbit is a nearly circular orbit around the Sun, providing a stability in a range of vital factors

40 The Anthropic Cosmological Principle John D. Barrow, Frank J. Tipler Oxford University Press, 1988

- Earth's orbit has a low inclination (its axis, tilted at 23.5 degrees) keeping its temperatures within a range permitting diverse ecosystems
- Earth's axial tilt is within a range that helps to stabilize our planet's climate. [Note: Our seasons change because Earth tilts on its axis, and the angle of tilt causes the northern and southern hemisphere to trade places throughout the year in receiving the sun's light and warmth most directly. If the angle was altered by only 3 degrees, the result would be catastrophic].
- The Moon's mass helps stabilize the Earth's tilt on its axis, which provides for the diversity of alternating seasons.
- The Moon's distance from the Earth provides tides to keep life thriving in our oceans.
- The Earth's distance from the Sun provides for great quantities of life and climate-sustaining liquid water. If the earth moved just a fraction closer or further from the sun, life would not be possible.

The Finely Tuned Parameters of the *Earth*

As if that wasn't enough, Barrow & Tipler add over 18 factors that are each finely-balanced to allow life on earth. Their list includes, but is not limited to:

- The Earth's surface gravity strength prevents the atmosphere from rapidly losing water to space.
- The Earth's just-right ozone layer filters out ultraviolet radiation and mitigates immense temperature swings.
- The Earth's spin rate on its axis provides for a range of day and nighttime temperatures that allow life to thrive.
- The atmosphere's composition (20% oxygen, etc.) provides for life's high energy requirements.
- If Earth's oxygen content were higher, forest fires would worsen; at 30%-40% the atmosphere could ignite.
- The atmosphere's pressure enables our lungs to function and water to evaporate at an optimal rate to support life.
- The atmosphere's transparency perfectly allows an optimal range of life-giving solar radiation to reach the surface.

An example of Fine-Tuning: Gravity

The force of gravity has been found to be tuned to the unfathomably perfect strength of one part in 10^{39} (1,000,000,000,000,000,000,000,000,000,000,000,000,000). This degree of perfection is required for the existence of stars that are capable of supporting life, such as our own sun. The mathematical probability of this occurring *by random chance* has been estimated to be 0.00000 00000 00000 00000 00000 00000 00000 00001. It would seem that only a fool would bet his life that there is no God.

According to Prominent Scientists –

Our sun is far from typical:

Guillermo Gonzalez (*American* astrophysicist) "While most textbooks discuss the Sun as if it were a typical star, it is a more massive star than 90 percent of the stars in the Milky Way. The Sun is anomalous in other ways, including its composition, brightness variation, and Galactic orbit. It can be plausibly argued that each of these characteristics must be exactly as it is for advanced life to exist on Earth."[41]

There are No blind forces working in the Universe:

Fred Hoyle *(British astrophysicist)*: "A common sense interpretation of the facts suggests that a super-intellect has monkeyed with physics, as well as with chemistry and biology, and that there are no blind forces worth speaking about in nature. The numbers one calculates from the facts seem to me so overwhelming as to put this conclusion almost beyond question."[42]

Paul Davies *(British astrophysicist)*: "There is for me powerful evidence that there is something going on behind it all ...It seems as though somebody has fine-tuned nature's numbers to create the Universe....The impression of design is overwhelming".[43]

Miraculous Complexity

George Ellis *(British astrophysicist)*: "Amazing fine tuning occurs in the laws that make this [complexity] possible. Realization of the complexity of what is accomplished makes it very difficult not to use the word 'miraculous' without taking a stand as to the ontological status of the word."[44]

Ed Harrison *(British cosmologist)*: "The fine tuning of the universe provides prima facie evidence of deistic design. Take your choice: blind chance that requires   multitudes of universes or design that requires only one.... Many scientists, when they admit their views, incline toward the teleological or design argument."[45]

The evidence for design appears quite overwhelming. It would seem that ignoring or rejecting these "coincidences" might require a far greater amount of faith (in this case, *blind* faith) than it would to follow the evidence to the most logical conclusion. However, we leave the conclusions up to the reader.

[41] Home Alone in the Universe by Guillermo Gonzalez

[42] Hoyle, F. 1982. The Universe: Past and Present Reflections. *Annual Review of Astronomy and Astrophysics*. 20:16.

[43] Davies, P. 1988. The Cosmic Blueprint: New Discoveries in Nature's Creative Ability to Order the Universe. New York: Simon and Schuster, p.203.

[44] Ellis, G.F.R. 1993. The Anthropic Principle: Laws and Environments. The Anthropic Principle, F. Bertola and U.Curi, ed. New York, Cambridge University Press, p. 30.

[45] Harrison, E. 1985. Masks of the Universe. New York, Collier Books, Macmillan, pp. 252, 263.

Lesson 3 Study Questions

1. Summarize the Teleological Argument: _____

   _____

2. Name 3 of the most interesting or persuasive conclusions that may be drawn (in your opinion) from the examples of fine-tuning in the universe, solar system, and earth.

   1)_____

   2)_____

   3)_____

3. In your own words, paraphrase the quotation on fine-tuning that you found to be the most convincing.

   _____

   _____

   _____

4. Read Genesis, chapter 1. Name as many specific items of creation mentioned in this chapter that you can find.

   _____

   _____

5. What can we learn about the characteristics of this Creator/Beginner by looking closely at the wide variety of everything created in Genesis 1? _____

   _____

   _____

6. What is the difference between rational faith and blind faith? Give examples _____

   _____

   _____

   _____

7. The strength of gravity was stated to be fine-tuned at 1 chance in

    1,000,000,000,000,000,000,000,000,000,000,000,000. Do you think that could have happened by coincidence?

    _____ Why? _____

    _____

8. Cars, wristwatches, and radios all have been designed by man. Can you name any living thing in creation

    that is not VASTLY more complicated than cars, wristwatches, or radios? If so, can you name one?

    _____ .

9. Why, then, do many seemingly rational persons believe that living things did NOT come from a designer?

    (see Romans 1: 18-32)

    _____

    _____

    _____

10. Read Psalm 139:13-14. What does this say about the design of Man?

    _____

    _____

    _____

11. How might this knowledge bring comfort and hope to all?

    _____

    _____

    _____

Lesson 4 - Arguments for Belief, Part 3

Three Arguments in Support of the Biblical Worldview (continued)

3. ## The Moral Argument.

The presence of universal moral laws presupposes a universal Law-Giver

All societies testify that there is a moral code built into everyone which is consistent among all ethnicities. This "code" says some things are right and some things are wrong. Whenever we get into discussions over right and wrong, we are actually appealing to a higher law that we assume everyone is aware of, and that this law doesn't change arbitrarily. Just the fact that we argue over what is right or wrong testifies to our innate awareness of a transcendent moral code. In fact, this is the apostle Paul's argument in Romans 2:1, "Therefore you are inexcusable, O man, whoever you are who judge, for in whatever you judge another you condemn yourself; for you who judge practice the same things." Paul's point is that every man makes moral distinctions; every man innately knows when he has been wronged by another. However, if we intuitively know when someone else has wronged us, then we also intuitively know when we have wronged others; thus, we condemn ourselves because we practice the same things. Indeed, Paul goes on to say that it is the conscience of man that bears witness to the fact that God has woven His moral law into the very fabric of mankind (Romans 2:14-15).

Now, man's innate ability to judge between right and wrong implies that there are *universal laws of morality*, and if there are universal laws of morality, then logically there must be a universal Lawgiver who transcends our human nature. Christianity claims that this Lawgiver is God.

Even the most remote tribes who are cut off from civilization observe a moral code of some kind, and very often their moral code is remarkably similar to those of more refined societies. From where does this innate moral knowledge come from? It comes from God, who created man to reflect His moral character as an image-bearer.

As we said earlier, Romans 1:18-21 and 28-32 emphatically states that all men are morally inexcusable because of the knowledge that they are born with; specifically, the knowledge that there is a God who is the righteous Judge of mankind. Additionally, all men are inexcusable because they are born with the knowledge of God's moral law, as Romans 2:14-15 says,

> " *Even Gentiles, who do not have God's written law, show that they know his law when they instinctively obey it, even without having heard it. They demonstrate that God's law is written in their hearts, for their own conscience and thoughts either accuse them or tell them they are doing right..*" (NLT)

In other words, even those who have never read the Bible know God's laws through the general revelation implanted in every human heart. Each of us has a conscience that speaks to us, confirming to us when we do right, and condemning us when we do wrong. We have to work to beat down, or suppress, our conscience; and unfortunately, we have an entire society around us trying to do just that. When a person assents to (is persuaded by and submits to) the proposition that there is no God, the result is a hard, calloused heart.

To conclude then, the moral law comes from an ultimate Lawgiver who is above man. He has made Himself known to all mankind so that they are without excuse, and the conscience of man attests to this truth.

Romans 1:21 (NIV): For although they knew God, they neither glorified him as God nor gave thanks to him, but their thinking became futile and their foolish hearts were darkened.

B. How can we *know* God?

General and Special Revelation:

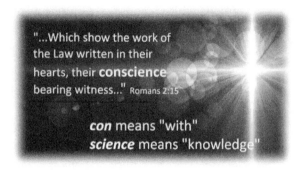

1. **General Revelation**. God has made Himself known to man both through general and special revelation. As we stated earlier, all men are born knowing certain things about God, and this innate knowledge falls under the category of general revelation. All men are born with the knowledge of God's existence; that He is holy and righteous; and that we fall short of His purity and perfection (the word SIN is an old-English archery term that meant "missing the bullseye;" thus, SIN is missing the mark of God's absolute purity and perfection). There is no person born who has an excuse for rejecting the belief that there is a God.

2. **Special Revelation**. God also reveals Himself to men through the Bible, and this is referred to as special revelation. 2 Timothy 3:16 states, "All scripture is given by inspiration of God" (is God-breathed) "and is profitable for teaching, rebuking, correcting, and training in righteousness." 2 Peter says, "His divine power has given to us all things that pertain to life and godliness, through the knowledge of Him who called us by glory and virtue". Our Bible has everything in it to guide us to abundant life and godliness. As we said in the last chapter, the Bible is trustworthy. It is confirmed by archeology, by historical records, and by the works of God in and around us. The scientific statements it makes are always accurate, dependable, and prescient (pre-science, or pre-knowledge - in other words, before we even gathered the knowledge, the Bible told us about it beforehand). It is *other-worldly*. It contains the highest moral standards of all other worldviews, religions, or ideologies. And these principles promise great success to all who embrace them.

This Book of the Law shall not depart from your mouth, but you shall meditate in it day and night, that you may observe to do according to all that is written in it. For then you will make your way prosperous, and then you will have good success. Joshua 1:8 (NKJV)

---

c. What is God Like? What does Special Revelation tell us about God?

We will divide the next section into three simple answers: He is **Ruler**, He is **Righteous**, and He is **Relational**. And later, when we look at the other religions, you'll see that their "god" lacks at least one, two or even three of these characteristics. We point this out to emphasize the huge difference between Christianity and all other worldviews, religions, or ideologies. All religions are *not* the same.

1. God is Ruler. The God of the Christian worldview consists of three persons - Father, Son, and Holy Spirit. He is the everlasting source of all things. He is: Omnipotent, Omniscient, and Omnipresent.

    a. Omnipotent. *Omni* means complete and total. *Potent* means powerful. He is absolutely, totally powerful. All power originates in Him, He is the source of all power. He is the creator and the sustainer of all life, and He is sovereign.

    b. Omniscient. All knowledge originates in the mind of God; His mind is the source of all knowledge. Therefore, any knowledge that you have has been generously revealed to your mind by the mind of God; your fund of knowledge has been loaned to you by the infinite bank of God's mind.

    c. Omnipresent. He is present everywhere at all times. If he wasn't present everywhere at all times someone could hide from him. But we are told in the Bible that we cannot. There is nowhere we can go outside of His presence (Psalm 139:7-12).

2. God is Righteous. What does that mean? He is holy, holy, holy. He is absolutely pure. He is always right, always true, and always good. He is the trustworthy Lawgiver and Judge.

    We know that our God is a God of love, but He is also a God of wrath. He cannot tolerate sin. That is why He sent His son to die for sinners. We have countless examples in the Bible that show God as being a God of wrath toward those who rebelliously flaunt His law. In the book of Jude it says,

> ## Pause and Consider
> ### How can a good God send people to hell?
>
> We live in a culture in which everyone believes that they are inherently deserving of special treatment or privileges (i.e., entitled). The question – *How can a good God send people to hell?* – reflects this type of entitlement mindset by assuming that everyone deserves heaven. But Romans 3:10-12 says, "There is none righteous, no, not one; there is none who seeks after God. They have all turned aside; they have together become unprofitable; there is none who does good, no, not one." Thus, God is not withholding special treatment or privileges (heaven) from those who deserve it, nor is He punishing people (sending them to hell) for something they don't deserve. The wages of sin is death (Romans 6:23). Therefore, the real question is how can a good God allow a single unrighteous, unprofitable, sinful person into heaven? How can a GOOD God **not** punish BAD people? We should not be amazed that God sends wicked people to hell; we should be amazed that He has made a way for wicked people to go to Heaven.

"I want to remind you, though you once knew this, that the Lord, having saved the people out of the land of Egypt, afterward destroyed those who did not believe" (Jude 5)

There is one thing He requires: Faith in Him. "And without faith it is impossible to please God, for whoever would draw near to God must believe that He exists and that He rewards those who seek Him" (Hebrews 11:6). Whoever rejects Him will experience the opposite of His presence. And that should cause one to fear such a rejection. Proverbs 9:10 states, "The fear of the Lord is the beginning of wisdom, the knowledge of the Holy one is understanding." A healthy fear of disobeying the laws of God is good for us all. After all, who would want to be eternally separated from the source of all *love, light, comfort, joy, and peace* – the source of *all good*?

3. God is **Relational**.

The Christian God is a *personal* God. He knows each of us intimately. After all, He "knit us together in our mother's womb" (Psalm 139:13). Scripture says that we are "fearfully and wonderfully made" (Psalm 139:14), and that He knows every hair on our head (Luke 12:7). Now, there are two sides to this coin. On the one hand, this intimate relationship means that He will never leave or forsake any who trust in Him (Hebrews 13:5). He is always with us. The rewards of this deep relationship with God are too numerous to count, and we will enjoy them into eternity as a result of placing our faith in Him. On the other hand, we are each personally responsible to Him for how we live our life (Hebrews 9:27). We are, in the end, only accountable to God, and our rejection of Him will have eternal consequences. It is a fearful thing to fall into the hands of the living God (Hebrews 10:31).

Psalm 51:4:
Against You, You only, have I sinned, And done this evil in Your sight—That You may be found just when You speak, And blameless when You judge.

Pause and Consider

Christianity isn't a religion, it's a relationship?

This phrase bears some consideration because it is widely repeated in Christian circles today and, we believe, has led to a watering-down of the essential message of Christianity. First of all, yes, it's a relationship. Thank God it is. It is the only worldview known to man that promotes a personal relationship with the living God. But it is also a religion, because a religion is essentially a set of ideas and principles that one believes in and lives by. Christianity certainly meets that description. After all, where would we be without God's commands to instruct and guide us? Moreover, James 1:27 tells us that, "Pure and undefiled **religion** before God the Father is this: to visit orphans and widows in their trouble, and to keep oneself unspotted from the world."

Lesson 4 Study Questions

1. Argument #3: The M_____ Argument. This states that "Because the _____ Law transcends (is above) humanity, this universal law requires a universal _____. "

2. Read Romans 2:1-16. What does this passage convey about the universal presence of a "conscience" in every human? (Who put it there? What does the conscience say to everyone? etc.)

   _____

   _____

3. Do you agree with the idea that *everyone knows* certain behaviors - like stealing, lying, cheating, or committing murder - are wrong? Why or why not? _____

   _____

4. The Christian worldview states that God is omnipotent, omniscient, and omnipresent. What would be the result if God was NOT any one of those three attributes?

   _____

   _____

   _____

How Can We Know God?

5. *General Revelation*. He is revealed *generally* to all men through inborn knowledge.

   1) Read Romans 1:18-23. What does this passage say about General Revelation?

   _____

   _____

   _____

6. *Special Revelation*. God is revealed *specifically* in the _____.

   1) Read 2 Timothy 3:16; 2 Peter 1:3; Hebrews 4:12. In your own words, where do the Scriptures come from, and what specific purposes do they perform?

   _____

   _____

   2) What do these passages say about the completeness of the Bible we have, and what does that mean in our complicated lives today? _____

_____

_____

3) What are some results if one chooses to not believe in ALL the words of the Bible? _____

_____

What is the God of the Bible like?

7. God is:

1) R _ _ _ _. Read Psalm 115:3; Prov. 16:9; Romans 8:28. What does this principle mean to you and how important is it?

_____

_____

2) R_ _ _ _ _ _ _ _. Read Psalm 119:137; Deuteronomy 32:4; Psalm 145:17. What does this principle mean to you and how important is it?

_____

_____

_____

3) R_ _ _ _ _ _ _ _ _. Read Gen. 1:18; Malachi 3:17; Matthew 14:14; John 3:16-18. What does this principle mean to you and how important is it?

_____

_____

_____

8. Christianity states that God is Ruler, He is Righteous, and He is Relational. What would be the result if God was NOT any one of those three attributes?

_____

_____

_____

_____

Lesson 5 – Compare & Contrast, Part 1

D. How does the Christian God compare to all the other gods?

First, let's define: What is a *Religion*?

Before we look at some important differences between Christianity and other major world religions, let's define *religion*. In this era of radically differing opinions and behaviors, religion can be best defined as the belief system from which one derives his or her values and moral standards. More simply religion is the set of ideas and principles that one believes in and lives by (one's worldview). These beliefs and ideas are what inform and prompt the decisions we make in our lives. The Bible declares this truth: "as a man thinks in his heart so he is." (Proverbs 23:7)

It is popular to say that Christianity is *not* a religion but a relationship. But if we say it is *only* a *relationship* and *not* a *religion*, we make it appear that our faith is purely emotional, having nothing to do with precepts and principles that we are called to believe and obey. This philosophy has led many to compartmentalize Christianity, placing false divisions between "sacred" and "secular", or "spiritual" and "material". But there is no aspect of life that isn't "sacred" or "spiritual". It would be far better, then, to say that Christianity is not *only* a religion, it is *also* a relationship. Christianity is a religion because it is indeed a belief system that informs values and moral judgments standards, by providing principles to live by. The God of the Bible requires obedience to His word in all things, always. There is no aspect of life that is outside the scope of Christianity. "Whether we eat or drink, or whatever we do, we are to do all to the glory of God." (1 Corinthians 10:31) The wonderful truth is, that though God requires obedience, He does so out of love for truth, and for us. Thus, Christianity is also a relationship. God loves us, desires relationship with us, and has made a way for that relationship to be possible. When we love and obey Him, that is a form of worship

Worship is inherent to human nature; man was created to worship. Because we were made to worship, everyone - even the self-proclaimed atheist—has an object of worship. And that is what religion is all about - worship, living our lives in devotion to someone or something. Sadly, as the Apostle Paul says in Romans 1:25, "they (mankind) exchanged the truth about God for the lie and worshiped and served the creature rather than the creator." Every single one of us has been guilty of that for at least some portion of our life. We have all sinned and fallen short of the glory of God. (Romans 3:2) We have missed the ultimate mark of absolute perfection and we have failed to worship God as the One True God. The Bible says, "The wages of sin is death." (Romans 6:23) This leaves us in a dire position; but leads us to the tremendous fundamental difference between Christianity and all other religions, or worldviews.

The Dividing Line: *The Doctrine of Sin*

Every religion man has ever imagined demands that man do certain things, meet certain requirements in order to reach the ultimate good, be that heaven, Nirvana, enlightenment, etc. Biblical Christianity places no such requirements on man. The Christian faith recognizes that man could never be good enough or work hard enough to earn his way to heaven. The unique truth of Christianity is that God Himself has done that work. He did this through His Son, Jesus, who sacrificed His perfect life to pay the penalty for our sins. The Christian's hope lies in Jesus, not in himself. When the spirit of God regenerates us, we turn from loving sin to loving God; we desire and are enabled to obey His commands. (John 3:5-8) Before regeneration, we were unwilling and unable to obey God's commands due to our sin nature. Romans 8:7-8, Ephesians 2:1-3) We did not truly worship the true God. But once we are born again, we receive a new nature that delights in keeping the law of God. (Romans 7:22) We now desire to obey out of pure gratitude for what he has done for us: His commandments are not burdensome. (1 John 5:3) They are not burdensome because we love Him, and to do His will is our reasonable act of worship. (Romans 12:2)

World Religions

Christianity makes up about 33% of all people who claim that they have a religion. This number includes all denominations that include Christ and the Bible within its key doctrine. Islam represents approximately one-fifth of the world's religious population; however, their numbers are increasing rapidly. The remaining religions each make up a much smaller percentage. Of these, we will focus on the most dominant of the opposing worldviews: Humanism, Islam, Buddhism, and Hinduism.

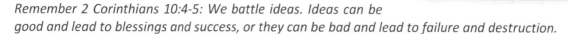

Remember 2 Corinthians 10:4-5: We battle ideas. Ideas can be good and lead to blessings and success, or they can be bad and lead to failure and destruction.

What Does Humanism Say About God?

Humanism is the dominant religion[46] of our country today; it pervades our public school system and the major media. Let's look at what Humanists believe.

The first Humanist Manifesto (there have been three) was written in 1933. Below is their statement of faith. We have listed the first ten doctrinal principles of Humanism – their statements of belief. The remaining five principles (not included for the sake of brevity) refer mainly to the effects which they predict this religion will have upon the world.

Religious Humanists believe…

1) The universe is self-existing and not created.
2) Man is a part of nature and that he has emerged as a result of a continuous process.
3) The traditional dualism of mind and body must be rejected.
4) Man's religious culture and civilization… are the product of a gradual development [evolution] due to his interaction with his natural environment and with his social heritage. The culture defines the individual.
5) The nature of the universe depicted by modern science makes unacceptable any supernatural or cosmic guarantees of human values… The way to determine the existence and value of any and all realities is by means of intelligent inquiry and by the assessment of their relations to human needs. Religion must formulate its hopes and plans in the light of the scientific spirit and method.
6) The time has passed for theism, deism, modernism, and the several varieties of "new thought".
7) Religion consists of those actions, purposes, and experiences which are humanly significant.
8) The complete realization of human personality is the end (purpose) of man's life and Humanism seeks its development and fulfillment in the here and now.
9) In the place of the old attitudes involved in worship and prayer the humanist finds his religious emotions expressed in a heightened sense of personal life and in a cooperative effort to promote social well-being.
10) It follows that there will be no uniquely religious emotions and attitudes of the kind hitherto associated with belief in the supernatural.[47]

---

[46] https://americanhumanist.org/what-is-humanism/manifesto1/

[47] americanhumanist.org

We see from this that Humanists believe that man is simply one part of nature. He emerged as a result of evolution; thus, he is no better than any other creature. They say there is no God and it is foolish to think so. It is important to note that Humanism is the religion of Marxism, Communism, and Socialism.

Socialism has taken over in western Europe and God has been rejected accordingly. Socialists are advancing the same agenda in America today and are near to accomplishing their purpose.

The Power of Bad theology

In chapter one, we saw that the formation of America was a result of the biblical worldview being embraced by the majority of our Founding Founders. But today, it appears that our nation—along with all of western Europe—has lost its biblical moorings. It would be wise, then, to investigate the cause of such a radical ideological shift—in view of the main thesis of this book, that **we battle ideas**. The following account reveals the degree of commitment and passion the enemies of Christianity—specifically the Religious Humanists— displayed in the years following the founding era. And note that this is only one small sampling of individuals who made it their life's work to turn America away from Christian theology to atheism.

A Plan to Undermine Christianity[48]

The Religious Foundations of Humanism
• All life is a product of unguided evolution.
• Only the material is real; there is no supernatural, spiritual realm.
• Man is purely a product of his environment; thus, he is not responsible for his behavior, society is.
• Reality is what science says it is.
• Typical religions that rely upon a supernatural god are outdated and foolish.
• The purpose of man begins and ends in this life.

Sept. 12, 1905

The year was 1905. Five men—Upton Sinclair, Clarence Darrow, Jack London, Thomas Wentworth Higginson, and J. Phelps Stokes (all devoted socialists)— assembled together in a small room above Peck's restaurant in New York to devise a plan to overthrow the Christian worldview as the dominant worldview in America. J. Phelps Stokes was a wealthy industrialist who had inherited his money and - like so many who find themselves rich but do not know God—wanted "to do what he thought was right". Clarence Darrow was a lawyer who later achieved fame as the defense attorney who represented the evolutionist teacher in the infamous Scopes "Monkey" Trial—which had the effect of making a mockery of the biblical creation model. Jack London was an extremely popular writer who contributed his tremendous influence through the media, along with Upton Sinclair—also a well-known writer of that day. Sadly, the church was represented by the Unitarian minister, Thomas Wentworth Higginson. At that time, the Unitarian church had become quite influential in American politics.

Here we see two very influential members of the media elite, a powerful financier, a prominent lawyer, and a minister from a cult masquerading as Christian, who were all united in their purpose to come against the ideas of God.

What was their plan? They set themselves upon a long-range strategy to take control of the education system by first infiltrating the universities—promoting *"an intelligent interest in socialism among college men and women".*[49] These men became disseminators of an idea passed onto them by a then obscure writer by the name of Karl Marx. Their purpose was to gain influence over the brightest young minds in the country as soon as they

---

[48] Marshall Foster and Mary-Elaine Swanson, *The American Covenant, the Untold Story.* ©1983 by the Mayflower Institute, p-xvii, xviii

[49] Paul W. Shafer and John Howland Snow, *The Turning of the Tides* (New Canaan, Connecticut: The Long House, Inc., 1962) p-1

left the umbrella of their parents. The five men began by establishing what first became known as the Intercollegiate Socialist Society. Within five years, they established 44 chapters in colleges across the country! Among those colleges was the University of Michigan, home of one of the most highly esteemed law schools of the day. By 1917, they had 61 chapters in colleges and graduate schools across the nation. They aimed at the cream of the crop of the youth – to sway them to their atheistic, socialist worldview – and they hit their mark.

In the early 1920's, the name of the organization was changed to *The League for Industrial Democracy* because the term socialism had begun to take on unfavorable connotations. By 1941, John Dewey—who was one of the authors of the original **Humanist Manifesto** and is considered to be the father of our modern progressive education system—had become their president. Dewey was a man who hated God and despised Christianity, and he became the father of the education system that America's children are imbedded in! At that time (1941), the League for Industrial Democracy boasted of 140 chapters and were active in every major graduate school in America.

1912 University of Michigan ISS Club
At front is future radical labor lawyer Maurice Sugar.

By the mid-20th century, Humanists controlled the state education system. Virtually all future teachers, legislators, U.S. presidents, and Supreme Court justices were now being indoctrinated to the godless Humanist worldview. In so doing, these five men had completely infected our country from the top down with their Godless worldview. This is what can happen when just a few dedicated people unite together behind a generational plan focused upon the education of the youth.

"Give me just one generation of youth, and I'll transform the whole world."
- Vladimir Lenin

"He alone, who owns the youth, gains the future." - Adolph Hitler

A study of the history of Russia and Germany in the first half of the 20th century, reveals that the ideas promoted by the atheistic worldview of Humanism led to the most murderous century in the recorded history of the world. Ideas have consequences and the ideas that come from Humanism have left a trail of hopelessness, hate, starvation, and death. What we believe about God affects everything in life; thus, our ideas about god (our theology) will either make us wise or make us fools. In other words, good theology produces wisdom and righteousness, while bad theology produces foolishness and wickedness.

The following is a quoted transcript from an interview with the renowned atheist and author of the book, The God Delusion, Richard Dawkins, by the noted economist, actor, and author Ben Stein, as recorded in the movie Expelled, No Intelligence Allowed.[50]

Ben Stein asks Richard Dawkins: "You have written that God is a psychotic delinquent invented by mad, deluded people".

"No", Dawkins replies. "I didn't say quite that. I said something rather better than that. I said *'The God of the Old Testament is arguably the most unpleasant character in all fiction. Jealous and proud of it. A petty, unjust, unforgiving, control freak. A vindictive, blood thirsty, ethnic cleanser. A misogynistic, homophobic, racist, infanticidal genocidal, filicidal, pestilential, megalomaniacal sadomasochistic, capriciously malevolent bully'"*

---

[50] 2008, Rocky Mountain Pictures

Stein responds: "Well, how did [the Heavens and the Earth] get created?"

[Dawkins:] "Well, um, by various slow processes... Nobody knows how it got started. We know what sort of event must have happened for the origin of life. It was the origin of the first self-replicating molecule."

[Stein:] "Right, and how did that happen?" [Dawkins:] "I've told you, we don't know."

[Stein:] "So you have no idea how it started?" [Dawkins:] "No, no, nor has anyone else."

[Stein:] "What do you think is the possibility that intelligent design might turn out to be the answer to some issues in genetics or in evolution?"

[Dawkins:] "Well, it could come about in the following way. It could be that at some earlier time, somewhere in the universe a civilization evolved by probably some kind of Darwinian means to a very, very high level of technology and designed a form of life that they seeded onto, perhaps, this planet."

We would comment that this only begs the question, "where did the aliens come from?"

Richard Dawkins

Psalm 14:1: "The fool hath said in his heart, There is no God."

Comparing Humanism to Christianity

	The Humanist View	**The Christian View**
God	Non-existent; a myth; "an opiate for the masses"	Uncreated loving creator. A personal, infinite, compassionate being
Man	Innately good	Innately sinful, dependent upon God's grace
The Human problem	Intolerance – a result of man-made religion (Christianity in particular)	Judgment caused by sin against the Holy Creator
Truth	There is no such thing	The Bible is all truth. All the words, principles, and precepts are true
Salvation	Only in this world by freeing oneself from religious restraints	Comes by faith in Christ's sacrifice. Freedom from the penalty of sin and death is assured
Heaven	The extinction of life	The fullness of life and joy with the fellowship of Jesus Himself along with believers of all time, and accompanied with enjoyable work to do
Christ	A myth. A distortion of a common man	The Son of God

Lesson 5 Study Questions

1. What does Humanism believe about God? _____

2. State at least one logical positive or negative result in an individual's life if he/she embraces this

   worldview? _____

   _____

3. From the highlighted beliefs of the religion of Humanism, can you explain what relationship religion has

   with politics and education, if any?

   _____

   _____

4. Name at least 2 results that might occur when a nation embraces Humanism over Christianity?

   1) _____

   _____

   2) _____

   _____

5. "Religious Humanists regard the universe as self-existing and not created; & believe that man is just one
   part of nature, the result of evolution."
   1) The foundational belief – the one upon which all the remaining beliefs of Humanism rest – is that
      everything in the universe – countless stars, comets, varieties of birds, flowers, animals with eyes that
      see, and, of course, human beings that can critically think – came about by chance, through an explosion,
      and without any intelligent designer. Do you see any evidence of this "something created from a chance
      explosion" in reality? _____. Does this seem logical to believe? Why or why not?

      _____

      _____

      _____

   2) List at least 4 dangerous consequences in the society around us that are the result of this worldview.

      (1)_____(2)_____

      (3)_____(4)_____

6. Read the Humanist Manifesto I @ http://modernhistoryproject.org/mhp?Article=HumanManifest. See the

   list of signers of the Manifesto at the bottom.

1) How many of the 34 signers were educators? _____.

2) How many were affiliated with religious denominations or organizations? _____.

3) What significance does this have and how might this affect us today?

_____

_____

_____

7. Read Roman 1:18-25 and 2 Corinthians 4:4. What is the result of believing in Humanism?

_____

_____

_____

8. From the section that spoke of the rise of the "Intercollegiate Socialist Society", why do you think they

were so successful in changing America's culture, and what lessons do they provide for the church today?

_____

_____

_____

9. Why do you think that many communist/socialist nations are Humanist in their worldview/religion?

_____

_____

10. In Humanism, who is ruler? _____ Can you count on righteousness to

rule in such a nation? _____. Why or why not? _____

_____

_____

11. In Humanism, can you expect the ruler(s) to be relational? _____. What difference would that make?

_____

_____

_____

Lesson 6 – Compare & Contrast, Part 2

Overview of the Religion of Islam

Islam is a monotheistic religious faith that developed in the Middle East in the 7th century. Islam, which literally means "surrender" or "submission," was founded on the teachings of the Prophet Muhammad. The Quran, the sacred text of Islam, contains the teachings of the Prophet that were claimed to have been revealed to him from Allah.

Essential to Islam is the belief that Allah is the one and true god with no partner or equal. There are several branches of Islam and much variety within those branches. The two major divisions within the tradition are the Sunni and Shi'a, each of which claims different means of maintaining religious authority. One of the unifying characteristics of Islam is the Five Pillars, the fundamental practices of Islam. These five practices include (1) a ritual profession of faith, (2) ritual prayer, (3) the zakat (charity), (4) fasting, and (5) the hajj (a pilgrimage to Mecca).

In the book titled "Unveiling Islam" (Ergon and Emir Caner, 118): "Allah's heart is set against the infidel (kafir). He has no love for the unbeliever, nor is it the task of the Muslim to "evangelize" the unbelieving world. Allah is to be worshiped, period. Any who will not do so must be defeated, silenced, or expelled. The theme is conquest, not conversion, of the unbelieving world. Allah has called the Muslim to ensure that the name of Allah alone is worshiped."

History

Retaining its emphasis on an uncompromising monotheism and a strict adherence to certain essential religious practices, the religion taught by Muhammad to a small group of followers spread rapidly through the Middle East to Africa, Europe, the Indian subcontinent, the Malay Peninsula, and China. By the early 21st century there were more than 1.5 billion Muslims worldwide.[51]

"Belief in jihad is a common thread to many Islamic sects. Although the exact meaning of the Arabic is difficult to express in English, jihad is most accurately translated as 'struggle' … Sometimes, the struggle can take the form of a physical war against non-believers. Although this kind of jihad is referred to in English as a 'holy war', most Muslims believe there is nothing holy about war and that wars should only be fought against oppressors and aggressors. A minority of Muslims, however, places great importance on holy war jihads. This minority feels that Muslims must wage war against all nonbelievers. It is this conception of jihad that inspires Islamic extremist terrorism."[52] However we would note that this "minority" is estimated in the

Like Founder, Like Faith

The simplest way to learn of a faith is by studying the life and words of its founder. As Christianity may be exposed by examining the life and words of Christ, so Islam can be defined by the life and words of the Prophet of Islam, Muhammad. History records that the establishment and growth of Islam began with – and has been characterized by – war. According to UShistory.org.: "Before his [Muhammad's] death…[in 629 A.D., following the capture of the city of Mecca] he *forcefully converted* most of the Arabian Peninsula to his new faith and built a small empire." (Emphasis ours) For more on the history of the beginnings of Islam, see the book, *The Truth About Muhammad*, by Robert Spencer (Regnery Publishing, September 15, 2006).

---

[51] https://www.britannica.com/topic/Islam

[52] USHistory.org (http://www.ushistory.org/civ/4i.asp)

millions of "fundamentalists" who are obedient to all the teachings of the Quran. Though a minority, theses extreme fundamentalists number in the millions.

What does Islam say about God?

Is He Ruler?

Allah is the name of the god almighty in the Arabic language. Allah is the personal name of god. The word *Allah* is never used for any other being or thing. He is the absolute ruler. He rules alone, which is one of the main differences between Allah of Islam and Yahweh (often translated "Jehovah" or simply by the capitalization of LORD in the Bible). The God of the Bible is triune. He is One God in three persons. Because He is three in one, all rule as one.

Is he Righteous?

This is where Islam takes a complete left turn. Allah "forgives whom he pleases, punishes whom he pleases, and deceives who he pleases." "Allah leads astray those whom He pleases..." In some 20 passages of the Quran, Allah is said to lead men astray.

These few quotes from the Quran reveal much about Allah's character. He commands:

- "Strike off their heads and strike from them every fingertip" (Surah 8:12).
- "Have no unbelieving friends. Kill the unbelievers wherever you find them" (Surah 4:89).
- "If the unbelievers do not offer you peace, kill them wherever you find them" (Surah 4:91).
- "Those who make war with Allah and his messenger will be killed or crucified; or, have their hands and feet on alternate sides cut off, or will be expelled out of the land. That is how they will be treated in this world, and in the next they will have an awful doom" (Surah 5:33).

Is He Relational?

Absolutely not. Never in the Quran is Allah spoken of as a god of love *as the Bible describes the Father's love for us*. Yahweh rules as three persons in one, and each loves one another; thus, Christianity's God can love *us*. A single person cannot know love because love is something shared by two or more persons. This helps explain why the holy book of Islam, the Quran, does not contain the word "love" as defined in the Bible (we'll see this in the quotes from the Quran below). *Agape* is the Greek term for God's love for His children in the Bible. Agape describes the sacrificial relationship between the Father and His children that results in a mutual bond between

Not a Religion of Peace

From the 19th through the 20th centuries, there appeared hundreds of "historical" accounts of the effect of Islam upon the Middle East and Europe from the 7th to the 12th centuries. Nearly all of these accounts were based in large part upon writings from Islamic historians which always shed favorable light upon Islam and a reflexive damning light upon Christianity. Thus, we see that many of our current history books are filled with this one-sided version of the past. However, archaeologic excavations over the last century have come to reveal huge discrepancies in these accounts. Most specifically, archaeologists recognize a mysterious gap beginning in the 7th century and continuing for 3 centuries (otherwise known as the "dark ages") where they find virtually no evidence of the classical Christian civilization that previously flourished in those regions. Though historians theorize in many directions, we believe that the most logical explanation is found best summarized in Emmet Scott's book "Mohammed & Charlemagne Revisited: The History of a Controversy". The central thesis of this book is powerfully demonstrated: The decline of Greco-Roman civilization seems to coincide with the rise of Islam. That is hardly coincidental. The historical pattern is very clear: Where Islam enters, civilization soon exits.

Scott shows quite convincingly that archaeological excavations paint a very clear picture of devastation brought by the Arab conquests throughout the entire Mediterranean region, from Syria to Spain, in the seventh century AD. From the 1st century through the 6th, Christianity had miraculously overcome the Roman empire and extended its influence throughout eastern and western Europe as a result of one of its central doctrines: "Love your neighbor as yourself". But with the Muslims, peaceful co-existence was never an option. These were the "unconvertibles" - men who were driven by their own religious zeal, and who waged war specifically to spread that faith. With the arrival of Islam, Mediterranean Europe was never again at peace. [53]

the God who loves and the child who gratefully responds in return... "For God so loved the world (He loved the world *in this way*) that He gave His only begotten Son, that whoever believes in Him should not perish but have

[53] Scott, Emmet. Mohammed & Charlemagne Revisited: The History of a Controversy. New English Review Press. Kindle Edition, Loc. 5138

everlasting life." (John 3:16) The distinction is clear. The God of the Bible calls people to believe in Jesus, receiving from Him the power to obey and to know the certainty of His unfailing love. On the other hand, Allah *demands* that his disciples perform works to earn his *conditional* love. Nothing in the Quran seems to indicate that Allah wants a relationship with humans.

Quite to the contrary, the Quran specifically denies that Allah is a father (112.3)

"…Allah intends man to pursue the relationship of a servant to his master, but not the relationship of a child with his father. Nowhere in the Quran does it suggest that Allah desires intimacy with humanity. We are not His beloved – just one of his creatures."[54]

Pause and Consider

Our battle is not against people

"For we do not wrestle against flesh and blood, but against principalities, against powers, against the rulers of the darkness of this age, against spiritual hosts of wickedness in the heavenly places" (Ephesians 6:12)

We recognize that many Muslims desire to live in peace, and do not subscribe to the violent tenets of Islam as recorded in the Quran. However, the violence which has historically characterized the religion undoubtedly has its roots in certain fundamental doctrines and principles spread throughout the Quran. It is those beliefs that we cannot naively ignore.

The following quotes from the Quran describe the conditional "love" that Allah will grant (italics added for emphasis):

• "Those who spend (freely), whether in prosperity or in adversity; who restrain anger and pardon (all) men; for Allah loves those *who do good*". (Surah 3:31)
• "How many of the Prophets fought (in Allah's way) and with them (fought) large bands of godly men? But they never lost heart if they met with disaster in Allah's way, nor did they weaken (in will) nor give in. And Allah loves those *who are firm and steadfast*". (Surah 3:146)
• "But seek with the (wealth) which Allah has bestowed on thee the Home of the Hereafter, nor forget thy portion in this world: but do thou good as Allah has been good to thee and seek not mischief in the land: for Allah *loves not those who do mischief*." (Surah 28:77)
• "Truly Allah loves *those who fight in his cause* in battle array as if they were a solid cemented structure". (Surah 61:4)

Allah loves his followers conditionally based upon their service and obedient submission to him, but he does not love unbelievers – he has no heart of mercy for them. By most conservative counts, the Quran contains over 100 passages that call Muslims to take up arms against unbelievers in the name of Allah.

For example:

• "Kill them [unbelievers] wherever you find them… And fight them until there is no more unbelief and worship is for Allah alone" (Surah 2:191-193).
• "The Messenger of Allah said: I have been commanded to fight against people till they testify that there is no god but Allah, and that Muhammad is the messenger of Allah" (Sahih Muslim 1:33).
• "Soon shall we cast terror into the hearts of the unbelievers, for that they joined companions with Allah, for which he had sent no authority". (Surah 3:151)
• "And fight with them until there is no more fitna (disorder, unbelief) and religion should be only for Allah" (Surah 8:39)
• "So when the sacred months have passed away, then slay the idolaters wherever you find them, and take them captive and besiege them and lie in wait for them in every ambush, then if they repent and keep up prayer and pay the poor-rate, leave their way free to them." (Surah 9:5)

Gregory Palamas, an Orthodox metropolitan, who was a captive of the Turks in 1354, stated: "These infamous people, hated by God and infamous, boast of having got the better of the Romans [Byzantines] by their love of God. They live by the bow, by the sword, and by debauchery, finding pleasure in taking slaves, devoting themselves to murder, pillage, spoil … and not only do they commit these crimes, but even – what an aberration – they believe that God approves of them." [55]

---

[54] 54 Nabeel Qureshi, *No God But One* (Grand Rapids: Zondervan, 2016).

[55] 55 Robert Irwin, "Islam and the Crusades: 1096-1699," in Jonathan Riley-Smith (ed.) Oxford History of the Crusades, p. 251

In stark contrast, the Christian gospel is for unworthy sinners and is rooted in God's grace – His unmerited favor in the place of merited wrath. Christianity's God became a man and took on that wrath for us – that's how relational He is.

But God demonstrates His own love toward us, in that while we were still sinners,
Christ died for us. (Romans 5:8 -NKJV)

God invites unbelievers and idolaters to turn away from sin and follow Him. He offers forgiveness, new life, and eternal love – all rooted in His grace. God desires relationship with all people and "is not willing that any should perish but all come to repentance." (2 Peter 3:9)

Whereas Christianity offers assurance of eternal life as a gift from God, in Islam *there is no assurance of heaven.* One may obey all the commands and perform all the works, but salvation is never absolutely promised. Though the Christian can be secure in his relationship with God, there is no such security with Allah.

The Consequences of Islam

A Sledgehammer to Civilization:
Islamic State's war on culture (7 April, 2015 – The Guardian.com)
"Isis has destroyed countless irreplaceable artefacts and heritage sites across the areas it controls of Iraq and Syria. As masked men with sledgehammers and drills stood amid priceless antiquities in Mosul museum in late February, a narrator on this Islamic state video read a justification for what was about to come. 'The prophet Mohammed took down idols with his bare hands when he went into Mecca. We were ordered by our prophet to take down idols and destroy them, and the companions of the prophet did this after this time, when they conquered countries.'"[59]

Even though Islam has proven to be able to destroy civilizations, it has yet to build one that lasts.[56] Islamic conquest follows a pattern in their subduing of nations:

1) The forced submittal of all (Islam means "submission")
2) A period of Islamic dominance and extortion through the plunder of the riches and knowledge of the conquered society
3) Loss of personal rights – especially among women
4) Ending with a slow Islamization until the riches have been completely drained.

It has been estimated that between the sixteenth and nineteenth centuries Muslim pirates based in North Africa captured and enslaved between a million and a million-and-a-quarter Europeans.[57]
Poverty and backwardness are typical in the Islamic world. Most of the Islamic nations rank in the bottom 40% of all nations in GDP per capita.[58]

The Historic characteristics of Islamic nations:
Fear, hatred, Jihad (war), loss of liberty, poverty, tyranny

---

[56] Scott, Emmet. Mohammed & Charlemagne Revisited: The History of a Controversy. New English Review Press. Kindle Edition, Loc. 4599-4613. See also Loc. 4692-4708: "The real ideological impression of Islam was not the enlightened thinking of Avicenna and Averroes, who were in any case rejected and expelled from the Muslim canon, but the darker thinking found in the Koran and the Haditha: the doctrines of perpetual war against non-believers; of holy deception (taqiyya); of death for apostates and heretics; of judicial torture; of slave and concubine-taking as a legitimate occupation. These were the teachings, and not those of the philosophers, which left an indelible imprint on medieval Europe. And this began right at the beginning."

[57] https://en.wikipedia.org/wiki/Barbary_pirates

[58] CIA - Net Wealth GDP per capita- https://www.cia.gov/library/publications/the-world-factbook/rankorder/2004rank.html; U.N. Human Development Report, 2016 (pdf)

[59] https://www.theguardian.com/world/2015/apr/07/islamic-state-isis-crimes-against-culture-iraq-syria

Comparing Islam to Christianity

	The Islamic View	The Christian View
God	Allah. One god who must be submitted to	Uncreated loving creator. A personal, infinite, compassionate being
Man	Born naturally good but must repent from his rebellion and submit to Allah	Innately sinful, dependent upon God's grace alone
The Human problem	Not submitting to Allah due to pride/ rebellion	Judgment caused by sin against the Holy Creator
Truth	A philosophy open to interpretation, but generally "Islam is truth"	The Bible is all truth. All the words, principles, and precepts are true
Salvation	Comes by works approved by Allah. Salvation cannot be assured	Comes by faith in Christ's sacrifice. Freedom from the penalty of sin and death is assured
Heaven	Like a garden in which there are beautiful women, flowing cups and juicy fruits, rivers of water, milk, wine and rivers of clear honey.	The fullness of life and joy with the fellowship of Jesus Himself along with believers of all time, and accompanied with enjoyable work to do
Christ	An enlightened man	The Son of God

Lesson 6 Study Questions
How does the God of the Bible compare to all other "gods"?

1. In relation to rulership, describe Allah? _____

   _____

2. Regarding Islam, what strikes you about the descriptions of Allah? _____

   _____

3. "Even though Islam has proven that it is able to d_ _ _ _ _ _ civilizations, it has yet to b _ _ _ _ one." Have

   you seen evidence of this in our world today? If so, give examples. _____

   _____

4. What dangers do we see proceeding from this worldview today? _____

   _____

5. Personal question: Why do you think Islam is growing at the rate it is? _____

   _____

What Does Islam Say About God? List the main points you believe answer each question.

6. Is he Ruler? _____ Why?

   a. _____

   b. _____

   c. _____

7. Righteous? _____ Why?

   a. _____

   b. _____

   c. _____

8. Is he Relational? ____ Why?

   a. _____

   b. _____

   c. _____

9. What have been the historical results of Islam in society regarding these 3 areas:

    a.   Economics

_____

_____

    b.   Personal Freedom

_____

_____

    c.   Hope of heaven

_____

_____

10. List 3 areas of difference between the Islamic worldview and the Christian worldview, and state why each

variance matters.

    a. _____

_____

    b. _____

_____

    c. _____

_____

Lesson 7 – Compare & Contrast, Part 3
Overview of the Religion of Buddhism

What does **Buddhism** say about god?

Buddhism recognizes supernatural spiritual beings, but there is no doctrine of god in Buddhism. Though Buddhists do not deny the existence of god(s), they simply don't find the existence of god(s) to be particularly important. In the Buddhist view, man must save himself from the "suffering", "pain", or "unsatisfactoriness" of life (the concept of *Dukkha*). How does man do this? By following the enlightened teachings of the Buddha. Hence, the existence of god(s) is completely irrelevant. One does not reach enlightenment by seeking divine guidance; one reaches enlightenment by seeking the guidance of the Buddha. Thus, it is not surprising that Buddha himself was an atheist, believing that there was no supreme god. Ironically, only a few hundred years after the death of Buddha, the Mahayana branch of Buddhism began to worship him as god and still do to this day.

Not only is there no doctrine of god in Buddhism, there is no developed doctrine of man. According to Buddhism, life is an illusion and is not actually real. Consequently, the fundamental problem of humanity is that we are constantly chasing after the things of this world – a world that is not actually real; we are continually yearning for that which is an illusion, trying to find fulfillment in a fantasy world. This inevitably results in a state of suffering (*Dukkha* – incapable of finding satisfaction; unable to attain true contentment) that is perpetuated through a cycle of birth, death, and rebirth – a cycle referred to as *Saṃsāra.* The notion of rebirth (reincarnation) is one of the central tenets of Buddhism, and it is intimately associated with the concept of *karma* – the idea that good intentions and good deeds plant the seeds of future good patterns of being, while bad intentions and bad deeds plant the seeds of future detrimental patterns of being. Desire for the impermanent, illusory things of this world produces negative karma that gets transferred into the next cycle of rebirth, and the only way to escape this vicious cycle of suffering (unsatisfactoriness) is to dispel one's cravings and ignorance by realizing the Four Noble Truths and practicing the Eightfold Path, thus attaining Nirvana. *Nirvana* literally means, "blown out", as in an oil lamp. Nirvana is therefore the cessation of existence in which the candle of life is blown out; it is liberation (salvation) from the cyclic rebirths of *saṃsāra.*

The goal of Buddhism is to reach Nirvana – the cessation of existence in which the candle of life is blown out.

Attaining nirvana is the only way to permanently escape suffering (unsatisfactoriness) and to free oneself from the illusion of this world. Thus, it is safe to say that Buddhists believe man is born basically good rather than morally corrupt and is responsible and capable of freeing or saving himself.

Buddhism:
- Explicitly rejects a creator
- Denies endorsing any views on creation

- States that questions on the origin of the world are worthless
- Teaches that IF there is a god, he is unimportant and uninvolved
- Does not teach that "God created man in His own image"
- Believes that liberation from suffering (unsatisfactoriness) is dependent upon man, not upon some deity
- Is associated with idealism and inaction
- Has no fixed special revelation, no written ideology or "bible". Rather, most "revelation" comes from within as a result of meditating upon the Buddha's principles of "the Three Jewels, the Four Noble Truths, and the Noble Eightfold Path.[60]

What is Buddhism?

Buddhism is a religion of about 300 million people around the world. The word *Buddhism* comes from "buddhi", which means, "to awaken". Buddhism has its origins about 2,500 years ago when Siddhartha Gautama, known as the Buddha, was himself awakened (enlightened) at the age of 35.

Buddhist practices, such as meditation, are means of changing oneself in order to develop the qualities of awareness, kindness, and wisdom. The experience developed within the Buddhist tradition is aimed to lead to a path which ultimately culminates in Enlightenment or Buddhahood. "An enlightened being sees the nature of reality absolutely clearly, just as it is, and lives fully and naturally in accordance with that vision."[61]

Is Buddhism a Religion?

To its disciples, Buddhism goes beyond religion and is more of a philosophy or 'way of life'. It is a philosophy because philosophy 'means love of wisdom' and the Buddhist path can be summed up as:

(1) To lead a moral life.
(2) To be mindful and aware of thoughts and actions.
(3) To develop wisdom and understanding.

The Spiritual Goal of Buddhism: to reach Nirvana

The term *nirvana* describes a state of freedom from suffering (unsatisfactoriness) and rebirth, but different Buddhist traditions have interpreted the concept in different ways[62], such as the absence of the weaving of activity of the mind, and the elimination of desire.[63] Typically, it represents the liberation from cycles of rebirth (reincarnation).

Consequences:
- Followers are more likely to be indifferent to the social/cultural issues of life because "Life is an illusion".
- As a result, Buddhist communities are easily controlled by tyrants (50% of all Buddhists live in China; 13% in Thailand).
- Buddhist communities are distinguished by their low standards of living and general poverty.

---

[60] 60 https://thebuddhistcentre.com/text/three-jewels

[61] *61* Buswell, Robert E.; Lopez, Donald S. (2013), The Princeton Dictionary of Buddhism, Princeton University) p-600

[62] 62 IBID

[63] 63 Steven Collins (1998). Nirvana and Other Buddhist Felicities. Cambridge University Press. P-9

One of the foremost practices of Buddhism is meditation, where the goal is to retreat from the unrealities of the world and dwell in the spiritual state of nirvana, attempting to deny pain and suffering (unsatisfactoriness). This type of intense introspection naturally gives way to social and cultural inaction, which is why we don't find many Buddhist hospitals, volunteer organizations, or missionaries. Buddhism revolves around individualism, and as a result, the governments of Buddhist nations are often defined by tyranny and oppression.

Comparing Buddhism to Christianity

	Buddhist View	**Christian View**
God	Unimportant impersonal force	Uncreated loving creator. A personal, infinite, compassionate being
Man	Born good, capable of self-salvation	Innately sinful, dependent upon God's grace
The Human problem	Suffering (unsatisfactoriness) caused by desire	Judgment caused by sin and the holiness of God
Truth	Man-made – the Tripitaka. Can change with time	The Bible is all truth. All the words, principles, and precepts are true
Salvation	Freedom from suffering and reincarnation. Attainable by meditation and rejection of material reality	Comes by faith in Christ's sacrifice. Freedom from the penalty of sin and death is assured
Heaven	The extinction of life	The fullness of life and joy
Christ	An enlightened man	The Son of God

Lesson 7 Study Questions

Buddhism

1. What Does Buddhism say about the idea of god? List the main points you believe answer each question.

   A. Does Buddhism have a God/Ruler? _____ What difference does this make to the individual and the

      culture?

      1) _____

      2) _____

      3) _____

   B. From today's lesson, does Buddhism contain written doctrines that define Righteousness? _____ What difference would this make to the individual and the culture?

      1) _____

      2) _____

   C. Does Buddhism promote a personal relational with a single god? _____ What difference would this make

   to the individual and the culture?

      1) _____

      2) _____

      3) _____

   D. What are the apparent results of Buddhism in society regarding these 3 areas:

      1) Economics _____

         _____

      2) Personal Freedom _____

         _____

      3) Hope of heaven _____

         _____

Lesson 8 – Compare & Contrast, Part 4
Overview of the Religion of Hinduism

Hinduism is among the world's oldest religions, with roots and customs dating back more than 4,000 years. With approximately 900 million followers, Hinduism is the third-largest religion behind Christianity and Islam. Roughly 95 percent of the world's Hindus live in India. Because the religion has no specific founder, it is difficult to trace its origins and history. Hinduism is unique in that it is not a single religion but a compilation of many traditions and philosophies.[64]

Each one of the depictions in the illustration represent a different god among the Hindu

What does **Hinduism** say about god?

Hinduism claims to be the world's oldest religion. It has no human founder. It is a mystical religion, leading the devotee to personally experience the "truth" within, finally reaching the pinnacle of consciousness where man and god are one. One can believe a variety of things about god, the universe, and the path to liberation and still be considered a Hindu. Most Hindus are devoted followers of one of the principal gods Shiva, Vishnu or Shakti, and often others besides, yet all these are regarded as manifestations of a single Reality. Perhaps the most well-known Hindu saying about religion is: "Truth is one; sages call it by different names." Hindus believe in the existence of an enduring soul that transmigrates from one body to another at death (reincarnation); and the law of karma that determines one's destiny both in this life and the next.

No United theology

Hinduism is a widely diverse system of thought. Most Hindus believe in an immense unifying force (Brahman) that governs all existence and cannot be completely known by humanity. Individual gods and goddesses are personifications of this cosmic force. In practice, each Hindu worships those few deities that he or she believes directly influence his or her life. By selecting one or more of these deities to worship, and by conducting the rituals designed to facilitate contact with them, a Hindu devotee is striving to experience his or her unity with that ultimate cosmic force, Brahman.[65]

The fundamental teaching of Hinduism, or Vedanta, is that a human being's basic nature is not confined to the body or the mind. Beyond both of these is the spirit or the spark of God within the soul. This spirit is within us and also within everything we see. All beings and all things are, in

Pause and Consider
Key Principle: Without Laws, Confusion Reigns

Without a "holy book" to define the fundamental principles and ideas of a religion or worldview, there will be little unity among the people.

Due to the differing ideas they subscribe to, they will be divided amongst themselves.

Christianity, which is grounded by the doctrines and principles contained in the Bible, is the most precise, clearly documented faith of all world religions.

---

64 64 https://www.history.com/topics/religion/hinduism
65 65 Smithsonian Institution http://archive.asia.si.edu/pujaonline/puja/basic_beliefs.html

their deepest essence, this pure or divine spirit, full of peace, full of joy and wisdom, ever united with God.[66]

> *Hinduism has no "bible", and as a result may be considered a mystical faith. There is no standard set of doctrines that define the religion, thus it is difficult to classify. Different sects have different gods or no gods at all. The Hindu "god" is complex and depends upon each individual and the tradition and philosophy followed.*

Hindus embrace...

a. Monotheism – One god
b. Polytheism – Many gods
c. Pantheism – The universe is god
d. Atheism – There is NO god
e. Agnosticism – god is, but he is unknowable
f. Gnosticism - god is only known by experiences

Brahma

The Most Prominent Deities
• Brahma: the god responsible for the creation of the world and all living things
• Vishnu: the god that preserves and protects the universe
• Shiva: the god that destroys the universe in order to recreate it
• Devi: the goddess that fights to restore dharma
• Krishna: the god of compassion, tenderness and love
• Lakshmi: the goddess of wealth and purity
• Saraswati: the goddess of learning[67]

Hinduism and Society

Hinduism divides society into four set castes based upon their karma and dharma. Each Hindu is born into a particular caste. This is called their Varna.

The Four Castes:
1. Brahmin: the intellectual and spiritual leaders
2. Kshatriyas: the protectors and public servants of society
3. Vaisyas: the skillful producers
4. Shudras: the unskilled laborers

The "untouchables" are a class of citizens outside the caste system and are considered to be in the lowest level of the societal hierarchy.

Today, the caste system still exists in India but is loosely followed. Many of the old customs are overlooked, but some traditions, such as Intermarriage between castes is so strongly disapproved of, there is very little chance of upward mobility or freedom. Varna even limits the jobs a Hindu may have since it is only appropriate for a Hindu to have a job that is suitable for his caste.

The Results of Hinduism

• One quarter of the world's poor (400 million+) live in India [BBC Aug 04]
• Two-thirds of people in India live in poverty
• 68.8% of the Indian population lives on less than $2 a day.
• Over 30% of the population live on less than $1.25 a day.

---

[66] 66 IBID
[67] 67 https://www.history.com/topics/religion/hinduism

- More than 800 million people in India are considered poor.
- Approximately 360 million in India live in abject poverty, more than the entire population of America.

Most of the 800 million poor live in the countryside and keep afloat with odd jobs. The lack of employment which provides a livable wage in rural areas is driving many Indians into rapidly growing metropolitan areas such as Bombay, Delhi, Bangalore or Calcutta. There, most of them expect a life of poverty and despair in the mega-slums, made up of millions of corrugated ironworks, without sufficient drinking water supply, without garbage disposal and in many cases without electricity. The poor hygiene conditions are the cause of diseases such as cholera, typhus and dysentery, in which children especially suffer and die.[68, 69]

Contrasting Hinduism with Christianity

	Hindu View	**Christian View**
Truth	Relative – revealed through experience and personal meditation	Absolute – Revealed in the Holy Bible
God	330 million gods	One God in 3 Persons
Jesus	Holy man, not a savior	Messiah, Son of God, Savior
Man's Problem	Ignorance of divine nature	Sin against creator
Solution	Enlightenment	Faith in Christ for salvation
Reincarnation	Yes	No
Goal	Merge with Universal Soul (Brahman)	Eternal Life with God in Heaven

Conclusion

Summary of the Lessons Learned in this Study of Theology

- When God is not defined, the results upon a nation and its people are catastrophic.

- Not all theologies/religions/worldviews (and their gods) are the same!

- The theology/religion/worldview of both a nation and its people has a strong influence upon the success or failure of both.

- The theology of a nation is a reflection of the worldview of its people. If the people have a high regard for God, the nation will display it to the world!

- Christianity is distinct among all other religions because God is well-defined: He is Love; He is Just; He is Righteous; He is Relational

---

[68] 68 https://www.uri.org/kids/world-religions/hindu-beliefs

[69] 69 https://en.wikipedia.org/wiki/Poverty_in_India

Lesson 8 Study Questions

Hinduism

1. Since there is not a single source – or holy book – that defines what ALL Hindus believe, what problems might arise because of this?

   _____

   _____

2. Imagine if there were many "gods", what problems might arise among those who followed them? _____

   _____

   _____

3. Can a Hindu have an assurance of "heaven"? _____ What difference might that make in a person's life?

   _____

   _____

4. What are the consequences of the caste system upon the people in Hinduism? _____

   _____

   _____

5. What are the apparent results of Hinduism in society regarding the following 3 areas:

   1) Economics _____

      _____

   2) Personal Freedom _____

      _____

   3) Hope of heaven _____

      _____

Subject Four: The Christian Worldview of Philosophy

Lesson 1 – Why Study Philosophy?

What Difference Does Your Philosophy Make?

Our philosophy of life is what guides all of our decision making, and the choices we make bring about blessings or troubles as a result. Thus, it is critical that we think through the ideas which make up our philosophy before we take serious life-steps in one direction or another.

Our philosophical outlook will determine the choices we make regarding:

1. A future spouse
2. Our friends
3. Our future career
4. Our work ethic
5. Our priorities in life
6. Our goals in life

One of the main objectives of the subject of Philosophy is to determine what is **right** and what is **true**

Every worldview leads to its own logical end. Thus, considering the end of a particular philosophy before we begin to follow it can save us much grief in the future.

In this chapter, we will compare and contrast the competing philosophies of the major worldviews/religions of today, and we will carry these opposing philosophical ideas out to their logical conclusions in order to see how they stand up in the light of critical questioning.

Defining Terms

As with each subject we discuss in this worldview series, there are certain words around which the subject of Philosophy revolves. Let's take a look at a few of these fundamental terms.

Noah Webster

The term **philosophy** comes from the joining of two Greek words: **phílos**, "a friend" (someone dearly loved in a personal, intimate way; a trusted confidant, held dear in a close bond of personal affection), and **sophía**, "wisdom".
Philosophy is therefore <u>the love of wisdom</u>.

• **Philosophy** (defined)
Noah Webster was a brilliant Christian who created the first American dictionary, published in 1828. Webster defined all words in the context of biblical interpretations whenever possible. His definition for philosophy was as follows:

PHILOSOPHY, noun [Latin philosophia; Gr. love, to love, and wisdom.] (condensed)

Literally, the love of wisdom… When applied to any particular department of knowledge, it denotes the collection of general laws or principles under which all the subordinate phenomena or facts relating to that subject, are comprehended. Thus, that branch of philosophy which treats of God, etc. is called theology; that which treats of nature, is called physics or natural philosophy; that which treats of man is called logic and ethics, or moral philosophy; that which treats of the mind is called intellectual or mental philosophy or metaphysics.[70]

- **Wisdom** (defined)

Again, Webster's 1828 dictionary defines wisdom as: (condensed)

The right use or exercise of knowledge; the choice of laudable (commendable) ends, and of the best means to accomplish them. It is the faculty of discerning or judging what is most just, proper and useful, and if it is to be considered as an acquirement, it is the knowledge and use of what is best, most just, most proper, most conducive to prosperity or happiness.[71]

In short, we might say that **wisdom is simply *the proper application of knowledge*.** And what is required for wisdom, the ability to properly apply knowledge? The fear of the Lord.

The fear of the LORD is the beginning of wisdom, and the knowledge of the Holy One is understanding. For by me your days will be multiplied, and years of life will be added to you. (Proverbs 9:10-11)

- **Knowledge** (defined)

"Knowledge" is not an easy term to define. This is because the words "knowledge" and "know" (along with their tenses and derivatives) are used in a variety of ways. Even in the Bible we see the words "knowledge" and "know" having a number of different meanings depending upon the context in which they are used. Nevertheless, we offer the following definition: **Knowledge – true thoughts of the mind**.

This definition works whether we are talking about God or man. God is omniscient (all-knowing), which means that all knowledge originates in Him – in His mind. Thus, to say that God is omniscient (all-knowing) is to say that <u>His mind is the origin of all true thoughts (knowledge)</u>. Now, if the mind of God is the origin of all true thoughts (knowledge), then where does all of man's knowledge come from? Obviously, from God, for where else could man's knowledge come from, since all knowledge originates in God? This is why we previously said (Chapter 3, Day 4, under the section, "God is Ruler"), "any knowledge that you have has been generously revealed to your mind by the mind of God; your fund of knowledge has been loaned to you

> **PAUSE and CONSIDER**
> A logical Implication of our Definition of knowledge is that *there is no such thing as "False Knowledge"*
> There *can* be pseudo or counterfeit knowledge – that which seems to be a true thought or has the pretense of being a true thought – but there *cannot* be false knowledge. Paul, for example, exhorts Timothy to avoid "what is falsely called knowledge" in 1 Timothy 6:20. Why is there no such thing as false knowledge? For the simple reason that all knowledge originates in the mind of God, and God can only think true thoughts; He cannot think false thoughts, as this would violate His nature. He is the Father of lights (truth), with whom there is no variation or shadow of turning (no falsehood). (James 1:17)

from the infinite bank of God's mind." Whenever you or I gain knowledge (true thoughts of the mind), it is God transferring the "currency" of His mind (knowledge) to ours. Accordingly, our definition of *knowledge* works whether we're talking about God or man – it is *true thoughts of the mind*.

---

[70] http://webstersdictionary1828.com/Dictionary/philosophy
[71] http://webstersdictionary1828.com/Dictionary/wisdom

Lesson 1 Study Questions

1. What does the term *philosophy* mean, and why is it important to think through our philosophy?

_____

_____

_____

2. How do you think **your** Philosophy might affect…

   a. Your occupation _____

   _____

   b. Your future education _____

   _____

   c. Your economic position _____

   _____

   d. Your future marriage (or not) _____

   _____

3. The topic of Philosophy deals in a large part with the questions: What is R__ __ __ __ and what is T__ __ __.

   Define, to the best of your ability, each of those terms:

   _____

   _____

4. Why do you think the meaning of these two terms has become so twisted in our culture today?

   _____

   _____

5. What results do you see in our society from the redefinition of these fundamental words?

   _____

   _____

   _____

6. Do you believe that <u>all</u> knowledge leads to wisdom? _____ Why or why not?

   _____

   _____

7. Define the term *knowledge.*

   _____

8. Explain what is meant by the statement, *Wisdom is the proper application of knowledge.*

   _____

   _____

9. List a few examples of what could be termed "pseudo or counterfeit knowledge"

_____

_____

10.   Read Isaiah 11:2. What words are used to describe the Holy Spirit in this verse?

_____ _____ _____ _____ _____ _____

11. Define what each of those words might mean to you personally. What difference would those qualities make in your life?

_____

_____

_____

_____

_____

_____

_____

_____

Lesson 2– Truth, Faith, and Philosophy

(NOTE: If using video series, there is no video for this lesson)

DIVING DEEPER: THE CHARACTERISTICS OF TRUTH

Above it was said that truth isn't merely an attribute of God, rather, truth is the essence of God's being. Let's investigate this statement further by considering some of the basic characteristics of truth.

1. Truth is **eternal**. Truth is not limited by time; it has no time constraints. Truth is always true – past, present, future, and even before time began. If one were to argue that, "truth is not eternal; today's truth may not have been true at some point in the past and may cease to be true at some point in the future," we can simply respond by saying, "if your argument is true today, it may not have been true at some point in the past and may cease to be true at some point in the future." Thus, in order to deny the eternality of truth, one would have to confirm the eternality of truth, which proves that truth is eternal.

    > Before the mountains were brought forth, or ever you had formed the earth and the world,
    > from everlasting to everlasting you are God. (Psalm 90:2)

    > Heaven and earth will pass away, but my words will not pass away. (Matthew 24:35)

2. Truth is **unchanging**. Truth never mutates; it is immutable. The statement "truth can change" could only be true if the truth of this statement never changed; thus, truth cannot change.

    > For I the LORD do not change. (Malachi 3:6)

    > Every good gift and every perfect gift is from above, coming down from the Father of lights,
    > with whom there is no variation or shadow due to change. (James 1:17)

3. Truth is **propositional**. A proposition is the meaning of a declarative sentence. Accordingly, there is no truth to declare without declarative sentences. If one were to contend that, "not all truth is propositional," we need only reply, "can you give me an example of a truth that is not propositional?" Any response at all proves that truth is propositional. Words are required to communicate truth, which is precisely why Jesus is called *the logos* (the Word) in John 1:1, "In the beginning was the Word, and the Word was with God, and the Word was God".

    > Now we have received…the Spirit who is from God, that we might understand the things freely given us by God.
    > And we impart this in words (i.e., propositionally) not taught by human wisdom but taught by the
    > Spirit, interpreting spiritual truths to those who are spiritual. (I Corinthians 2:12-13)

4. Truth is **intellectual**. If words are required to communicate truth, then truth necessitates an intellect or a mind, for one cannot form or communicate words/propositions without a mind. The argument, "truth does not require a mind," is only true if it can be argued without a mind, which is impossible. Hence, truth requires a mind. Truth is rational; it demands cognition, reasoning.

    > Come now, let us reason together, says the LORD. (Isaiah 1:18)

    > "For who has understood the mind of the Lord so as to instruct him?"
    > But we have the mind of Christ. (I Corinthians 2:16)

5. Truth is **inerrant**. It is error-free, infallible, perfect, pure, always right, never incorrect, etc. The claim, "truth is not always free of error," could only be true if truth is always free of error, which proves that truth is inerrant.

    > Every word of God is pure; He is a shield to those who take refuge in Him. (Proverbs 30:5)

    > The words of the LORD are pure words, like silver refined in a furnace…purified seven times. (Psalm 12:6)

In summary, truth is eternal, unchanging, propositional (must be declared), intellectual (requires a mind), and inerrant (error-free). Truth, therefore, must originate from an eternal, unchanging, inerrant, declarative, mind. This is God. More specifically, this is the essence of God's being as revealed in the Bible.

- **Faith** (defined)

Many people today would define faith as "A trust, or a belief, in something that is not necessarily based on proof or evidence." [72] However, this view makes faith out to be irrational, which is most certainly <u>not</u> the biblical view of faith. Webster's 1828 dictionary defines faith as "The assent of the mind to the truth of a proposition, advanced by another, by a belief, or by probable evidence of any kind." [73] Let's dig a bit deeper.

The word that is translated as "faith" in the Greek New Testament is "pistis", which comes from the word "peitho", meaning, "to be persuaded". The concept of *persuasion* entails the mind being presented with a certain proposition, weighing the proposition, and agreeing with or assenting to the proposition. In other words, biblical faith is intellectual assent to understood propositions.

Key Principle
Faith/belief: Intellectual assent to understood propositions.

"Faith" is synonymous with "belief" or "trust". To intellectually assent to an understood proposition is to place one's faith in the truthfulness of the proposition, to be persuaded that the proposition is true, to believe it, to trust it.

Why Study Philosophy?

The study of philosophy has always been a fundamental requirement in liberal arts education programs since the Reformation. This was certainly true of the first universities founded in America between 1640 and 1790, which were nearly all established by Christian denominations to "advance learning and perpetuate it to posterity; dreading to leave an illiterate ministry to the churches, when our present ministers shall lie in the dust." [74]

Although it is commonly recognized that these universities were established first and foremost for the purpose of preparing future ministers for service in Christian churches, very little is noted about the vast number of graduates from these institutions that went on to be leaders in law, politics, education, economics, science, and so on. These students not only learned to read the Bible in its original languages and to expound theology, but they also studied mathematics, astronomy, physics, botany, chemistry, philosophy, poetry, history, and medicine through a biblical lens. One authority describes the initial tradition at Harvard as one in which *"there was no distinction between a liberal and a theological education, and its two sources were first, the Holy Bible, and second, Aristotle."* [75]

ASSENT: DEFINITION

Assenting to is agreeing with and trusting in, to the point of belief in a certain idea or proposition. *Faith is not meant to be blind or passive!*
In Romans chapter one, it is made very clear that we all know there is a God and we have no excuse for denying Him (Romans 1:18-20). He has provided such an abundance of evidence in creation to support the General Revelation present in our souls, that to ignore this knowledge is deemed foolish. When the Bible states "without faith it is impossible to please God", we are to understand that He expects us to take that step based upon good reason and sufficient confirmation. We cannot separate faith from reason. God always gives us ample verification of Himself before He asks us to place our faith in Him.

---

[72] https://en.wikiquote.org/wiki/Faith

[73] http://webstersdictionary1828.com/Dictionary/faith

[74] http://www.constitution.org/primarysources/firstfruits.html, https://hds.harvard.edu/about/history-and-mission

[75] J. W. Ashley Smith, p. 71. Morison, Intellectual Life, similarly concludes that "Puritanism in New England preserved far more of the humanist tradition than did non-puritanism in the other English colonies" (p. 17).

It's critical to understand that one's philosophy is derived from his or her theology – his or her view of God. Philosophy flows out from theology (remember, the beginning of wisdom is the fear of the Lord). With this in mind, the philosophy which dominated the learning environment in those early universities was grounded upon the theology of Christianity, centered around the Bible. For example, one rule observed at Harvard was:

Harvard

Let every student be plainly instructed and earnestly pressed to consider well the main end of his life and studies is to know God and Jesus Christ which is eternal life, John 17:3, and therefore to lay Christ in the bottom, as the only foundation of all sound knowledge and learning. [76]

It is obvious that the Puritans – who founded Harvard - would be shocked by secular education devoid of religious purpose. In their view, such an education would lack the most essential ingredient. Cotton Mather expressed it thus:

"Before all, and above all, tis the knowledge of the Christian religion that parents are to teach their children…The knowledge of other things, though it be never so desirable an accomplishment for them, our children may arrive to eternal happiness without it. But the knowledge of the godly doctrine in the words of the Lord Jesus Christ is a million times more necessary for them." [77]

Education aimed at equipping the whole person

The distinguishing mark of the early colonial universities can be likened to the idea of bringing together many di<u>verse</u> areas of thought under one <u>uni</u>fying central theology (unifying a diversity of subjects is the central idea behind the term, ***university***). This philosophy of education combined biblical knowledge and extra-biblical knowledge, spiritual thought with material applications. The goal was not only to educate in a wide variety of academic fields, but to ensure that the virtues of biblical morality governed in all areas of life – doing all things with excellence and piety intermixed. The overarching philosophy of biblical morality enjoined with practical application was the target.

Samuel Willard summed up the ideal by asserting: "The Word of God and rule of religion teach us, not to destroy, but to improve every faculty that is in us…to the glory of God who gave them to us." All this integration was possible ultimately because of the Puritans' view of truth. In their view, God was the source and end of all truth. There is thus no dichotomy between biblical and extra-biblical truth. Samuel Willard's description once again serves as a fitting conclusion: "All streams do naturally lead down to the ocean; and all divine truths do as certainly carry us home to God himself, who is the essential truth. As truth comes from God, so it leads back to God." [78]

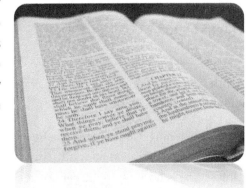

---

[76] New England's First Fruits Published 1643),[Miller/Johnson, 2:702].Ryken, Leland; Ryken, Leland. Worldly Saints: The Puritans As They Really Were (Kindle Location 3474). Zondervan. Kindle Edition

[77] Ryken, Leland; Ryken, Leland. Worldly Saints: The Puritans As They Really Were (Kindle Location 3485). Zondervan. Kindle Edition

[78] Heavenly Merchandise [Lowrie, p. 205]. Ryken, Leland; Ryken, Leland. Worldly Saints: The Puritans As They Really Were (Kindle Locations 6251-6252). Zondervan. Kindle Edition

Lesson 2 Study Questions

1. Read Psalm 19:7-9 (English Standard Version). How does David describe the Word of God (Scripture), and what does the Word of God do for those who believe it?

    1) The _____ of the LORD is _____ , _____ .

    2) The _____ of the LORD is _____ , _____ .

    3) The _____ of the LORD is _____ , _____ .

    4) The _____ of the LORD is _____ , _____ .

    5) The _____ of the LORD is _____ , _____ .

    6) The _____ of the LORD is _____ , _____ .

2. Now refer to the "DIVING DEEPER: THE CHARACTERISTICS OF TRUTH" section. What are the 5 characteristics that are listed? Truth is: _____ .

3. How do these 5 characteristics of truth compare to the 6 words that David uses to describe the Word of God in Psalm 19:7-9 (i.e., perfect, sure, right, pure, clean, true)?

    _____

    _____

    _____

4. If Philosophy deals in a large part with the questions – what is RIGHT and what is TRUE? – how important is the Word of God in developing our philosophy, especially when we consider Psalm 19:7-9?

    _____

    _____

5. If truth requires a mind that is eternal, unchanging, inerrant, and declarative, can truth exist apart from the God of the Bible? Put another way, is there any other philosophical belief system/religion that meets all these criteria of truth? _____

    _____

6. Truth is propositional, and a proposition is the meaning of a declarative sentence. Below are some examples of biblical propositions:

    In the beginning, God created the heavens and the earth.
    The greatest commandment is to love the Lord your God with all your heart, soul, mind, and strength.
    Unless one is born again, he cannot see the kingdom of God.
    No one can serve two masters.

    Give 5 more examples of propositions from the Bible.

    _____

    _____

    _____

_____

_____

7. Not all propositions are true. List some false propositions (bad ideas). For example: Life originated from non-life; God does not exist; etc.

_____

_____

_____

8. Our philosophy of life is based upon our IDEAS & BELIEFS about God. As Christians, it is vital that our ideas and beliefs about God are supported in Scripture. For example, what might be the result:

   a. If professing Christians believed that God would never send anyone to hell because God is love?

_____

_____

_____

   b. If professing Christians believed that God required them to do good works in order to receive eternal life?

_____

_____

_____

Lesson 3 – Philosophy and Culture

An Amusement-centered Society: Dumbing Us Down

Unfortunately, today we are surrounded by a culture that is primarily focused upon amusement, rather than upon learning. In an age that is dominated by television, video games, the internet, and other forms of electronic media, most young people today are far more interested in being entertained than in developing and cultivating their God-given gifts and talents. Our country's general philosophy of life has changed from *"be all you can be in preparation for this life and the next"*, to *"eat, drink and be merry because this life is all that there is."*

> ### PAUSE and CONSIDER
>
> It's important to note that when the first settlers came to America, the **average life span was less than 40 years**. When life is short and fraught with peril, people tend to take life more seriously, and to soberly consider what comes after death. However, with the average life span today estimated at close to 80 years, many have adopted a "put off until tomorrow" mentality. Thus, today we live in a culture that doesn't consider the pursuit of biblical knowledge and wisdom to be a high priority. That's just too much work (and it's boring). However, as we learned in the first chapter, it was our Puritan forefather's powerful work ethic and high regard for a biblical education that resulted in drastically raising the standards of living that we now enjoy. It's a general principle that honoring God's Word and working hard in the midst of hardship leads to blessing, while dishonoring God's Word and living complacently in the midst of ease leads to the removal of blessings.

If we don't aggressively address this 21st century imbalance between work and leisure, education and entertainment, we will suffer the consequences in the years to come.

The philosophy of the youth today will result in the society we will either enjoy – or be forced to endure – tomorrow.

The Aim of Christian Philosophy

The Christian God wants us to pursue His wisdom, to learn about Him. To study His ways and learn His will. If we believe that God is the omnipotent Creator of the universe and all of the life within it, then it is wise for us to seriously consider a few critical questions: *what is true*; *what is right*; *what matters in this life*? Even if one hasn't accepted the proposition that there is an infinite, all-powerful Creator, it's still wise to ponder the same inquiries. In today's colleges and universities, the prevailing philosophy regarding these questions goes something like this: "There's no such thing as absolute truth, everything is relative. You determine what is true and what is right and what matters."

> The word **AMUSE** is the joining of the word *muse*, which means "to deeply contemplate or think upon something", and the prefix *a*, which means "not". Thus, the word *amuse* conveys the idea of *not thinking or deeply contemplating*.

But Christianity is diametrically opposed to such relativism. Absolute truth exists because there is an absolute God who reveals truth (the essence of His being) in His Word. Thus, biblical truth is worth pursuing and living because without it we are like *"children, tossed to and fro and carried about with every wind of doctrine, by the trickery of men, in the cunning craftiness of deceitful plotting"* (Ephesians 4:14). And because we don't want to be deceived, we consider it essential to seriously ponder life's fundamental questions – the questions everyone would *muse* upon if they weren't so busy *a-musing* themselves to death.

Four Basic Questions of Life

There are 4 fundamental questions that any philosophy must answer:

---

1. Where did I come from?
2. Why am I here?
3. Where am I going?
4. How do I get there?

These are important questions that are worthy of our time and attention. As we progress through this chapter, we will examine competing philosophies to determine which one provides the most trustworthy answers to those four questions. It is vital that our lives be guided by a reliable philosophy!

Don't be Fooled!

Key scripture for this subject: Colossians 2:8
Beware lest anyone cheat you or take you captive through philosophy and empty deceit according to the tradition of men, according to the basic principles of the world, not according to Christ

---

To emphasize the importance of discerning the validity of philosophies and choosing which one will guide our lives, consider the following example.

The picture on the right was taken in a New York subway train several years ago. Notice the statements the advertisers are making.[79]

"Holidays come and go. Clothes wear out, bank accounts go up and down. But philosophy lasts a lifetime. This course, *Philosophy Works*, reveals how wisdom leads to happiness, shows how to live more consciously with greater purpose, and teaches how to harness the power of attention and realize one's potential." Sounds pretty appealing, doesn't it? You can imagine a lot of people saying, "I'll sign up for that. 10 lessons and I can turn my life around. Just pay them $120 bucks and take this class." But what is the source of the philosophy they are promoting?

A look at their website revealed the following: "*Philosophy Works* encourages everyone to access their inner happiness, wisdom, and strength. The premise is that there is "an inexhaustible source of strength and energy inside all of us" that is just waiting to be tapped into. Put another way, there's an inexhaustible (eternal) source of strength and energy <u>within</u> us that can give us all the answers, wisdom, understanding, and well-being that we desire. "The classes put students in touch with this inner resource." This certainly sounds intriguing, but it's completely at odds with the Christian worldview, which states that God alone is the inexhaustible (eternal) source

---

[79] https://philosophyworks.org/who-we-are/

of strength and energy Who can give us all the answers, wisdom, understanding, and well-being that we desire. Thus, as Christians, we don't look <u>within</u> ourselves for direction, we look <u>outside of</u> ourselves to God.

Again, what is *Philosophy Works* based upon? According to their website: "The curriculum is inspired by the philosophy of *Advaita* ("not two"), and embraces a wide range of philosophical ideas, tapping into the wisdom of the great minds of East and West, including Plato, Socrates, the Buddha, Shakespeare, Emerson and Shri Shantananda Saraswati." *Philosophy Works* is what might be called a New Age religion – a hybrid of several different philosophies.

So, does *Philosophy Works* actually deliver, does it really work? Remember, all philosophies stem from a theology, even if that theology states that God is unknowable or is nonexistent. In the case of *Philosophy Works*, their philosophy isn't based upon a single, all-knowing, wise God whose laws and standards are well-defined and clear. Thus, without an ultimate standard of truth from which to derive knowledge, what might we expect to be the results of a life devoted to such a philosophy? Consider the following scripture:

2 CORINTHIANS 10:4
For the weapons of our warfare are not of the flesh [carnal; of the world], but have divine power to destroy strongholds.

What is a stronghold? In this context, a stronghold is a bad idea that "captures" our mind and leads us into an intellectual dungeon. Bad ideas take away our freedom. Our job, then, is to "destroy [philosophical] arguments and every lofty opinion [bad idea] raised against the knowledge of God, and take every thought captive to obey Christ." (2 Corinthians 10:5) We are to <u>measure</u> every philosophical argument/opinion against Scripture, and any philosophical argument/idea that doesn't <u>measure up</u> to Scripture is to be rejected. In this way, we bring every thought into captivity to the obedience of Christ. We don't want any thought to be "captured" by the enemy, for any such thought is disobedient to Christ and binds us in an intellectual dungeon; rather, we want to "capture" every thought and make it obedient to Christ. We are constantly striving to discipline our minds to think like Christ.

Another key verse states,

ROMANS 12:2
Do not be conformed to this world, but be transformed by the renewal of your mind, that by testing you may discern what is the will of God, what is good and acceptable and perfect.

Here are 3 conclusions we may draw from this critical verse:

1. We are <u>not</u> to be conformed to the philosophies of this world

2. We are commanded to align the thoughts of our mind with the thoughts of the Mind who created us

3. In doing so, we come to the truth, for by definition, *truth* is that which conforms to the mind of God (*the essence of His being*)

The Tree of Your Life

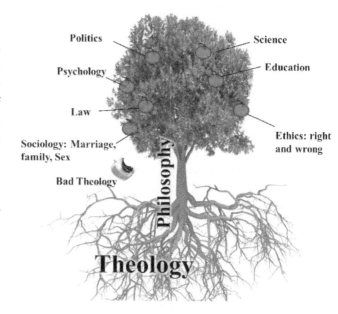

Figuratively speaking, your philosophy is the trunk and branches of the tree of your life, and your theology is the root system of this tree. The depths of the roots correspond to the depths of what you know and believe about God. Who is God? What does He say is good and right? What does He say is wicked and wrong? What are His laws? Your philosophy – what you determine to be true and worth pursuing, plus what you determine to be untrue and not worth pursuing – springs up from your theology. Thus, the more you study the Word of God, the healthier your theological root system will be. A healthy root system naturally leads to a healthy trunk and branches (philosophy), which in turn produces the highest quality fruit.

Good theology → good philosophy → produces sweet, wholesome, pristine, fresh fruit.
Bad theology → bad philosophy → produces rancid, contaminated, corrupt, rotten fruit.

Consider the words of Christ:

> ### LUKE 6:43-45
>
> For no good tree bears bad fruit, nor again does a bad tree bear good fruit, for each tree is known by its own fruit…The good person out of the good treasure of his heart produces good, and the evil person out of his evil treasure produces evil, for out of the abundance of the heart his mouth speaks.

Jesus is saying that the nature of a tree is what determines the fruit it will bear. If the nature of a tree is bad, it will bear bad fruit, and if the nature of a tree is good, it will bear good fruit. Likewise, a heart with good treasure <u>inside</u> (good roots) produces good <u>outwardly</u> (good fruit), and vice versa. But how do we get a heart with good treasure inside? We need good theology. If we want a good heart filled with good **treasure**, we must come to Christ, "in whom are hidden all the **treasures** of WISDOM (pure philosophy) and knowledge (pure theology)." (Colossians 2:3)

Notice that the fruit produced by "The Tree of Your Life" corresponds to the subjects that we're covering in this curriculum.

* **Sociology**. Sociology is the study of society and what makes it work. What makes it thrive or fail? Marriage and family are at the very center of the study of sociology in a Christian worldview. Our beliefs about sex and how we deal with sex in marriage and society are critical to the health and happiness of both.
* **Psychology**. This subject is of huge importance today. Why is our mind broken, and how do we fix it? Our beliefs about sin and the nature of man will dictate how we go about answering these questions. Here again, the Word of God is indispensable in order to obtain the correct diagnosis and treatment plan for the broken mind of man.

- **Politics**. Whether a person votes or not, he or she is playing a part in the political process in America. Our positions on political issues matter because we are responsible for the leaders we choose (or don't choose) to represent us – those who will create laws that will either be beneficial or harmful to us and to our society. How do we know which side of a particular political issue we should be on? How do we know if a particular law is good or bad? Well, does this particular law agree with the moral laws of God found in the Bible. We must look to the Word of God (because good theology produces good philosophy, right?).
- **Science, Education, Ethics, etc**. Our philosophy will affect all of these areas of life. Did human life ultimately come from non-living processes? Is man made in the image of an animal, or is he made in the image of God? Is it the government's responsibility to educate children? What does the Bible have to say about the parent's role in educating their children? If parents send their children to Caesar (the government), should they be surprised when their children come home as Romans (godless, statists)? How do we determine what is ethical or not? Do ethics depend on the given situation that we find ourselves in (situational ethics), or are there fixed, absolute ethical standards?

Bad theology (bad roots) in any one of the above worldview categories can potentially spread to corrupt the whole tree. Diseased roots in one area can eventually diffuse and infect the entire root system, causing the entire tree (philosophy) to be corrupted and all of its fruit to go rotten. Worse still, the rotten fruit that falls from your philosophical tree of life can be picked up and eaten by somebody else, which transfers your disease to their root system and can possibly corrupt their entire tree as well. The bad ideas that take hold in your life don't just affect you; they impact your friends, your family, and anyone else you might share them with. Bad ideas are like intellectual viruses. One virus (one bad idea) can take down the entire host (an individual's entire philosophical tree of life), and can also use that host to gain access to a host of others. For this reason, we must be vigilant to take every thought captive and make it obedient to Christ.

Lesson 3 Study Questions

1. What does the word *amuse* mean?

   _____

2. In your opinion, what are some of the consequences of a society that becomes amusement-centered?

   • _____

   • _____

   • _____

3. Read Eph. 5:15 and Phil. 4:8. What does the Bible say about how we are to spend our time and what we should be thinking upon? (Note: This is not to say that amusement does not have a place in our lives; we simply should not let the seeking of pleasure and amusement control our lives)

   _____

   _____

   _____

4. What are the four main questions everyone asks, and why are they important to muse upon?

   a. W_ _ _ _ did I come from?

   _____

   b. W_ _ am I here?

   _____

   c. W_ _ _ _ am I going?

   _____

   d. H_ _ do I get there?

   _____

5. Read 2 Corinthians 10:4-5. What does Paul mean when he says that the weapons of our warfare are not of the flesh (carnal, worldly)?

   _____

   _____

   What type of war does Paul have in mind (hint: we are in battle over _ _ _ _ _ _)?

   _____

6. If our weapons of warfare are not carnal, then what are the weapons of our warfare? (Hint: read Ephesians 6:10-18a, and don't forget about prayer.)

   _____

   _____

   _____

7. Read Romans 12:1-2, Proverbs 1:20-33, and Proverbs 24:7. According to these verses, why should it be a priority in every Christian's life to focus on the "renewing of our minds"? State 5 reasons why this is considered wise?

    1) _____

    2) _____

    3) _____

    4) _____

    5) _____

8. Read Luke 6:47-49. Compare Jesus' analogy of building a house to our "Tree of Your Life" analogy. How are the two analogies similar?

    _____

    _____

    _____

9. How important is it to come to Jesus, hear His words, and do them? Do these verses confirm our statement that good theology leads to good philosophy, which produces good fruit? Explain.

    _____

    _____

    _____

    _____

    _____

    _____

Lesson 4 – The Christian View

A Christian View of Philosophy: Foundation & Benefits

Christian Philosophy is based upon the eternal, unchanging Word of God

It's imperative that we understand that our philosophy *must* be based upon the word of God (theology). Why? Because philosophy is the love of wisdom, and wisdom is the practical application of knowledge. Wisdom is walking according to true thoughts of the mind (knowledge). And how do we obtain true thoughts of the mind (knowledge)? From the mind of God – the source of all knowledge. God must reveal the thoughts of His mind to our mind if we are to have true thoughts (knowledge), and once we obtain true thoughts of the mind (knowledge), we want to apply those thoughts practically in our daily lives (wisdom).

We want a philosophy that will keep us <u>sure-footed</u>, <u>safe</u>, and <u>headed in the right direction</u> as we walk through life. In order to be sure-footed, we need a constant source of light with no variation or shadow due to change (James 1:17), a perpetually burning lamp for our feet and a continuous light for our path (Psalm 119:105). To ensure constant safety and guidance, we need a moral compass that always points us in the direction of true north. In other words, if we want to be sure-footed, safe, and headed in the right direction, we need <u>rules (ordinances)</u> for walking the path of life that are **true**, **righteous**, and **everlasting**. Is there a philosophical flashlight and road map that we can trust?

*The sum of Your word is **truth**, and every one of Your **righteous** <u>ordinances</u> is **everlasting**.* (Psalm 119:160)

Wisdom is guided by principles that are rooted in eternal moral laws that never change. Said another way, wisdom is established upon truth, and as we've already learned, truth is eternal and unchanging. Thus, anyone who puts his or her trust in a philosophy that is not founded upon fixed laws and principles will be like a wave of the sea that is driven and tossed by the wind. By contrast, those who trust in the Word of God to be their anchor will be philosophically buoyed, regardless of the force of any opposing winds of the world.

> *[The LORD] will be the sure foundation (stability) for your times, a rich store of salvation and wisdom and knowledge; the fear of the LORD is the key to this treasure. (Isaiah 33:6)*

Why is the God of the Bible a sure foundation? Why does He provide stability for all our days? Because His Word never withers, fades, or passes away; it stands forever.

> *The grass withers, the flower fades, but the word of our God stands forever. (Isaiah 40:8)*
> *Heaven and earth will pass away, but My words will not pass away. (Matthew 24:35)*

No other philosophy/worldview/religion makes such bold, unconditional statements about its foundational writings. But the Bible doesn't just make these statements, it backs them up. The truth claims of the Bible are consistently confirmed – both throughout history, and when applied to our present reality. We will discuss this point in greater depth later in this chapter.

Christian philosophy practiced in real-life promises blessing

Psalm 128:1-2 and 4 says,
"Blessed is everyone who fears the LORD, who walks in His ways!
You shall eat the fruit of the labor of your hands; you shall be
blessed, and it shall be well with you….Behold, thus shall the man
be blessed who fears the Lord."

This is a promise by the Creator of the universe to you, individually.
But it's not an unconditional promise. What's the condition? You must fear the LORD, you must walk in His ways. If you desire the blessings of this promise, your philosophy needs to be the result of searching after the wisdom of God, not searching after the "so-called" wisdom of the world (1 Corinthians 3:18-19). We reap what we sow. In order to reap a healthy produce of blessing, we must sow the seeds of Biblical wisdom in the fear of the Lord. Accordingly, everything (every thought) needs to be run through the filter of the Bible (taken captive and made obedient to Christ) because we are told that everything we need to know for life and godliness is contained in Scripture. (2 Peter 1:3)

Christian Philosophy is Realistic

As we have said before, one of the main objectives of the subject of philosophy is to determine what is right and what is true. There are many competing philosophies that we may choose from, and though each will have something to say regarding what is right, they can't all be true. In fact, we would contend that Christian philosophy *alone* is true. How can we be so confident that Christianity, and *only* Christianity, owns the entire philosophical market of truth? Is there some sort of philosophical litmus test that can be used to weed out phony philosophies? It turns out that there is. The litmus test of philosophy is <u>physical reality</u>. Consider the following:

---

*For everyone practicing evil hates the light and does not come to the light,
lest his deeds should be exposed. But he who does the truth comes to the light,
that his deeds may be clearly seen, that they have been done in God.*
(John 3:20-21)

This passage states that those who walk in wickedness try to conceal it because they don't want to be seen for what they are – immoral; whereas the one who walks morally upright (does the truth) has nothing to hide. Note the direct correlation here between truth and morality, which confirms what we said earlier – *truth is moral*.

We can infer a general principle from these verses → physical reality exposes us for who we are.

We cannot hide our philosophical assumptions about what is right and what is true, though we might try. As the saying goes, "it will all come out in the wash" eventually. Our ideas of what is right and what is true don't sit dormant in our heads, they get put into practice by our hands. The question is, what happens when our philosophical rubber hits the road of physical reality? Do our philosophical tires hold up, or does reality cause us to skid off the road and over a cliff? Are there gaping holes in our philosophy – do our tires immediately go flat the moment they touch concrete reality? The point we're <u>driving at</u> (get it?) is that *truth will always be confirmed in our physical reality*.

There are innumerable bad ideas being promoted in this world that are taught as fact, even though our physical reality tells us otherwise. With a little critical thinking, we can use our physical reality as a means of testing the validity of ideas –both our own and the ideas of others. Ideas that are inconsistent with our physical reality can be rejected as bad ideas.

Sadly, most people consume ideas uncritically; they simply accept everything that is being fed to them via news channels, entertainment, social media posts, etc., and swallow it whole. It's been said, "You are what you eat." Imagine this applied to the uncritical mind that eats anything it's given – including massive amounts of junk food and worse still, lethal poison! Proverbs 14:15 says, "The simple believes everything, but the prudent gives thought to his steps." This is just another way of saying that it's absolutely foolish to take in ideas uncritically. Why? Because...

Ideas have consequences

It would be foolish to jump off of a 30-story building without some kind of parachute or safety net. Why? Because the law of gravity predicts that we would likely not survive such an experience. This idea is easily verified in the real world. Thus, it is wise to obey the physical law of gravity.

Similarly, reality confirms the idea that it's wrong to commit murder. How? The conscience. Every one of us is born with a conscience that convicts us of immorality, and our bodies can actually *feel* the conscience convicting us. The idea of murder – the unlawful premeditated killing of one human being by another – is a concept that the conscience condemns as being immoral, and society reinforces this innate moral law and this natural conviction of the conscience by punishing those who violate it. Thus, it is wise to listen to our conscience and to obey the innate moral law, "you shall not murder." Moreover, both of these ideas – that we are all born with a moral law written on our heart (including the law that murder is wrong), and that we are born with a conscience that convicts us when we break this moral law – are entirely consistent with what the Bible teaches (Romans 2:14-15). Thus, these Biblical ideas are validated by what we see in reality. The Bible makes many such truth-claims that can be tested in the real world, and when tested, they are never found wanting – they are always authenticated.

The point is that ideas have consequences, and those consequences are borne out in our physical reality. There are consequences for disobeying God's moral laws just as there are consequences for disobeying His physical laws. However, the consequences for disobeying His moral laws are far worse than the consequences for violating His physical laws. Luke 12:4-5 states, "I tell you, my friends, do not fear those who kill the body, and after that have nothing more that they can do. But I will warn you whom to fear: fear Him who, after He has killed, has authority to cast into hell. Yes, I tell you, fear Him!"

Lesson 4 Study Questions

1. Why is it imperative for us to understand that our philosophy *must* be based upon the word of God?

   _____

   _____

2. Reread the very 1ˢᵗ paragraph of this Lesson 4 section.
   a. How many definitions of key philosophical terms can you spot in this 1ˢᵗ paragraph? _____
   b. What would be the result if we didn't have clear definitions, especially with regard to key philosophical terms?

   _____

   _____

   _____

3. Our philosophy is the result of our fundamental beliefs about God, and those beliefs will guide us in every major decision we make.
   a. What should be the source of a Christian's philosophy? _____
   b. Do you think most Christians understand the weight of this principle? Explain your answer.

   _____

   _____

   c. What would be the result if Christians mixed their philosophy with other philosophies?

   _____

   _____

   _____

4. *We want a philosophy that will keep us sure-footed, safe, and headed in the right direction as we walk through life. What does our philosophy need to have in order to accomplish this?*

   _____

5. If everyone who fears the LORD and walks in His ways is promised blessings, what do you think is promised to those who don't fear the LORD and walk according to their own ways? Give 3 Scriptures that support your answer.

   _____

   _____

   _____

6. What is the philosophical litmus test that can be used to weed out phony philosophies? _____

7. Why is it so important to critically think through the ideas that are presented to us, and what can happen if we fail to do so?

   _____

   _____

   _____

   _____

Lesson 5 – Compare and Contrast

Two views of reality

In our society today, there are two primary (and fundamentally opposed) interpretations of what constitutes reality.

1. *Reality is only physical.* This is the view of Materialism/metaphysical Naturalism, which states that matter is the fundamental substance in nature, and that all things, including mental aspects and consciousness, are results of material interactions. Put simply, matter is all that matters; only what can be observed by the senses – what we can taste, touch, see, smell, and hear – is real. Thus, belief in Materialism/metaphysical Naturalism automatically rejects any notion of a spiritual reality. This is the prevalent philosophy in most universities and colleges.

   Can we test this view? Sure. Simply ask the proponent of Materialism/metaphysical Naturalism if ideas are real. What is the atomic mass of the idea, "only what can be observed by the senses is real"? How long is this thought in centimeters? Clearly, ideas are not made up of protons, neutrons, and electrons; neither is the concept of "mind" or "knowledge" or "truth". What is the melting point of truth, and if truth does melt, is it still true?

   Such questions prove that the idea – *reality is only physical* – is inconsistent with our physical reality. Matter is unable to explain ideas, minds, thoughts, knowledge, truth, etc. Thus, reality must be more than meets the eye, it must be more than purely physical. We shall revisit and further unpack this in our chapter on science.

2. *Reality is both physical (natural) and spiritual (supernatural).* This is the Christian worldview. We see this idea conveyed in the very first verse of the Bible. Genesis 1:1 declares, "In the beginning, God..." God is not physical, He is spiritual; He is not natural, He is supernatural. And what did God do in the beginning? He "created the heavens and the earth" – the physical universe. Right out of the gate, the Bible affirms that there is both a natural (physical) and a supernatural (spiritual) reality. Thus, the Biblical account of reality explains both the material (protons, neutrons, electrons, etc.) as well as the immaterial (ideas, minds, thoughts, knowledge, truth, etc.).

Which of these two views of reality is more reasonable?

Remember, our God is rational. He doesn't expect us to accept His Word uncritically – quite the opposite, in fact. God encourages us to reason with Him (Isaiah 1:18). Indeed, the Bible repeatedly commands us to love God with all our heart, soul, and *mind*.

Four Main Questions

In Day 2 of this chapter, we said philosophy must answer these four fundamental questions: *Where did I come from? Why am I here? Where am I going? How do I get there?*

Let's look at these questions and see which worldview/religious philosophy has the best answers. Remember, a philosophy is only *reliable* if the answers that it provides to these questions are *rational* and *realistic* (i.e., confirmed by our physical reality).

HUMANISM

The Oxford English Dictionary defines *Humanism* as: *a system of thought that considers that solving human problems with the help of reason is more important than religious beliefs. It emphasizes the fact that the basic nature of humans is good.* Humanism has been the core philosophy of our national education system for nearly the past century. As a result, humanist philosophy has become the predominant worldview of our society. How does Humanism answer our four fundamental questions?

Where did I come from?

The humanist's rejection/denial of religious beliefs necessarily leads to an affirmation of evolution. Therefore, the humanist answer to the question – *Where did I come from?* – is prebiotic soup. Ultimately, you and I are the result of accidental pond scum; we're simply highly evolved animals. Look at the monkey over there. He's your ancestor. One Christian apologist stated, "From the goo, to the zoo, to you."

Why am I here?

If life is simply the product of an unintelligent, unguided chemical pinball machine, then obviously human life has no special significance. Random chance, by definition, is something that occurs in the absence of any purposeful decision-making process or conscious design. Hence, there is no underlying reason or purpose to your life.

Where am I going?

Again, if you and I are here by random chance events, then we're going *nowhere*. Randomness has no goal or objective, and chance is in direct opposition to planning. The final destination of life is death, pure and simple. Our destiny is to break down into a chemical slushy, to go back to where we came from – meaningless chemistry.

How do I get there?

How do you get where? You're not going anywhere because your life is meaningless. The universe didn't have you in mind because the universe doesn't have a mind. So just eat, drink, and be merry, for tomorrow you die! Or don't do any of these things, it doesn't really matter in the end.

If these are the answers that Humanism has to offer, why do so many subscribe to this depressing philosophy? Perhaps because Humanism requires no individual accountability or personal responsibility. All that is required is to suppress the built-in knowledge of God; to make man the measure of all things in place of the everlasting moral law of God. But at what cost? Only the significance of your entire existence.

ISLAM

As mentioned in the previous chapter, Islam is the world's second largest religion. Let's see how Islam answers our four fundamental questions:

Where did I come from?

The Quran does not provide a unified creation narrative. There is nothing in the Quran that is comparable to the opening chapters of the book of Genesis in the Bible. Rather, the Quran contains a smattering of scattered verses with regard to the creation of the world and the creation of man. For example, regarding the creation of man, Surah 32:7-8 reads,

"He [Allah] originated the creation of man out of clay, then he fashioned his progeny of an extraction of mean water, then He shaped him, and breathed his spirit in him."

It's quite clear from these verses that the Quran's version of the creation of man has been taken from the Bible since this passage is nearly identical to Genesis 2:7. In other words, the Quran's version of the creation of man is unoriginal. However, there is a huge difference between the Bible and the Quran concerning the purpose of man - why man was created. The Quran does not say that man was uniquely created in the likeness of God for the purpose of imaging God upon the earth. The Bible does.

Why am I here?

Islam teaches that man was made to submit to Allah's authority, nothing more and nothing less. Indeed, the word *Islam* comes from Arabic *'islām* 'submission', from *'aslama* 'submit (to God)'. Thus, according to Islam, the chief end of man is not to glorify God and to love Him forever (as it is in Christianity), the chief end of man is to bow down in submission to Allah. You solely exist to be subjugated – to be brought under the domination and control of Allah by way of conquest.

Where am I going?

The Quran promises paradise (heaven) to its followers, and eternal damnation (hell) to unbelievers: "Those who disbelieve – there awaits them a terrible chastisement; but those who believe, and do deeds of righteousness – theirs shall be a great wage." (Surah 35:7) The "great wage" that is promised to Muslims is paradise – "Gardens of Delight" – where they will recline on luxurious couches while being waited upon by immortal youths, and will enjoy sensual pleasures of choice food and drink, fine clothing and jewelry, and beautiful virgins (Surah 56:12-37).

> ### REMEMBER
> *Every worldview rests on one or more foundational axioms or 1st principles, and an axiom, by definition, is not proved. However, an axiom <u>must be defensible</u>. In order for a worldview to be trustworthy, its axioms must pass the tests of logic and reason and be consistently confirmed in reality.*

Incidentally, those who believe in the Bible are referred to as "the People of the Book" (i.e., Jews & Christians), and are considered "the worst of creatures". Thus, those who believe that the Bible alone is the Word of God go to hell, whereas those who reject that the Bible alone is the Word of God, and believe the Quran and do good works, go to heaven:

"The unbelievers of the People of the Book and the idolaters shall be in the Fire of Gehenna, therein dwelling forever; those are the worst creatures. But those who believe, and do righteous deeds, those are the best of creatures; their recompense is with their Lord [Allah] – gardens of Eden, underneath which rivers flow, therein dwelling for ever and ever." (Surah 98:5-8)

How do I get there?

Islam is entirely a works-based religion. Therefore, in order to go to paradise, you must obey the Quran, and your good deeds must outweigh the bad: "...those whose scales are heavy [with good deeds] – they are the prosperous, and those whose scales are light [with good deeds] – they have lost their souls in Gehenna dwelling forever, the fire will scorch their faces and they will grin therein with their lips displaced." (Surah 23:102-104) Unfortunately, nobody, except for Allah, knows just how many good deeds are enough to cancel out the bad deeds; therefore, the Quran never explicitly guarantees paradise for anyone. Entrance into paradise is wholly dependent upon whether or not Allah will grant mercy to an individual based upon his or her performance. "To Allah belongs the kingdom of the heavens and of the earth; he forgives whom he will, and he punishes whom he will..." (Surah 48:14) The bottom line is this: if you want to reach paradise, you need to be good enough in the eyes of Allah, but the tally of your good works vs. bad is known only to him. Not to worry though, Allah is said to be "all-forgiving" and "all-compassionate."

BUDDHISM

Where did I come from?

At the heart of Buddhism is the concept of *Saṃsāra* (Sanskrit for "flowing on" or "passing through") – a <u>beginningless</u> cycle of repeated birth, life, death, and rebirth. Saṃsāra is a cycle of conditioned existences (reincarnations) that is perpetuated by the accumulation of Karma, and terminates only if/when Enlightenment or Nirvana is reached. Thus, according to Buddhism, you came from a past life, of a past life, of a past life, etc., etc., *ad infinitum*. Ultimately, your existence never really "began" because this cycle of existences (reincarnations) that you are currently stuck in is a cycle that had no beginning. You may be wondering how a cycle can begin if it has no beginning? How indeed.

Why am I here?

Buddhism lacks a doctrine of creation because all of life is merely an illusion that results in suffering; therefore, the goal of Buddhism is to escape reality, not study it. One of the weaknesses of Buddhism as a viable philosophy is that it simply does not deal with the major questions relating to the origin and purpose of life.

Where am I going?

The ultimate goal of Buddhism is to reach Nirvana: the cessation of existence in which the candle of life is blown out. Thus, until you're able to attain this state of nirvana (where you cease to be), you aren't really going anywhere. You're simply trapped in a karma-driven cycle of existences (reincarnations) – a cycle that had no

The Buddhist Wheel of Life

beginning – and the only way out of this cycle is to cease to exist. In other words, Buddhism can't explain how you came to be (exist), but your being (existence) is a problem, and the only solution to this problem is for you to stop being (existing). *Where am I going?* Buddhism answers: You're going to a "place" (nirvana) in which you are no longer anywhere because the candle of "you" has been completely snuffed out, the flame of your life has been extinguished. Buddhism can therefore be thought of as the "going, going, gone" philosophy. You're going, going (round and round the cycle of birth, life, death, and rebirth), until you're finally gone (reach nirvana and cease to exist).

Here we can see how Buddhism's philosophical diagnosis of man leads us to an entirely different treatment plan when compared to Christianity. Christianity defines the human problem as sin, whereas Buddhism defines the human problem as suffering brought about by desire, which gives rise to the effects of karma, which in turn results in samsara. In the Buddhist view, "salvation" means the escape from desire and from the cycle of birth, life, death, and rebirth; while the Christian view of salvation is to escape the wrath of God brought upon us by sin, and to enjoy the fullness of life that results from being reconciled to God through the birth, life, death, and resurrection of Christ. In Buddhism, the goal is to stop being reborn; whereas in Christianity, the objective *is* to be reborn (born again).

"Salvation" in the Buddhist sense, is the exact opposite of Christian doctrine.

How do I get there?

The only way to escape the vicious cycle of suffering (unsatisfactoriness) is to dispel one's ignorance and cravings (via meditation) by realizing the Four Noble Truths and practicing the Eightfold Path, thus attaining Nirvana.

Lesson 5 Study Questions

A. Briefly define and explain the two main views of reality in our day. 1) _____

_____

2) _____

B. Which view seems more reasonable, and why? _____

_____

C. The 4 Main Philosophical Questions of Life

1. Humanism: Briefly explain how Humanism answers our four main philosophical questions.

    a) Where did I come from? _____

    b) Why am I here? _____

    c) Where am I going? _____

    d) How do I get there? _____

2. What problems or benefits, if any, do you find in the answers that Humanism provides to our four main questions?

_____

_____

_____

_____

3. Islam: Briefly explain how Islam answers our four main philosophical questions.

    a) Where did I come from? _____

    b) Why am I here? _____

    c) Where am I going? _____

    d) How do I get there? _____

4. What problems or benefits, if any, do you find in the answers that Islam provides to our four main questions?

_____

_____

_____

_____

5. Buddhism: Briefly explain how Buddhism answers our four main philosophical questions.

    a) Where did I come from? _____

    b) Why am I here? _____

    c) Where am I going? _____

    d) How do I get there? _____

6. What problems or benefits, if any, do you find in the answers that Buddhism provides to our four main questions?

_____

_____

_____

_____

Lesson 6 – Compare & Contrast, Part 2

Four Main Questions (cont.)

HINDUISM

The answers that Hinduism gives to our four main questions are very similar to the answers provided by Buddhism. This makes sense when we understand that Buddhism originated from and has close ties to Hinduism. Indeed, the founder of Buddhism, Siddhartha Gautama, was raised to believe as a Hindu, but chose to reject the teachings of the Hindu Vedas. Thus, even though Gautama Buddha rejected the Hindu scriptures and the gods of Hinduism; nevertheless, he was still influenced by the Hindu worldview in which he was raised.

Where did I come from?
Like Buddhism, Hinduism believes that we are all caught in a beginningless cycle of birth, life, death, and rebirth referred to as Saṃsāra. Thus, you came from a past life, of a past life, of a past life, etc., etc., *ad infinitum*.

Why am I here?
Although there is a Hindu creator god (Brahma), Hinduism (like Buddhism) lacks any definitive doctrine of creation. Hindus do not believe in a personal creator God as do Christians, they believe that the multitude of gods in the world make up one impersonal, ultimate reality – Brahman. They believe that Brahman inhabits all life forms and that we are identical with the ultimate reality or spiritual force that represents this divinity. Therefore, because there is only an impersonal ultimate reality or spiritual force, rather than a personal creator God, there is no reason for our being here. There is no significance to your life because significance can only be defined by a mind – a person – which Brahman is not.

Where am I going?
Similar to Buddhism, the chief aim in Hinduism is to gain release from the cycle of reincarnation caused by karma – the consequences of past actions, in this or in previous lives. However, unlike Buddhism, there are actually four goals of life that are permissible to Hindus. Hinduism recognizes that in the course of many lifetimes people may legitimately give themselves to any of these four goals. The first is the goal of pleasure or enjoyment, particularly through love and sexual desire. This is called *kama*. The second legitimate aim in life is for wealth and success, which is known as *artha*. The third aim in life is moral duty or *dharma*. One who gives himself to dharma renounces personal pleasure and power in order to seek the common good. The final (and ultimate) aim in life, however, is *moksha* – liberation from the cycle of lives in this material world, and the attainment of nirvana.

The Hindu concept of nirvana (moksha) is not identical to the Buddhist concept of nirvana. For the Hindu, nirvana does not entail a complete loss of *existence*, it entails a complete loss of *personality*. The person of the Hindu "dissolves" into the impersonal, ultimate reality of Brahman. The Hindu version of nirvana is more like a droplet of water merging into the ocean (of Brahman) than it is a candle being finally blown out.

How do I get there?
Hindus recognize three possible paths to moksha, or salvation.
1. **The first is the way of works or *karma yoga*.** This is a very popular way of salvation that emphasizes the idea that liberation may be obtained by fulfilling one's familial and social duties, thereby overcoming the weight of bad karma one has accrued. The Code of Manu lists many of these rules. Most important among them are certain rituals conducted at various stages of life.
2. **The second way of salvation is the way of knowledge or *jnana yoga*.** The basic premise of the way of knowledge is that the cause of our bondage to the cycle of rebirths in this world is ignorance or *avidya*. According to the predominant view among those committed to this way, our ignorance consists of the

mistaken belief that we are individual selves and not one with the ultimate divine reality called Brahman. It is this ignorance that gives rise to our bad actions which result in bad karma. Salvation is achieved through attaining a state of consciousness in which we realize our identity with Brahman. This is achieved through deep meditation, often as a part of the discipline of yoga.

3. **The third and final way of salvation is the way of devotion or *bhakti yoga*.** This is the way most favored by the common people of India as it satisfies the longing for a more emotional and personal approach to religion. It mainly involves self-surrender to one of the many personal gods and goddesses of Hinduism. Such devotion is expressed through acts of worship (*puja*) at the temple, in the home, through participation in the many festivals in honor of such gods, and through pilgrimages to one of the numerous holy sites in India. In the way of devotion, the focus is on obtaining the mercy and help of a god in finding release from the cycle of reincarnation.

CHRISTIANITY

What does Christianity say? How does the Bible answer our four main philosophical questions?

Where did I come from?
Unlike the other worldviews that we have investigated, the Bible provides a detailed account of creation, including the creation of man. The first chapter of the book of Genesis states that God created the material universe by the power of His Word, apart from any previously existing materials. Regarding the creation of man, the Bible states that, "the LORD God formed the man of dust from the ground and breathed into his nostrils the breath of life, and the man became a living creature." (Genesis 2:7) Similarly, in the book of Job we read:

> The Spirit of God has made me, and the breath of the Almighty gives me life. (Job 33:4)

> But there is a spirit in man, and the breath of the Almighty gives him understanding. (Job 32:8)

The breath of life that God personally breathed into Adam's nostrils was what authenticated man as being the unique image-bearer of God, and this concept of image-bearing provides a perfect segue to our next question. One could say that our lives began with a Divine kiss from our Heavenly Father.

Pause and Consider

The Christian answer to the question – Why am I here? – is incredibly profound. Man was made to righteously represent the Creator of the universe as His designated prophet, priest, and king upon the earth! Is there any higher privilege or honor that could be bestowed upon a creature?!

Why am I here?
The Westminster Shorter Catechism begins with the following question: *What is the chief end of man?* This is just another way of asking: *Why am I here?* And the catechism famously answers: *Man's chief end is to glorify God (I Corinthians 10:31; Romans 11:36), and to enjoy Him forever (Psalm 73:25-28).*

Of all of God's creatures, only man has been made to reflect the very image of God (Genesis 1:26-27). Thus, you and I are here – we were made – to glorify, worship, and enjoy God as His unique image-bearers. But this just begs the question – *What does it mean to bear the image of God?*

Many learned theologians have tackled this question, and a variety of answers have been put forth for consideration. A common approach is to answer the question of image-bearing by focusing on the distinguishing characteristics of man that separate him from the lower creatures (e.g., rationality, morality, creativity, etc.) This approach attempts to answer the question of image-bearing by looking at the nature of man. However, the concept of image-bearing primarily has human <u>identity</u> in view, rather than human nature.

Prophet, Priest, and King

Questions of identity have to do with meaning; i.e., why am I here? Therefore, with this in mind, we would argue that **to bear the image of God is to find one's identity (significance and security) in the God of the Bible (Yahweh); to worship and glorify Yahweh by reflecting His moral character as a representative prophet, priest, and king.**

Adam (man) was made to represent God upon the earth through the offices of prophet, priest, and king. In other words, Adam (man) was made to speak the truth (as a prophet), to pray and sacrificially intercede for others in truth (as a priest), and to rule according to the truth and to guard and defend the truth (as a king).

Though Adam failed to reflect God when he sinned in the garden; nevertheless, man's purpose and significance as an image-bearer was not revoked or rescinded. Man did not lose his identity as a result of the fall; sin simply introduced an identity crisis for man. This is why the second Adam (Christ) came to earth – to resolve man's identity crisis by doing what the first Adam failed to do; to perfectly represent God upon the earth as a prophet, priest, and king:

> ...in these last days He [God] has spoken to us by His Son [**prophet**], whom He appointed the heir of all things, through whom also He created the world. [3] He is the radiance of the glory of God and the exact imprint of His nature [**the perfect image-bearer**], and He upholds the universe by the word of His power. After making purification for sins [**priest**], He sat down at the right hand of the Majesty on high [**king**]. (Hebrews 1:2-4)

Having accomplished this mission, Christ is now able to restore the identity of anyone who believes in Him. Jesus unites the Christian to Himself so that the Christian becomes a righteous prophet, priest, and king, just as He is.

> But you are a chosen generation, a royal [**kings**] priesthood [**priests**], a holy nation, His own special people, that you may proclaim [as **prophets**] the praises of Him who called you out of darkness into His marvelous light... (I Peter 2:9)

Where am I going?
The Bible teaches that every man is appointed to die <u>once</u> and then face judgment (Hebrews 9:27); thus, there is no concept of reincarnation in Christianity. Upon death, every man will be judged by Christ according to whether or not he or she repented and believed in Christ and His gospel (Matthew 25:31-46). Those who rejected Christ and His gospel (unbelievers, non-Christians) will be sentenced to eternal damnation in hell (Revelation 20:14-15),

and those who were granted repentance and given the gift of faith to believe in Christ and His gospel (Christians) will enjoy living in the presence of God forever and ever in the new heaven and the new earth, where:

> He will wipe away every tear from their eyes, and death shall be no more, neither shall there be mourning, nor crying, nor pain anymore, for the former things have passed away. (Revelation 21:4)

How do I get there?

Christianity is the only religion/worldview that is **not** works-based. Christianity teaches that man is utterly unable to save himself. In fact, unbelievers are at enmity with God; they do not and cannot submit to God's laws, and thus can do nothing to please God. (Romans 8:7-8)

So, if man cannot save himself, how then is he saved? Through repentance and faith in Christ. However, man cannot repent and believe in Christ on his own. Repentance must be granted by God (2 Timothy 2:24-25), and faith is a gracious gift of God, lest any man boast.

> For by grace you have been saved through faith. And this is not your own doing; it is the gift of God, [9] not a result of works, so that no one may boast. (Ephesians 2:8-9) Thus, we come to another key principle of Christianity:

Key Principle

Thus, salvation is by grace alone, through faith alone, in Christ alone. *Salvation is entirely of the Lord!*

Lesson 6 Study Questions

1. Hinduism: Briefly explain how Hinduism answers our four main philosophical questions.

    a) *Where did I come from?* _____

    b) *Why am I here?* _____

    c) *Where am I going?* _____

    d) *How do I get there?* _____

2. What problems or benefits, if any, do you find in the answers that Hinduism provides to our four main questions?

    _____

    _____

    _____

    _____

3. Christianity: Briefly explain how Christianity answers our four main philosophical questions.

    a) *Where did I come from?* _____

    b) *Why am I here?* _____

    c) *Where am I going?* _____

    d) *How do I get there?* _____

4. What problems or benefits, if any, do you find in the answers that Christianity provides to our four main questions?

    _____

    _____

    _____

    _____

5. How important do you consider these 4 main philosophical questions to be? Have you ever put much thought into any or all of them? Why or why not?

    _____

    _____

    _____

6. Which of the 5 philosophical religions/worldviews seemed the most logical? _____ Why?

    _____

    _____

    _____

7. Which of the 5 philosophical religions/worldviews seemed the most illogical? _____ Why?

_____

_____

_____

_____

8. In what ways is the Christian worldview <u>unique</u> when compared to the other 4 religions/worldviews?

_____

_____

_____

9. What does it mean to bear the image of God?

_____

_____

10. Do you find the Christian concept of image-bearing to be a good answer to the question – *Why am I here?* Does the concept of image-bearing provide significance/meaning/purpose to your life? Explain your answer.

_____

_____

_____

_____

Lesson 7 – Testing the Faiths

All philosophies are based upon faith in a fundamental set up principles and propositions. But faith in principles that don't hold up in reality is what we have defined previously as *blind* faith, and no reasonable person wants to discover the hard way that the principles he has built his philosophy of life upon *fail* when put to the test. With this in mind, we will be spending the rest of our time in this chapter putting each of the five main religions through three tests to see if they work in reality. These three tests are:

1. The Common Sense test
2. The Scientific Validation test
3. The Historical Collaboration test

This procedure is simply an exercise in critical-thinking, a very necessary discipline for everyone to develop that brings great rewards to all who practice it regularly. Critical thinking requires testing and is a fundamental necessity in the Christian faith.

"Does not the ear test words, as the palate tastes its food?" (Job 12:11)

Before we begin the testing of the faiths, let's look at how Christianity views the art of thinking critically.

A Reasonable, Intelligent Faith

Key Principle: *Christianity says that the Bible is true because its truths can be tested.*

Christianity is the most clearly defined religion/worldview in human history because its entire philosophy is spelled out in one book that defines its doctrines explicitly and consistently. Two scriptures in particular convey this thought:

2 Timothy 3:16-17 – *"All Scripture is God-breathed, and is profitable for doctrine, for reproof, for correction, for instruction in righteousness, that the man of God may be complete, thoroughly equipped for every good work."*

2 Peter 1:3 – *"His Divine power has given to us all things that pertain to life and godliness, through the knowledge of Him…"*

By these scriptures we understand that the Bible claims to contain *everything* we need for clear doctrine (our beliefs) as well as instruction for all areas of life. In other words, the Bible is the Christian handbook for living. This means that through the Bible we can learn *what is true* and *how to apply those truths in real life*.

Christianity and Critical Thinking

Christians as well as all people are required to think critically. The God of the Bible calls us to reason with Him (Isaiah 1:18). Up until the mid-20th century, educating students to critically think had always been a central part of the school curriculum in America. But that goal has been eliminated from public education over the last sixty years. Today, most schools require strict adherence to the official views of the politically correct ideas of the day.

Critical thinking requires the presence of contrasting ideas or views. For example, how would we ever appreciate or understand light if there was no darkness? If there was no presence of loneliness, how could we appreciate or understand love? Contrast is what enables us to distinguish one thing from another – whether physical or non-physical. Accordingly, contrasting ideas are necessary for us to determine whether or not a particular idea is logical, beneficial, and trustworthy.

Beginning Our Critical Thinking at The Beginning

Analyzing and evaluating the axiom(s) of a particular philosophy/religion/worldview is always the best place to begin our critical thinking. Every philosophy/religion/worldview begins with (is founded upon) certain 1st principles or axioms; thus, where better to begin than at the beginning?

We've already introduced the idea of an axiom, but let's take some time to elaborate upon this vital philosophical term. An **axiom is a proposition that is assumed to be true without proof; a truth that is considered to be self-evident**. It is essential that we understand that **an axiom cannot be proved**. If a first principle could be proved by appealing to a prior principle, then that prior principle would be the first principle. The only thing "before" a <u>first principle</u> is infinite regression, which is no principle at all. Therefore, <u>to demand that everything be proved is an **irrational** demand</u>.

For example, let's say that our starting point is axiom Z, and someone says, "prove it." If we appeal to something "greater" than axiom Z, say axiom Y, then clearly axiom Z was not our starting point.

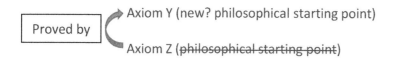

But even if we appeal to axiom Y, someone will say, "prove it." And if we appeal to something "greater" than axiom Y, say axiom X, then once again it is clear that axiom Y is not our starting point.

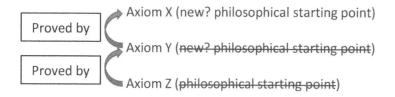

Obviously, this could go on *ad infinitum*, in which case nobody would ever be able to begin any kind of meaningful discussion about anything. Thus, <u>to demand that everything be proved is an **irrational** demand</u>. One does not argue *for* an axiom; one argues *from* an axiom.

Again, every philosophical system must be allowed a first principle – an unproved beginning or starting point; otherwise, there cannot be a second, third, or fourth principle, etc. Hence, critically thinking through a philosophical worldview should always begin at the beginning, which is to say, by testing the validity of a worldview's philosophical axiom(s). Though an axiom is never *proved*, nevertheless, an axiom must be *defensible*; it must be coherent (logical and consistent).

Testing the World Religions. What is True? What makes sense to live by?

Let us now test the first principles/axioms of the five major religions we have been examining in order to see which worldview leads to the most logical philosophy to live by. Remember, as we test the rationality of each religion, we always want to keep in mind what we learned in the "Tree of Your Life" section back in day 2 of this chapter: Your philosophy – what you determine to be true and worth pursuing, and what you determine to be untrue and not worth pursuing – springs up from your theology.

Good theology → good philosophy → produces sweet, wholesome, pristine, fresh fruit.

Your philosophical fruit is only as good as your theological root. In other words, where you begin determines where you will end. A bad first principle/axiom will inevitably lead to bad fruit. Hence, we need to be philosophical fruit inspectors. If we consistently find bad fruit being produced from a particular religion, it means that the root system is bad and the first principles/axioms of that religion should therefore be rejected.

Test #1: Common Sense and Observation

Humanism

The fundamental axiom of Humanist philosophy begins with rejecting God and embracing evolution; thus, man becomes his own god. However, this rejection of God does not match the innate beliefs of the vast majority of human beings. (see below).

The observable result: This philosophical base promotes socialism, communism or Marxism and has ruled in Stalin's Russia, Hitler's Germany, Castro's Cuba and Mao Tse-Tung's China – all of which displayed tyranny at the highest level.

Islam
The foundational axiom of Islamic philosophy is that God – Allah – is one God, creator of the universe, and wholly independent of creation. Quran – the holy book of Islam - defines Islam and is considered the source of truth. However, the doctrines contained in the Quran and descriptions of the character of Allah are often cloudy and contradictory, leading to deep divisions over the most fundamental issues of life, such as peace and war, the sanctity of life, life after death, and the sanctity of marriage.

The observable result: The greatest threat of terrorism to nations worldwide has come from Islam in the last 30 years because their holy book, the Quran, promotes Jihad (holy war) with the objective of forcing all people to submit under the domination of Allah. All the while, many vehemently claim that Islam is a religion of peace. Additionally, women are widely treated as 2nd class citizens, at best.

Buddhism
The axiom of Buddhism is difficult to define. Buddhists do not believe in a god and have no single holy book which defines its doctrine. Rather than encouraging unity with and service to one another, Buddhism promotes withdrawal from others and the world. Thus, the religion has little or no affect upon the nation or the culture at large.

The observable result: Because the religion promotes withdrawal from reality, the followers are easily controlled by tyrants. Over 80% of Buddhists live in four communist/socialist countries: China, Thailand, Vietnam, and Myanmar. [80] Nearly one-third of all Buddhists live in China, which is currently the most aggressive nation in the world with an agenda to dominate all others.

Hinduism

Similar to Buddhism, there is no clear foundational axiom present in Hinduism. Their basic doctrines or principles are found in a whole host of texts passed down through the ages, each with no named author. God is either one or more of many available gods or is not necessary at all – depending on the sect. There is no single holy book to define doctrine, encouraging wide variances in their beliefs. Because each can choose his/her own "god", there is no clear instruction to unify and guide the lives or the society of Hindus. 97% of all Hindus live in India.

The observable result: Due to the absence of a sound platform of clearly articulated doctrine and a deeply divisive caste system, Hindus have few unifying principles, allowing them to be easily controlled by those with the riches and power. For these reasons, the poor remain poor and the rich remain rich. There is virtually no middle class and no mobility between the classes.

Christianity

The central axiom of Christianity is stated in Genesis 1:1, "In the beginning God created the heavens and the earth." It is further developed within the first three chapters in Genesis where the fundamental doctrines of the Trinity, original sin, and the plan for salvation are articulated.

The Bible not only declares a clear, consistent belief system, but proclaims that He has made Himself known to all people, stating: "God has placed eternity in our hearts"(Ecclesiastes 3:11), and "what may be known of God is manifest (made clear) in them, for God has shown it to them." (Romans 1:19) These principles are typically affirmed by studies which conclude that nearly 90% of all human beings believe in a god or a higher power. Barely 10% assent to atheism. But unlike the god of Islam, Christianity's God does not force humanity to submit to His domination. He not only reveals Himself to every man, but He gives everyone an opportunity to either personally respond to His call to believe and repent (turn from rejecting God to loving and obeying Him), or to remain as they are. Romans 2:4 states this principle clearly: "…do you show contempt for the riches of His kindness, forbearance and patience, not realizing that God's kindness is intended to lead you to repentance?"

The observable result: The near universal belief in God has always verified the fundamental truth statements of the Bible. And because the doctrines of biblical Christianity are spelled out so clearly, it has provided a firm foundation upon which to build a society that values human life, promotes individual freedom and opportunity, and enjoys the safety and stability that comes when the fundamental laws and rational doctrines of morality govern the people.

Although no nation is capable of perfection due to the presence of sin in all mankind, the unity created by the principle beliefs of the Bible influenced the creation of the most powerful, influential, charitable society in history.

---

[80] https://www.buddhanet.net/e-learning/history/bstatt10.htm

Lesson 7 Study Questions

Testing the Faiths

1. Critical thinking requires the presence of contrasting thoughts or ideas coupled with the freedom to think those ideas through to their logical conclusions. Humanistic methods restrict the freedom to consider contrasting ideas, but Christianity strongly encourages such examination. List 3 ideas prevalent in today's world along with both sides of the argument.

    1) _____

    _____

    2) _____

    _____

    3) _____

    _____

2. The Axiom – which can also be called the philosophical root – of a religion or belief system will eventually lead to "fruit" in the form of consequences (good or bad) in our life. Name the axiom – or root idea – at the foundation of the 5 religions and the fruit it has produced.

    1) Humanism _____

    _____

    2) Islam _____

    _____

    3) Buddhism _____

    _____

    4) Hinduism _____

    _____

    5) Christianity _____

    _____

3. Comparing these 5 faiths, why do you think Christian society seems the most more free and prosperous than the civilizations that have grown from the seeds of the other religions?

    _____

    _____

    _____

    _____

Lesson 8 – Testing the Faiths, Part 2
Test #2: Scientific validation

Humanism
From the 1850s, this philosophy claimed to have the "high ground" in knowledge -- that they were the ones who knew what was true and what was not true because *science was their god*. The foundation of their philosophical belief system states that man evolved, he was not created or designed.

- Modern science now supports the view that the entire universe – especially man – screams of design.
- The 2nd Law of Thermodynamics says that the Universe had a beginning, and it is winding down toward an end. Everything is suffering entropy – the move from order to disorder. Common sense tells us that If we park a Volkswagen on the street and leave it to sit for 20 years, it doesn't become a Cadillac. It becomes rust. But yet, Humanists claim that evolution is true and that everything is improving. This completely contradicts the 2nd law.

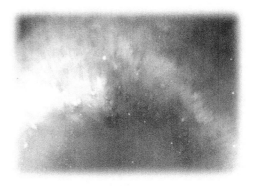

- The idea of spontaneous generation – or life coming from non-life – cannot be found in creation. Yet this is what many scientists believe to be true.
- Modern science does not validate evolution.

Islam
The foundation of Islam's philosophical belief system states:

- Man was created by water and clay *over time*; i.e., by evolution. "We created man from sounding clay, from mud molded into shape..." (Surah 15:26).
- There is no attempt to explain where matter and energy came from in the Quran. "Allah has produced you from the earth, growing (gradually)" (Surah 71:13-17).
- The Quran describes that Allah "made from water every living thing" (Surah 21:30). Another verse describes how "Allah has created every animal from water. Of them are some that creep on their bellies, some that walk on two legs, and some that walk on four". (Surah 24:45) These verses agree with the evolutionary theory that life began in the Earth's oceans.
- This has all been invalidated by science

Buddhism
The foundation of Buddhism's philosophical belief system:

- Proposes no theory or doctrine to explain how life began
- Rejects the idea that a god created man. Man is simply the product of reincarnation.
- Topics such as the existence of god, the afterlife, or creation stories are ignored in Buddhism because this life is treated as an illusion that is to be vigorously ignored.
- The key to happiness is emptying oneself of any consciousness of internal or external awareness.
- These ideas have no scientific foundation

One would think that because fundamental Buddhist philosophy denies the value of science (which is the study of the material world) altogether, that its ideology would be rejected by modern scientists; however, a modern and modified form of Buddhism has been embraced by a great number of today's scientists because its purpose is to deny reality, which seems to fit in comfortably with the doctrine of Darwinian evolution.

Hinduism
The fundamental philosophical beliefs of Hinduism are in many ways similar to that of Buddhism:

- There is no doctrine regarding the creation of life by any god, but reincarnation is assumed. There is no substantive argument given to support reincarnation.

- There is no foundation upon which to answer the fundamental questions of life
- The multiple gods that populate the Hindu religion provide no continuity of thought and fall far short of providing a sound moral and legal system upon which to build a civilized culture
- The philosophy that evolves from such a "theology" cannot possibly be reliable, measurable, or consistent. This is clearly observed when viewing the myriads of Hindu gods.[81]

Christianity

The most fundamental axiom of the Christian worldview is this: <u>The Bible is the Word of God</u>. As an axiom, this proposition is assumed to be true without proof; a truth that is considered to be self-evident. It is the unproved starting point of the Christian worldview. Accordingly, if one were to demand that the Christian prove that the Bible is the Word of God, this would be an *irrational* demand, for not everything can be proved.

The foundation of Christianity's philosophical belief system states with utmost clarity:

- The universe is the product of mathematical law, order, design, and beauty conceived by a brilliant, loving and creative Mind. We find this clearly stated in the first chapter of Genesis, first chapter of John, and first chapter of Colossians.
- Life came from life. This is scientifically observed occurring billions of times a day in all life around us.
- Life came by design, not by accident. Science testifies that there is more information in a molecule of DNA than there are in all the libraries in the entire world, validating the intelligent design argument. If there is information, there must be an informer. This information was programmed so precisely in the cell, it strongly points to a programmer. Thus, the Bible describes reality perfectly like no other worldview. John 1:1 states "In the beginning was the Word..." The term *Word* in the Greek is *logos*, which is interpreted to mean: *the mind, reason, thought, wisdom, intelligence, the master idea, the law, order, purpose, design*. All those words are synonyms for the word *logos*. John 1:3, "All things were made through Him, without Him nothing was made." Again, the Bible describes reality: Life came from Life. Mind came before matter...see John 1:1, Hebrews 11:3. God came before man: Genesis 1:1. Plan and design came before Creation. This is consistent with observable reality. Without a mind to design such an intricate universe, there could be no Universe. The Bible claims that He (Christ) "holds the Universe together by the power of His Word."

Sir Francis Bacon	*Johannes Kepler*	*Rene Descartes*	*Isaac Newton*	*Dr. Francis Collins*
Christian philosopher. Established the scientific method of inquiry based on experimentation and inductive reasoning. His goals were "discovery of truth, service to his country, and service to the church." He viewed science as a way to learn deeper truths about God. He wrote: "A depth in philosophy brings men's minds about to religion."	A German astronomer who established the laws of planetary motion. Kepler was an extremely sincere and pious Lutheran, whose works on astronomy contain writings about how space and the heavenly bodies represent the Trinity.	French mathematician and philosopher. The "Father of modern philosophy". One of his notable works was titled "Meditations on First Philosophy, in Which Is Proved the Existence of God and the Immortality of the Soul"	English mathematician, physicist, astronomer, theologian, and author. Considered one of the most influential scientists in history. A devout but unorthodox Christian, Newton is responsible for the laws of motion and universal gravitation; also known as the discoverer/inventor of calculus	Francis Collins, one of the world's foremost geneticists, led the landmark Human Genome Project, culminating in the completion of a finished sequence of the human DNA instruction book. Describing himself as a serious Christian, he wrote the book "The Language of God: A Scientist Presents Evidence for Belief"

---

[81] https://en.wikipedia.org/wiki/List_of_Hindu_deities

Lesson 8 Study Questions

Scientific Validation – Testing the Faiths

1. How does modern science confirm or deny the foundational axioms of each major religion?

    1) Humanism _____
    _____

    2) Islam _____
    _____

    3) Buddhism _____
    _____

    4) Hinduism _____
    _____

    5) Christianity _____
    _____

2. How adequately or inadequately does each faith answer some of the fundamental questions of life (Where did I come from? Why am I here? Where am I going?). Be specific. (for example, "Buddhism gives no explanation of how life began"). Give more than one example if you can.

    1) Humanism _____
    _____

    2) Islam _____
    _____

    3) Buddhism _____
    _____

    4) Hinduism _____
    _____

    5) Christianity _____
    _____

3. Name the main scientific contribution of each of the scientists below as listed in today's study

    1) Sir Francis Bacon
    _____

    2) Johannes Kepler
    _____

3) Rene Descartes:

_____

4) Isaac Newton:

_____

5) Dr. Francis Collins:

_____

4. Personal question: Based upon the question above and after reading Joshua 1:8 and Proverbs 2:1-8, do you believe God is ready and able to inspire you in the areas He has gifted you? _____

And what is necessary for you to receive that inspiration, according to those scriptures?

_____

_____

_____

Lesson 9 – Testing the Faiths, Part 3

Test #3: Historical Collaboration

Humanism:

Has become the dominant ideology in western Europe and America over the last 100 years. In that time, we have seen:

- The schools, the media, and the societies that have embraced Humanism devolve, not evolve (see sidebar at right)
- The socialist revolution in Russia resulted in millions of deaths and the abolition of freedom for the people.
- Hitler's embrace of Darwinism resulted in the Holocaust and World War II.
- Europe's embrace of Humanism and subsequent rejection of Christianity has opened up Europe to the embrace of globalism, leading to the invasion of the continent by millions of militant Islamicists in this century, causing civil unrest and social breakdown throughout the continent.
- In America in particular, we have seen the sanctity of life devalued with millions of abortions occurring annually and legislation brought forth to allow infanticide up to and even after birth.

Islam: Since its inception in the 7th century, Islam has been responsible for

- The decimation of the once great and prosperous Persian culture
- The leveling or plundering of many European cultures that had been built up by Roman influence
- The destruction of countless invaluable books, manuscripts, and monuments of antiquity
- The introduction in the 21st century of the barbaric, vicious and senseless holy wars that are reaping havoc among the nations of the world today – even within Muslim nations.

Buddhism:

The fundamental philosophy of Buddhism calls for complete rejection of the reality of the material world and withdrawal away from it. The results of this philosophy have revealed:

- Although the religion promotes peace, it does not get involved in the culture, leaving the culture in the hands of others
- Due to the policy of individual non-involvement, the nations that are predominantly Buddhist are among the most tyrannical countries in the world
- Buddhism is not known for promoting or supporting hospitals and care for the poor and the sick

---

Effects of Humanist Philosophy in America since 1962

The 1962 Engel v. Vitale Supreme Court decision removing prayer from schools marked **the ascension of Humanism as the standard for civil law in America.** From that point it is observed that within 20 years of this decision:

- Teen pregnancies doubled [82]
- Teen suicides tripled [83]
- Teen murder arrests doubled [84]
- Abortions increased from 292 in 1962 to 1.5 million in 1982 [85]
- Divorce rates nearly tripled [86]
- Single Parent households doubled [87]
- SAT scores dropped by 8% [88]
- STD's (Sexually Transmitted Diseases) doubled [89]
- Violent crime tripled [90]
- Prison population doubled [91]

(Statistics based upon per capita of population)

---

[82] Heritage.org, 2010
[83] Centers for Disease Control and Prevention, National Center for Health Statistics (Teen suicide)
[84] Basic Data: U.S. Dept. of Justice, FBI
[85] http://www.johnstonsarchive.net: Historical abortion statistics, United States
[86] National Center for Health Statistics, 1962 and 1982 Divorce Statistics Anaysis
[87] U.S. Census Bureau, 11/17/16
[88] https://www.erikthered.com/tutor/historical-average-SAT-scores.pdf;
[89] U.S. CDC https://www.cdc.gov/nchs/data/hus/hus82acc.pdf
[90] http://www.disastercenter.com/crime/uscrime.htm U.S. Crime rates 1960-2017
[91] Justice Policy Institute Report: The punishing decade, & U.S. Bureau of Justice Statistics Bulletin NCJ219416 – Prisoners in 2006

- In Buddhism there is no acknowledgement of sin. The root cause of human suffering, they teach, is considered to be "ignorance" (unsatisfactoriness), which can only be remedied through meditation. Law and order in the society is not a priority to be enforced
- Buddhism is not known for the promotion or support of schools or universities
- Buddhist nations are among those with the lowest standards of living

Hinduism:

With no written single theology or philosophy to ground the religion, there can be no platform upon which to build a clear belief system. Therefore, Hinduism provides no specific, uniting, coherent set of moral laws or standards of behavior. The historic result has been:

- No involvement in the culture
- The Hindu culture is still plagued by the caste system which divides society into a hierarchy of classes where those toward the bottom are limited or prohibited from holding meaningful jobs
- Few policies for taking care of the poor and the sick among all people
- Hinduism is not known for promoting or developing schools and universities available to all
- Women in the Hindu culture typically have limited freedom in a culture dominated by males
- The predominantly Hindu nation of India is among the poorest in the world

Christianity:

In the 2,000 years that have passed since Christ, the basic philosophical ideas that emanated from the faith have benefitted Christian nations in countless ways:

- Individual freedom is a hallmark of the faith. The principles of equal liberty and justice for all, first applied in America, continue to bring benefits to the entire world.
- Slavery has been ended in Christian-based nations, while it still exists in various forms in most other nations
- Women's freedom and dignity is established. In contrast, women are still treated as second class citizens in the majority of world nations
- Hospitals and healthcare available for all abounds in Christian nations
- Education for all began with Christianity
- Free economic market principles featuring the right to private property ownership has dramatically raised the standard of living in the nations that have embraced it. This is in direct contrast to those nations that live under communism, socialism, and Marxism.

We must repeat that - as with all other worldviews - many have professed to be of the faith who in deed misrepresented Christ and the teachings of the Bible. This is the unfortunate effect of the innate sin nature in all mankind and can only be corrected through diligent education and discipleship. However, we must not allow these bad examples to define the entire faith. That is another reason why critical thinking is vital to determine what is true.

What About the Crusades?

Many outside Christianity claim the faith "is responsible for more wars than any other religion" and they point to the Crusades of the middle ages as their proof. Our response is two-fold:

1. The Crusades were primarily a defensive response by Christians to the barbaric invasion of Christian nations in Europe by the Muslims.

2. Much of the violence attributed to Christianity was perpetrated by those who falsely claimed to be Christian but in fact proved by their actions that they were not. Christian means "follower of Christ", but nowhere in the Bible does one find Christ promoting wars of aggression. However, Muhammed, the one whom Muslims are commanded to follow not only promoted violent aggression but participated in many such wars.

Logical Conclusion

The fundamental principles of Christianity are confirmed in real life to be applicable and trustworthy by common sense and observation, by science, and by history. The fundamental principles of all the other religions are proven by the same tests to be illogical, inapplicable, untrustworthy and in many cases, dangerous.

An Abbreviated Overview of the Basic Principles of the Christian Worldview

Based upon the principle that **the Bible contains all truth from the mind of God and the logical implications of those truths**, Christianity lays out clear principles to guide the believer in all walks of life. The following chart conveys the basic philosophical ideas that Christianity promotes in the 11 major areas of life that we are all involved in to one degree or another. This list is by no means exhaustive but is meant as a simple overview. As we progress through this worldview series, we will investigate each of these principles in greater detail.

Subject	Basic Principles
Theology	God is Creator, Ruler, Righteous, and Relational; Omnipotent, Omniscient, and Omnipresent. He is the God of love and mercy. and the God of pure grace balanced by perfect justice.
History	God is the *Author* of all History, He is *Above* all History, and He is *Involved* in all History. Every Christian is born with a purpose to do the works for which God created them.
Philosophy	The Bible is the source of all truth, and belief in that truth leads to salvation by grace through faith and promises success (as defined by God) in all we do.
Economics	God is our provider. Man is made to be responsible for his God-gifted talents and to be free to work and to serve others with those gifts and talents.
Science	All knowledge is revealed by the mind of God to the mind of man for God's glory. Creation reveals God's glory. Science is extremely useful but must be overseen by biblical wisdom (morality).
Psychology	Because of sin in us, we must transform our minds to conform to God's so that we may be in our right mind.
Ethics	Right and wrong are defined by Scripture. Man is to be truthful and honest; walking in virtuous integrity and character.
Sociology	Marriage and Family are the foundations of society. Healthy societies require morally responsible individuals. Every individual is personally accountable to God.
Law	God is the Lawmaker. The 10 Commandments are the foundation of God's law, and are for our benefit
Politics	Laws and policies of nations are best when flowing from biblical principles. All secular laws legislate morality, defining right and wrong. Christians are responsible to be involved.
Education	Is the responsibility of parents and the church. Knowledge cannot be divorced from morality, but rather must be guided by biblical morality.

Lesson 9 Study Questions

Historical Collaboration – Testing the Faiths

1. Using human history to test the end results that proceed from the ideas of each faith is a powerful tool for evaluating all. List at least 3 results from each worldview that are obvious from the historical records presented in this chapter and state and why those results either support or suppress individuals and nations.

    1) Humanism

    _____

    _____

    _____

    2) Islam

    _____

    _____

    _____

    3) Buddhism

    _____

    _____

    _____

    4) Hinduism

    _____

    _____

    _____

    5) Christianity

    _____

    _____

    _____

2. After reading the sidebar above titled *What About the Crusades?,* what do you think is the most critically important answer for those who cite the Crusades to support the frivolous claim that Christianity is responsible for as many violent acts as Islam?

    _____

    _____

    _____

    (See https://thefederalist.com/2015/03/04/like-most-people-president-obama-gets-the-crusades-wrong/ for further research if you wish)

Subject Five: The Christian Worldview of Economics

Lesson 1 - Why Study Economics?

Why Should Christians (or anyone) Study Economics?

Howard L. Dayton, Jr., founder of Crown Financial Ministries, stated in his book *Leadership*,

> "Jesus talked much about money. Sixteen of the thirty-eight parables were concerned with how to handle money and possessions. In the Gospels, an amazing one out of ten verses (288 in all) deal directly with the subject of money. The Bible offers 500 verses on prayer, less than 500 verses on faith, but more than 2,000 verses on money and possessions."[92]

The most obvious reason for this abundance of instruction on riches and possessions is due to the fact that our possessions can so easily become a replacement for God in our lives. Because we are born into a material world, the material can capture our attention, cause worry and anxiety, and distract us from pursuing what really counts. While the Bible does not condemn monetary success, it is clear that God wants us to avoid the traps that will result from an imbalanced view of the material world.

According to Webster's dictionary, the study of economics deals with *the production, distribution, and consumption of goods and services*. Thus, it is intimately concerned with defining how wealth (goods, possessions, or resources) is generated, obtained or spread among individuals and nations. The economic policies of a nation will either lead to a rich economy or a poor one and will affect every citizen of that nation. As we studied in the first chapter – "What is a Worldview and Why Does It Matter?" – the Biblical worldview of early America not only brought tremendous benefits to U.S citizens, but also to the nations throughout the world; and it is safe to assume that much of that success was based upon the economic philosophy established by the Founding Fathers at the very start.

In this age, many are questioning the economic system of capitalism (free market economics) and more are embracing socialism as the "fairest" way of governing the public wealth. Throughout this chapter, we will examine the differences between these two worldviews by contrasting the capitalist system, which was established by our founders here in America, against the socialist, communist, Marxist views that are prevalent in most of the

countries in the world today. As we do so, we will also compare the biblical views of charity, poverty, and welfare programs with those of socialism. Hopefully, by comparing and contrasting these opposing worldviews, students will be better equipped to decide for themselves which makes more sense.

Please note that we will also make extensive references to America, simply because it is the only nation in history to have fully embraced a free market economic system based upon ideas presented in the Bible.

---

[92] Howard L. Dayton, Jr., Leadership, Vol. 2, no. 2

The Foundations of Biblical Economics

To begin, biblically-based economics is grounded upon the fundamental principle of human freedom, as stated in our Declaration of Independence, that rights come from God alone and that man is to be free to pursue his dreams with the least amount of government interference, as long as he follows God's moral laws. The result of America embracing this principle at its founding was, as we highlighted in chapter one, a virtual five-thousand-year leap in human progress and prosperity as never seen before in history. In the short span of only two hundred years from the signing of the Constitution, this new free market enterprise system fueled a landslide of ideas and inventions that catapulted America and the Western world into a level of prosperity never dreamed of before.

Freedom encourages creativity, because those who own property and have the ability to develop it with the least amount of government interference will use their time, their energy, and their resources much more efficiently than those who have nothing to gain from the same investments.

One of the most obvious results of this precept can be seen in the fact that the number of American inventions from the 1800s until today dwarf those of every other nation. The comparative chart below illustrates this point based upon the most recent information available.

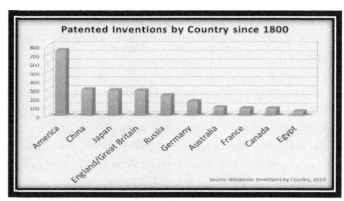

Source:https://en.wikipedia.org/wiki/Category:Inventions_by_country 2019

To further drive home this point, see the list of American inventions in the sidebar to the right. As you do so, imagine where the world would be without these miniature and monumental miracles.

Not Your Average Country

America is an exceptional nation. In the charts on the following page, you'll see that free market America produces roughly one quarter of all the goods and services in the world, yet we have less than 5% of the population. On the other hand, Communist China produces one third less than what America does, and they have over four times the population. This means that the average citizen in America produces over 10 times the amount of goods and services as the average citizen of China.

AMERICAN INVENTIONS

An Abbreviated List

Cotton gin, telegraph, water tower, rubber tire, barbed wire, diving machine, cash register, sewing machine, electric iron, subway, revolver, oil well, coffee pot, safety pin, skyscraper, copy machine, bandages, blue jeans, bread slicer, calculator, CD's, chocolate chip cookie, coca cola, defibrillator, disposable diapers, dental drill, the escalator, frozen food, aerosol can, the revolving door, Scotch tape, microwave, mini-computer, nuclear sub, nylon, optical fiber, product bar code, radio astronomy, the space shuttle, air conditioning, toilet paper, the zipper, the airplane, the threshing machine, the tractor, the telephone, bifocal glasses, the combined harvester, assembly line production, ether anesthesia, the phonograph, the radio, refrigerator, polio vaccine, electric motor, the incandescent light bulb, digital computers, GPS, the heart lung machine, the Hubble telescope, transistor, the integrated circuit, the jumbo jet, the liquid fueled rocket, the computer operating system, the Internet, the artificial heart, the laser, the cell phone.

Source:https://en.wikipedia.org/wiki/
Category:American_inventions2019

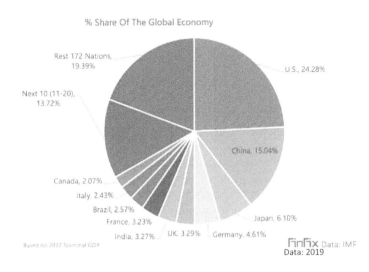

Scientific Citations

Scientific achievement can be measured by the number of scientific citations a nation receives in comparison to the rest of the world. And by that method, we see that the US outperforms the next six highest ranking nations in the world *combined* in scientific creativity.

The Bottom Line

As we can verify in reality, the American worldview of economics taken from biblical principles has made a huge difference in the lives of virtually all of humanity. But why? What makes the biblical worldview so extraordinary? And what distinguishes it from other views?

Remember, our foundational Scripture is 2 Corinthians 10:4-5 -- *we battle ideas*. Only two economic ideas rule in this world today and they produce radically opposite results. The first, free market economics or *capitalism*, which always results, as you'll see, in greater freedom and opportunity. The second is government owned or controlled markets, such as socialism, communism, or Marxism, which inevitably result in the loss of freedom and opportunity. We will take a closer look at these opposing economic philosophies in the next section.

International Science Ratings
by % of Scientific Citations, 1996-2016

Lesson 1 Study Questions

1. Why do you think money (economics) plays such a large part in the Bible?

   _____

   _____

2. Define *economics*

   _____

   _____

3. How do the economic ideas you embrace affect your life? Name a few examples.

   _____

   _____

4. From this segment on American inventions, can you state what the relationship is between personal freedom and the explosion of creativity it brings about?

   _____

   _____

5. Similarly, why might the dynamic of a free-market economy contribute to an explosion in scientific discoveries? (Consider the words *competition* and *profit*)

   _____

   _____

6. Look up on the Internet: *AFA.net - How Socialism Nearly Destroyed the Pilgrims* – What further evidence does this provide that demonstrates the Biblical principles of free market economics?

   _____

   _____

7. Read Psalm 119:98-100. What does this scripture say is the key for anyone who desires to be creative and innovative?

   _____

   _____

   _____

Lesson 2 – Fundamental Principles

Eight Principles of Biblical Economics

Let's begin by examining the biblical view of free market enterprise, and then we'll look at the contrasting views and you can decide for yourself which one you think is best.

Free Market Economics

The Christian view of economics begins with the understanding that...

1. God has made man to be free.
2. God has entrusted man with gifts and blessings in the form of property or resources or talents. And even an idea is considered by law to be your personal property.
3. God has designed man to be productive.
4. God requires all men to be good stewards of those gifts and blessings that he's given us.
5. God has made man to be responsible and accountable for the management of his property and resources.
6. God has made man to enjoy the fruits of his labor.
7. God has made men to bless others with the fruits of his labor.
8. Lastly, but critically important, man is sinful.

These concepts are illustrated in two of Christ's fundamental teachings on the subject of economics. The Parable of the Talents in Matthew and the Parable of the Minas in Luke. We'll focus on the parable of the talents, found in Matthew 25:14-30.

The Parable of the Talents

Here we find a man that is leaving his property in the care of his servants while he goes on a trip, and he calls them in and gives each of them a portion of his money to manage until he returns. One gets five talents, another gets two, another gets one. The story specifically points out that each man is given talents according to his own ability. By the way, one talent was worth a huge amount of money in those days. And our English word for talent is derived from that Greek word as well.

The story continues when the owner returns and asks for an accounting from each of the men. The man who was entrusted with five talents doubled them, as did the man who was given two. They both were applauded and honored by the owner and given great promotions. But the man who was given one talent did nothing with his, stating that he believed the owner to be a hard, unfair man. Now, the owner did not take the rewards from the man who worked hard and invested wisely and give those rewards to the man who didn't. Instead, the man who refused to put his talent to work had his money taken away from him and given to the ones who worked. The closing line brings the jarring point home, "for to everyone who has, more will be given, and he will have an abundance. But from him who does not have, even what he has will be taken away. And cast the unprofitable servant into the outer darkness, where there will be weeping and gnashing of teeth."

Lessons from this parable

As we saw in the beginning, each man was given talents, money or gifts *according to his ability*. Not everyone was given equal income or gifting, but all had equal opportunity. Each one had the freedom to use the talents as he chose best. All had equal responsibility to bring fruit or a return from what each had been entrusted with. Those who used their talents diligently on the investment were rewarded with more. The man who did nothing with his investment lost everything. In fact, in the Parable of the Talents, he lost Heaven. Not because he didn't earn it, but because he didn't believe in the righteousness of God. He actually attributed evil motives to God. He didn't have faith. And without faith, Scripture says, it's impossible to please God.

Now this shows that our faith in God, as one who is a rewarder of those who are diligent, is seen by the fruit that we produce in our lives. The Bible says, you'll be known by your fruit.

> ## Pause and Consider
>
> ### What was the value of a Talent?
>
> In Jesus' time, one talent was made up of 6,000 Denarii, and one Denarius was the average wage for a day of labor; therefore, it would take 6,000 work days – or 19 years - to earn just one talent. At a wage of $10/hour, a Denarius would be worth $80/day and a talent would be valued at nearly a half million dollars!

https://en.wikipedia.org/wiki/Parable_of_the_talents_or_minas]

To sum this up, we've all been entrusted with special gifts by our Father. And we're expected to develop them to the best of our ability. And this is for our blessing and for the blessing of others, as well.

Private Property and Personal Responsibility

The Bible teaches an economic system of private property and individual responsibility. Private ownership and stewardship or personal responsibility of property is assumed to be the design of God throughout the Bible. The Commandment "thou shalt not steal" specifically implies individual ownership of property. This right to property stems from our duty to work. Proverbs 10:4 says, "whoever works with a lazy hand becomes poor, but a diligent hand brings riches." The Bible shows that God worked six days and then rested. When he completed the work at the end of each day, he looked at his work and said, "this is good". We're made in God's image, thus, we're designed to work with what we've been given – our talents, so to speak. We can create, invent, and build using our talents. Everyone, therefore, can be productive in some way or another. And when we're finished with whatever task we have performed, we too can look at what we've done and feel good. We can be proud of who we are and what we've accomplished. It gives meaning and brings fulfillment to our lives. It's good for us to work diligently. God has designed a world in which the existence of private property encourages people to be responsible and fruitful.

Who Should Manage Your Property?

The best use of property to benefit ourselves and to serve others can only occur in a society in which property is privately owned. The fact is, men and women who own property will almost always take better care of it than those who don't own property. Publicly owned property destroys a person's sense of responsibility to use his possessions, his time, and his talents diligently, because there is little or no incentive for a hardworking - or even a lazy person - to treat property responsibly. If a man is not personally invested in the property, he simply won't respect it as will the one who owns property.

The Principle of *First, Second, and Third Party Purchases* [93]

Who will manage your money better, you or the government? You or someone who doesn't even know you? This isn't a trick question. There are three ways that something can be purchased.

1. <u>First Party Purchase</u>. This is when you purchase something for yourself. Now, if you buy for yourself, you care about both price and quality. You're going to spend your hard-earned money according to how much you have and the quality of what you buy. You budget and you shop wisely. You don't want to waste your own money; thus, your money goes a lot further.

2. <u>Second Party Purchase</u>. Here, you purchase something with your own money, but for someone else; or someone buys for you and he picks up the tab. If you're buying for someone else, you care about price, but not necessarily quality. If someone is buying for you, you care about quality but not so much about price, because you're not paying for it. It's their treat. "Oh", you say, "I can order *anything* on the menu? You're paying? Okay, I'll have the prime rib!" You see, you care about quality because you're going to be consuming it, but you don't care about the price. Someone else is paying for it.

3. <u>Third Party Purchase</u>. This is when a person uses someone else's money to buy something for someone else. That person cares a whole lot less about both price and quality. He's paying for products and services that he won't necessarily use, and he's spending someone else's money to buy it. By this example, we see that all government purchases are third party purchases; which means that waste and overspending are guaranteed. That's why the control of money or property is best kept in the hands of those who have earned it, are personally responsible for it, and are most closely connected to it.

... and climbing!

---

[93] Ohio Congressman Bob McEwen, www.unitedinpurpose.org at Rediscover God in America conference, 2011

Lesson 2 Study Questions

A. The Biblical View: Free Market Enterprise

Eight principles of God's Economics

1. Man is made to be free. Read Jer. 34:12-22. Is individual freedom for every man and woman a priority to God?

_____   What punishments are promised to those who enslave others? _____

_____

2. God has entrusted man with gifts and blessings (property or Resources) Read Gen. 11:1-9, esp. verse 4. Babylon was judged by God. Why was He displeased with the people of Babylon, and what might this teach us about the reasons for a country's economic success or failure?

_____

_____

3. God has made man to be productive. Read Matt. 25:26-30. What are the consequences that come from wasting your natural gifts and talents?

_____

_____

4. God requires all men to be good stewards of those gifts and blessings. Read Matt. 24:45-47. What are the rewards God promises for faithful stewardship?

_____

_____

5. God has made man to be responsible and *accountable* for the management of his property/resources. Read Matt. 24:48-51. What consequences will come to the unfaithful one?

_____

6. God has made man to enjoy the fruits of his labor. What can we learn from Eccl. 5:18-19; Prov. 10:4-5; Prov. 12:11; Prov.13:4, :11 regarding this principle?

_____

_____

7. God has made man to bless others with the fruits of his labor. Read Luke 6:38 and 12:16-21. What physical and spiritual results come from being generous or selfish with the fruit of our labor?

_____

_____

8. Man is sinful. Read Rom. 3:23; Gen.6:5; Jer.17:9. Is there any area of life that sin does not affect?_____ Why, then, do you think a system that encourages integrity and courtesy might help control our sin nature ?   _____

_____

B. Lessons from the Parable of the Talents (Matt. 25:14-30).

1. Each man was given talents – (money, "gifts") *according to his ability*. What is significant about that last phrase, and how does this apply in your life? _____

_____

2.   All had equal responsibility – to bring fruit – or a return – from what each had been entrusted with. In Matt. 25:26,

how did his lord describe the unprofitable servant? _____

_____

3. Those who used their talents to bring a return on the investment were rewarded with more! What were the fruitful

   ones promised? _____

4. He who did nothing with the investment lost everything. In this parable He lost Heaven. Not because he didn't earn it,

   but because he actually attributed evil motives to God. He did not have faith, and without faith, Scripture says, it is

   impossible to please God. Read Matt. 25:16 and Colossians 3:22-24. Name some ways we can reveal our faith in God in

   the workplace? _____

   _____

   _____

5. Our faith in God as one who is a rewarder of those who are diligent is seen by the fruit we produce in our lives. Read

   Deut. 11:13-15; Prov. 13:4. What are the promised results of doing all our work diligently "as unto the Lord"?

   _____

   _____

6. Explain the difference between 1st, 2nd and 3rd party purchases. _____

   _____

   _____

Lesson 3 – Comparing and Contrasting

Considering the Sin Nature

No other economic system is grounded upon the core belief that man is sinful by nature. The founders of America firmly believed this. That was the expressed purpose for the three divided branches of government to provide checks and balances for each other. Because of this selfish nature in man, the most desirable economic system for the average person is one which protects the rights of individuals from being taken advantage of or bullied by others. In other words, it gives everyone equal opportunity to succeed - not just the nobility, the rich, or the powerful. In short, it must be a *just* system. If all people were inherently good, no one would steal the property of

The Biblical Precedent for 3 Divided Branches of Government of the U.S.
Isaiah 33:22...
For the Lord is our Judge,
The Lord is our Lawgiver,
The Lord is our King;...

others, or be so lazy and uninterested in working that they would lay down on the job and force others, like you or me, to have to work harder and longer just to get the job done. But we know that in the real world, people are not inherently righteous. You'll never find a child who has to be taught to lie and to act selfishly. We actually spend much of our time trying to teach them *not* to lie or to be selfish, and often, we're not very successful.

The Principle of Economic Competition

Christianity is the only worldview that takes into account the sin nature of man, and it is a fundamental in every way we look at life. So of course, it applies to our view of economics. Sin is a reality, and we want to live in reality. Therefore, because man can't be trusted to always behave righteously in the best interest of others, the best economic system must contain checks and balances. There must be some ingredient in the system that forces a fair and balanced playing field. That's where competition comes in. The Bible calls for men to compete with each other in the marketplace to encourage fruitfulness. When this biblical principle is applied, it turns out to be very practical. Economic competition provides the checks and balances that we need in a free market economy, because competition counterbalances man's sinful tendencies.

Why? Because *impolite behavior equals lost customers*. So does shoddy work or lazy attitudes. A good business person must consider the customer's best interests, or the customer will go to the competition. Economic competition forces people who may not be polite or responsible by nature to act polite and responsible in order to stay in business or to simply keep their job. It forces self-control and discipline upon everyone who provides a good or service. However, when a company has no competition in the marketplace (often found in government-operated monopoly businesses such the Post Office, the Department of Motor Vehicles, etc.) the virtues of diligence, courtesy, and efficiency might be set to a far lower standard or may not be required at all.

The Principle of Comparative Advantage

When we use our best talents and interests to provide a service that benefits others, we will enjoy greater advantages, which benefits everyone. When a society is allowed to promote free enterprise, the result will be greater blessings to the people of that society because every person has an opportunity to choose an occupation that he or she loves; and because they love it, they'll put more into it. They will not be forced to do something that they dislike or disinterested in. This encourages everyone to apply themselves in the area where they are gifted. They can pursue an occupation that they enjoy and love. And through hard work and diligence, they'll have greater opportunity to succeed. That's why we have so many people are constantly banging at the door to get into America.

To conclude this point, let's look at how these principles of private property, personal responsibility, economic competition, and comparative advantage all support our conclusion that free markets help everyone to enjoy a better life. Clearly, there's a relationship between the type of economy a society chooses, and the amount of freedom that the individual will enjoy or sacrifice.

Quality of Life and Economic freedom.

If you could choose to live in one of the countries among the two lists below, which list would you choose? The wise answer would most likely be List A. Why?

2017 World Economic Freedom Rankings	
LIST A	**LIST B**
Hong Kong	North Korea
Singapore	Venezuela
New Zealand	Cuba
Switzerland	Republic of Congo
Australia	Eritrea
Estonia	Zimbabwe
Canada	Equatorial Guinea
United Arab Emirates	Timor-Leste
Ireland	Algeria
Chile	Djibouti

2017 Index of Economic Freedom: U.S. Score Declines Further as World Average Increases [94]

Comparing Canada, which is #8 on List A, to Cuba, Canada's poverty rate[95] is less than 20% of Cuba's[96] and less than 10% of Venezuela's[97]. As a matter of fact, every one of the countries in List A are better off than those in List B. The income per person is 10 times higher on average in those countries in List A. These lists, however, aren't organized by income. They're organized by economic freedom. What sets List A apart from List B is that those in List A have the most free economies in the world. List B are the least free.[98]

Everywhere in the world we look, we find a strong relationship between economic freedom and the quality of life the people enjoy. For instance, people in the most free countries earn on average over eight times more than people in the least free. The poor earn 10 times more. People in the most free countries are happier. They have better protected civil rights, cleaner environments, and the average person lives 20 years longer. The freest countries also have less corruption, less infant mortality, less child labor, and less unemployment. So if you care about improving people's lives, then you really care about economic freedom.

And having economic freedom means your property is protected under an impartial rule of law. You're free to trade with others for what you need and want. Your money keeps its value because your national currency is

stable. And government stays small relative to the size of the economy.[99]

As a note, prior to 2006, the United States was always among the top three in List A [100] (the most economically-free nations in the world); but by 2017, it fell to seventeenth[101], signifying that size of government has been growing dangerously fast. This verifies our proposition that the larger the size of government, the less freedom for the individual.

https://www.fraserinstitute.org/studies

---

[94] https://www.heritage.org/international-economies/impact/2017-index-economic-freedom-us-score-declines-further-world-average

[95] https://www.statcan.gc.ca/eng/topics-start/poverty

[96] https://borgenproject.org/what-is-the-poverty-rate-in-cuba/

[97] https://www.weforum.org/reports/the-global-competitveness-report-2018

[98] https://www.facebook.com/EconomicFreedomNetwork, https://www.charleskochinstitute.org/   Economic freedom and Quality of Life, Charles Koch Foundation, 2011.

[99] https://www.fraserinstitute.org/sites/default/files/EFW2005-newsrelease-cda.pdf

[100] https://www.facebook.com/EconomicFreedomNetwork, https://www.charleskochinstitute.org/   Economic freedom and Quality of Life, Charles Koch Foundation, 2011.

[101] https://www.heritage.org/international-economies/impact/2017-index-economic-freedom-us-score-declines-further-world-average

Lesson 3 Study Questions

1. Why is it good to develop a strong work ethic? Name at least 3 ways this will benefit you.

    1)_____
    2)_____
    3)_____

2. Name at least 2 ways a poor work ethic might hurt you.

    1)_____
    2)_____

3. Why are we assured of getting a lower quality product at a higher price when government controls it?

    _____

4. What might be the results in your life if you and others did not have the freedom to choose your own
    occupation? _____

5. Read Ex. 20:15, 17. How do the 8th and 10th Commandments imply private property ownership?

    _____

    _____

6. Read Gen. 23:10-17 and 2 Sam. 24:18-24. Why do you think Abraham and David insisted upon paying for
    property even when they were offered it for free?

    _____

    _____

7. God designed a world in which the existence of private property encourages people to be responsible and
    fruitful. Read Prov. 31:13-31. How does this woman make full use of her property?(Name at least 3 ways

    1)_____
    2) _____
    3)_____

Economic Competition

8. What core Christian belief is the reason for the 3 divided branches of government and the idea of "checks
    and balances" in America? (see Romans 3:23; Jeremiah 17:9, Isaiah 33:22)

    _____

9. Why does economic competition force people to be polite, responsible, and diligent on the job?

    _____

    _____

10. What are the usual results in terms of the (1) quality of service, (2) price, and (3) performance at a company
    that has no competition?

    _____

    _____

    _____

The principle of Comparative Advantage

11. What happens to personal productivity when a person works at a job he or she loves?

    _____

    _____Why?_____

12. When we use our best talents and interests to provide a service *that benefits others*, we're rewarded as
    well. How? (Read and compare Romans 12:4-8 and Luke 6:38 _____

    _____

Lesson 4 - Fairness, Justice & Wealth

A Common Objection

Some people attempt to biblically justify a socialistic or communistic economy by citing Acts 2:44-45, where the early of church bonded together and sold their goods, creating a sort of communal system. But as we read through the book of Acts, we find that this system didn't last. Why not? Looking at the story of Ananias and Sapphira, we find that communism fails because man is sinful. Some people will lie or cheat. Some people will hold back.

Big Government to the Rescue

Some people still insist that the Bible teaches a form of economic Marxism, often simply referred to as economic justice. A current popular term for this is *liberation theology*. The underlying belief is that socialism will somehow usher in a Kingdom of Heaven, like a utopia - a perfect society. Economic justice is the belief that all men deserve equal riches. Unfortunately, in reality it turns out that in socialism some are simply more equal than others – those who are high in government standing live in luxury while everyone else suffers. The middle class dissolves because socialism inhibits the common person from using his or her gifts, talents, energies and resources to their full potential; and this constricts economic growth, leading to virtual bankruptcy, as evidenced by the fall of the Soviet Union in the '90s, and the current economic failures of many of the European and South American social states such as Greece and Venezuela.

It's All About Fairness?

What is Social Justice?

A simple definition is: *The state-enforced distribution or redistribution of income and society's advantages and disadvantages*. This term is used today to mean that the government should take property (money, real estate, or personal and business assets of any kind) from those who have more than others and redistribute it among those who have less. The main questions attached to this redistribution process are "What is Right?" and "What is Fair?"

One argument that social justice advocates give to justify government control over social programs is what might be termed the *tug-on-your-heartstrings* argument. People say, *oh, we have to feed the poor and provide healthcare for everyone because healthcare is a right and it's fair*. But we have two questions for them. The first is, *where do those rights come from? Who created them?* America's founding legal documents state that all rights come from our Creator. If men can arbitrarily create rights, then what's to stop them from arbitrarily taking away rights? Where in the Bible, the Constitution, or the Bill of Rights does it say that the poor should never be poor? Or that everyone has a right to free healthcare at the expense of another? The second question is, *who determines what's fair?* Shouldn't we be more concerned about *what is right or just, not what is fair?* After all, is life always fair? Everyone is born with different talents and abilities. Some are born strong and healthy. Others are born with debilitating birth defects. No, life is not fair, not when judged in human terms. *Fair* is a subjective term. It depends upon the opinion of the subject – or person – who is judging what is fair and what is not. But what is *fair* to person "A" might not be *fair* to person "B" ...or person "C" or even person "D".

Biblical Justice

Biblical economics is based upon justice. Biblical justice prefers no person or class over another. As it says in Galatians 3:28, "there is neither Jew nor Greek, there is neither slave nor free, there is neither male nor female. We are all one in Christ." And in 2 Thessalonians 3:10, it again says, "he who is not willing to work, he should not eat." Any law, therefore, that gives an advantage in the economic sphere to anyone, rich or poor, violates biblical justice. Why? Because biblical justice requires equal rights before the law, *not equal outcomes*. True economic justice is not based on equal income, but on *equal opportunity*.

Where does wealth come from?

There are two opinions on where wealth comes from.

1. Free market economics says, *anyone who provides a service to another is creating wealth, adding prosperity to the world.* Wealth can be created by simply developing an idea. Steve Jobs designed the I-phone based on idea which led to a product that enriched the lives and fortunes of millions.

2. Keynesian economics (the philosophical economic system of socialism) says: *There is a fixed amount of riches in the world and those who have more simply have it because they took advantage of others - in effect, stealing it from those who are now poor.* Therefore, they contend that it is perfectly justifiable to allow everyone's income to be controlled and redistributed by a few elite, wise central planners. The politicians shame us into giving the government control over welfare programs for the poor, because they accuse the rich of extracting their wealth from the poor. Unfortunately, this view just simply doesn't match reality. In free market economics, the wealthy ordinarily create more wealth for everyone. In fact, anyone who works will create wealth.

Wealth Creation

American conservative political commentator and video producer Bill Whittle states that *wealth* simply means having more than one needs to survive. In his video *Wealth Creation*,[102] Mr. Whittle debunks this idea of *a fixed amount of riches in the world and those who have more simply have it because they took advantage of others.* He states that conservatives [and we add, those who hold to a biblical worldview] see this very differently.

> "We believe that wealth can be created from thin air; that people can, through creativity, invention and hard work, physically create new wealth essentially out of nothing. For us, the rich man with the car, the houses and the Learjet is not a villain at all. On the contrary, he's a hero. Not a good man, necessarily. That depends on the individual. But his personal wealth is just a small percentage of the much larger wealth that he has produced, which translates directly into hundreds or thousands or tens of thousands of new jobs and valuable products or services that wouldn't exist otherwise."

Mr. Whittle points out that the entire federal budget in 1862 was $530 million. In 2010, that number was $3.55 trillion. That's 3,550 billion dollars! It's an increase in wealth of about 300 times more - even adjusting for inflation. But if the U.S. population is only ten times greater, the Socialist's theory doesn't begin to explain the prosperity that has come to America. Where did the money - the excess wealth - come from to turn America from towns with unpaved roads traveled by horse and carriage and lit by gas lamps, into the richest nation in history in less

---

[102] Bill Whittle - https://billwhittle.com/what-we-believe-part-3-wealth-creation/

than 150 years? What 'Pot of Gold' somewhere supplied the money necessary to create and build all the shops, the restaurants, the 7 Elevens, the manufacturing plants, and the endless rows of houses, each with automobiles, air conditioning, widescreen TV's, computers and all the rest? Mr. Whittle the adds another exclamation point, saying,

> "Oh by the way, this is a nation where the poorest people have things that the richest people in 1862 never had or could have dreamed of. Things like antibiotics, electricity, cell phones, and a thousand other common everyday miracles. Where did all of this spectacular increase in wealth come from?"

Free trade vs Controlled Economies

Mr. Whittle answers the question by explain three basic principles: Creativity, Complexity, and Free Trade, the last of which he states is, by far, the main driver of all wealth creation. He relates the following example.

> Let's say you're a member of a hunting tribe up in the mountains. Your tribe is great at making spears. They are solid, they're straight, and they've got a strong flint spearhead. But you don't get to do much gathering, so your baskets look like old bird's nests. Meanwhile, down in the valley is a gatherer tribe. Their baskets are woven tight enough to hold water, but their spears are a little better than wobbly sticks. One day a guy from the Hunter tribe meets a guy from the Gatherer tribe, and together they agreed to trade one of the Hunter's excellent spears for one of the Gatherer's top-notch baskets. The question now is which one of them is wealthier? They both are! And that's the miracle. They both are returning with things that they and their tribe prize more highly than what they gave away, simply because they are harder to obtain. They're rarer.

> But that's just the beginning. See, the expert spear-maker then realizes that if he gets up early and stays up late, he can make more spears than he needs for just himself, and he can trade that extra work for something he considers valuable - a basket, let's say. It motivates him to do more than he needs. The exact same thing is true of the basket weaver. And pretty soon, both of them are employing their idiot sons-in-law, manufacturing spears and baskets. Yes, the guy making and trading with spears gets relatively rich, but the fact is, everybody wins. The idiot son-in-law, the guys making the Flint spearheads... The entire Hunter tribe gets the kind of baskets that they would never have had otherwise. And likewise for the gatherers with their awesome new spears.

> Now for our progressive friends who feel that all wealth has to be stolen, yes, the guys with the spears could come out and kill the gatherers and take all the baskets - and then there'd be no more baskets!

> *Free trade Is non coercive.* Both parties only get wealthier when both parties willingly trade what they have for what they want.

Lesson 4 Study Questions

1. Economic Justice is a term that means redistributing income from those who have more to those who have less. Read Exodus 30:15. What does God say about taxing some more than others? _____ _____

2. Name several natural consequences to a society when everyone is guaranteed the same income no matter how diligent or lazy the person. _____ _____ _____

3. In your own words define Social Justice and state why you think these policies might hurt a hard-working person who has earned a higher wage or position than another. _____ _____ _____

4. Biblical justice requires that everyone receive equal *opportunity*, not equal income. Why would this principle encourage an individual to work harder to attain his/her dreams? _____ _____ _____

Where does Wealth Come From?

5. In Free Market Economics (Capitalism), where does wealth come from? _____ _____

6. Keynesian Economics (modern Socialism) says wealth comes from a large, but fixed "pot of gold" in the world. Do you agree? ____Why? _____ _____

7. Why can the idea of government-mandated wealth redistribution programs be considered stealing? _____ _____

8. Can you name some of the programs currently imposed on Americans that promote wealth redistribution for the sake of "fairness"? _____ _____

9. From the last 3 paragraphs in Mr. Whittle's story of the 2 tribes – Gatherers and Hunters – why does Free Trade (Capitalism) create wealth, but Controlled Markets (Socialism, Communism, Marxism) strangle wealth creation? _____ _____ _____ _____

Lesson 5 - The Results of Socialism at Work

Keynesian Economics

The Bible promotes an economic system that respects private property, rewards the work ethic, and requires personal responsibility. A dominant feature of capitalism is economic freedom, which is simply the right of people to exchange things voluntarily, free from force, fraud, and theft. Socialism, on the other hand, seeks to replace the freedom of the market with a group of central planners who exercise control over the entire marketplace. John Maynard Keynes was the man responsible for the idea of what is called Keynesian Economics which heavily influence the aggressive theories that promote strong government control over the economic policies of a nation. Early in the 1900s when socialism was gaining momentum in the universities in America, the word *socialism* didn't go over well with the public, so those who held to these Keynesian theories changed their terminology and began calling themselves *progressives*. Now whenever we see a political group identifying itself as *progressives*, we know that they are coming from the socialist/Keynesian ideology.

By the end of the 20th century, however, these ideas had spread and taken hold in virtually every western democratic country. Keynes' version of socialistic economics is in direct contrast to that of free market capitalism. Listen to what Keynes himself writes to describe one of the ways socialism collects the money it needs for its entitlement programs. He wrote, "By a continuous process of inflation" (inflation often occurs when the government simply prints more money, resulting in the lowering of the value of the existing money in circulation) "governments can confiscate, secretly and unobserved, an important part of the wealth of their citizens. And while this impoverishes many, it actually enriches some. The process engages all the hidden forces of law on the side of destruction and does it in a manner that not one man in a million can diagnose."[103]

In other words, the government can steal our property without our even knowing that it's happening until it's too late.

> ### Entitlement Program
>
> Definition: *a government program that guarantees certain benefits to a particular group or segment of the population.*
> The most obvious examples of entitlement programs at the federal level in the United States would include Welfare, Medicare, and Medicaid, most Veterans' Administration programs, federal employee and military retirement plans, unemployment compensation, food stamps, and agricultural price support programs

In America, those who promote the Keynesian economic theory believe that the best way to convince the population to give government more of its money, property, or personal rights is to create a crisis that is concerning enough to frighten the people into allowing wholesale changes to be made in the government of the country. If the people are fearful enough, they'll turn over more power to the government to do things they wouldn't normally be allowed to do if not for the crisis. Citizens who are not properly informed by the politicians or the media often end up granting the federal government power to take control of the largest banks, corporations, and industries, ...industries like healthcare. Then, with power concentrated at the federal level, free market capitalism can be squelched and with it, personal freedom. Now the government can redistribute income as they please. Unfortunately, redistributing income is like stealing, and it is expressly forbidden by the laws of God because of the harm it causes to individuals and to society.

In socialist societies, the individual is forced to give over to the government much of the control of his or her life, virtually making them slaves. We conclude then, that the bigger the government, the poorer the people, and the smaller the government, the richer the people.

---

[103] https://www.goodreads.com/work/quotes/2919954-the-economic-consequences-of-the-peace

The Results of High Taxation

Consider the following illustration.

Imagine that you're given a check for $300 for a few day's work at your job, and you decide to head to Best Buy and spend that money on whatever you choose. You figure that you're absolutely free to buy whatever you want up to that $300. But what happens if - after you cash the check and you're walking from your car to the store - someone pulls a gun and demands the $100 bill that you had in your wallet? Now when you go to shop, you have less freedom to choose. That means you'll have to settle for the 32" off-brand TV instead of the 49" name-brand Smart TV. You have less buying power; thus, you have less freedom to choose.

Now suppose that you weren't robbed in the parking lot but went first to cash your check and found that the government took 33% or $100 in taxes from your check. What's the difference? You still have fewer choices, which means you have less freedom. Or what if the government took 50% in taxes as they do in Belgium, for example? That's a whole lot fewer choices you'll have. You'll have less personal freedom to enjoy what you've worked hard for, ...AND, you'll most likely be a lot less happy.

Clearly, the bigger the government, the less freedom you'll enjoy. The smaller the government, the greater the freedom.

The Biblical View of Health Care – the Parable of the Good Samaritan
(Luke 10:25- 37)

When asked by a lawyer how to inherit eternal life, Jesus asked him what the two great commands were. After he recited, "Love God with all your heart, mind, soul, and strength, and to love your neighbor as yourself." The lawyer then asked, "Who is my brother?" Jesus then illustrated the meaning of the phrase "loving your neighbor as yourself". He told a story about a man traveling from Jerusalem to Jericho who was robbed, beaten, and stripped of his clothes, and left half-dead. A priest and a Levite each saw him, but they passed by on the other side of the road. However, a Samaritan, a despised man by the Jews, saw him and scripture makes a point of saying that the Samaritan had compassion toward the stranger. He then proceeded to bandage his wounds, pour medicine on him, put him on his animal and take him to an inn where he spent the night taking care of the man. The next day, he left the innkeeper with enough of his own money to pay for the man's room and board and any further treatment that he might need for his recovery, and then promised to return and repay the innkeeper if it cost him anymore than he was already given.

John W. Robbins from *The Trinity Review* gives a great summary of the lessons from this parable.[104]

A. First, the political religious establishment, the priest and the Levite, seemed to be uninterested in actual healthcare because they passed on the other side of the road. This brings up the question, *is the church as involved today in taking care of the poor as they were 150 years ago or 100 years ago? Or have we given up most of the control of this over to the government?* (see sidebar on the next page)

---

[104] John W. Robbins, *The Ethics and Economics of Health Care* http://www.trinityfoundation.org/journal.php?id=266

B. The Samaritan businessman paid the innkeeper for his trouble. He apparently didn't think that the innkeeper had an obligation to help him or the crime victim without being paid. The Good Samaritan didn't hold the belief that just because someone has a need, it means he is entitled to the property of someone else. In other words, just because a person is injured, it doesn't mean someone else is obligated to give free services to him.

C. The Good Samaritan acted out of compassion, not out of compulsion. He didn't try to compel anyone else to be kind. The Samaritan businessman spent the night in the inn with the victim, making sure that the man would recover. And after the emergency had passed, he continued on his trip, leaving the victim in the care of the innkeeper who agreed to the compensation offered by the Samaritan.

D. The Samaritan man displayed a touching level of personal involvement and care toward the injured stranger. It was an open display of love which no doubt brought great pleasure to the injured man and to the Samaritan, and it was a great example to the innkeeper as well. The Good Samaritan didn't organize a lobby to agitate for a National Healthcare Plan because that has nothing to do with loving your neighbor, because loving your neighbor is a personal issue.

E. This traveling Samaritan was a good neighbor by sharing both his own goods and his own time with the crime victim. And it's his example, not that of the political and religious leaders, that Christ commands us to imitate.

A BRIEF HISTORY OF CHRISTIAN CHARITY

In his essay, *A History of Charity in the Church*[105], Nicholas Placido writes:

Many of the original foundations of benevolence and charity have their beginnings in Christianity.

"The roots of social compassion go deep into the soil of the Judeo-Christian tradition"[106]. From the beginnings of the biblical narrative, we find the concept of loving and caring for others. "The Old Testament law specified how the community should provide care and to whom"[107] The Law addressed hospitality to strangers and foreigners[108], allowing the poor to glean the field to obtain grain [109], and the provision of care for widows and orphans[110]. The New Testament "added a new and more challenging idea of the care of the poor"[111].

Early Christians saw it as part of their calling to model the life of Christ in their conduct and attitude toward those with fewer resources. "One cares about others, especially the poor, not because it brings benefit but because that person in need is made in the image of God".[112]

The early Christians were noted for their charity to each other. The early church in 4th century was noted for caring for the poor via feeding programs, and obtained "money, property and other goods from the rich to distribute to the poor"[113]. The writings of the day focused on the duty and the right to be of assistance to the poor

The concept of Christian charity "blossomed into an important force within western Christianity in the twelfth century."[114] Monasteries in the middle Ages provided employment, and the development of shelters, almshouses, hospices, and leprosaria occurred during this period.[115] However, "religious charity was not just a set of institutions: it encompassed an ideology that describes a distinctive version of the Christian life in the middle ages"[116]

The great revival movements of the 19th century lead to a "dynamic Christian faith that would change society as a whole"[117]. Many social activities developed as a result of this revival movement. This included the establishment of orphanages by George Mueller, and the development of the Salvation Army, YMCA, YWCA, and Volunteers of America.

The Bible has much to say about the Christian's privilege and responsibility for caring for the poor and the sick. Jesus made the ultimate statement when He says that the righteous will show their love for Him by feeding the

---

[105] https://www.nacsw.org/Convention/PlacidoNAHistoryFINAL.pdf A HISTORY OF CHARITY AND THE CHURCH By: Nicholas Placido
[106] Karger & Stoesz, 2008, p. 39
[107] Poe, 2008, 106
[108] Exodus 22:21, Hebrews 13:2
[109] Leviticus 19:9-10, Ruth
[110] Deuteronomy 14:28-29, 26:12
[111] Poe, 2008, p. 107
[112] IBID
[113] Brandsen & Vliem, 2008, p.62
[114] Brodman, 2009, p. 43
[115] IBID
[116] Brodman, 2009, p. 9
[117] Poe, 2008, p. 111

hungry, welcoming the stranger, clothing the poor, and taking care of the sick, thereby fulfilling the call "love thy neighbor". (Matthew 25:34-46; 22:39)

A final observation: One of God's greatest attributes is that He loves to care for His children. John 3:16 says that He showed his great love for us by giving the most precious gift *ever* in order to heal us. We are made in His image; therefore, *one of the greatest blessings we can enjoy is to follow His example by giving to others unselfishly*. When we surrender the privilege of taking care of others to an impersonal, unaccountable government, everyone suffers.

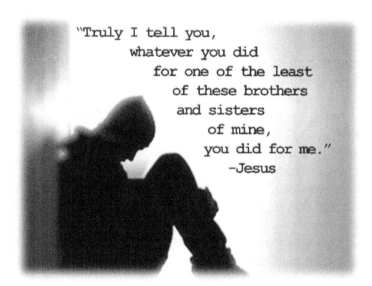

Lesson 5 Study Questions

1. The Bible is much more supportive of an economic system that...

    a. Respects private property. Read Ex. 20:15,17; Ex.22:1-4. Name several things these scriptures say about respecting private property._____

    _____

    b. Rewards the work ethic. See Prov. 12:11; Ruth 2:1-8; Prov. 31. How is hard work rewarded?

    _____

    c. Requires personal responsibility. Read Luke 19:11-26. How is God's attitude illustrated in this parable?

    _____

2. Read Genesis 2:2a, 2:15, Exodus 20:9, 31:17a. According to these scriptures, what is one of the primary purposes we were created for, which is also a common trait of God? _____

    _____

3. Consider the principle: "The smaller the government, the richer the people. The bigger the government, the poorer the people" Is this true?_____ Why or why not? _____

    _____

4. What might happen if an individual is taxed at a higher rate than others based upon his personal success, and why? _____

5. Define *entitlement program* and state your views of such programs _____

    _____

    _____

Lessons from the Parable of the Good Samaritan (Read Luke 10:25-37)

1. What are the 2 greatest commandments?_____ _____
2. What was the attitude of those in the religious establishment of Israel toward the unsaved one in need?

    _____

    _____

3. Do you think, from this parable, that Jesus is implying that the church (corporate and individual) has a responsibility to care for the poor more so than the state (government)? _____
4. Name several actions (at least 3) that the Samaritan businessman displayed which exemplify what it means to "love your neighbor as yourself"._____
5. Name two results of the "social justice" belief that the State is responsible to care for the poor. 1) _____ 2) _____
6. Is Jesus saying that our primary way showing our love to our neighbor is to lead him/her to say the sinner's prayer?* _____ If not, what IS our primary responsibility? _____

    _____

7. Read 1 Corinthians 3:6-7; 1 Timothy 1:15; 2 Timothy 1:8-9. Who is responsible for saving a soul? _____

    _____

*NOTE: We are certainly not advocating that leading another to Christ is not a part of our calling, as God moves and provides opportunities. We are simply pointing out Christ's definition of loving one's neighbor, and the central part this should play in all our lives. Could it be that the church has emphasized personal evangelism to such a point that we have forgotten our first duty: to simply love the lost? Examine Jesus' example in **Romans 5:8**.*

Lesson 6 – Caring for the Sick and Poor

The Christian View of Charity vs. Government-run Social Programs

The socialist term for charity is *economic* or *social justice*, and it states that regardless of anyone's work ethic, their moral choices or attitude, everyone has a right to anything that's available in that society, and that it's the government's responsibility to disperse everyone's property equally among the people. In other words, government should take from those who have and give to those who don't have. The traditional American biblical standard regarding charity or welfare is much different, though. Before the 20th century, the notion that the poor are somehow entitled to the property of others had no place in America. The Bible itself teaches no unconditional duty to help others simply because they need help. Paul commands, "he who does not work, neither shall he eat." Paul knew that there's always plenty of work to be done. Even if you're not getting paid, you can always do something to contribute to the welfare of others by simply working to help out others. Paul says that there is no duty to support anyone who can work but chooses not to. The Bible knows nothing of either legal or moral entitlements to the property of another, simply because someone needs help.

Paul's command here obviously does not fit in with today's social justice policies that call for government-forced wealth redistribution. If the Bible's policies were obeyed then, it would mean the immediate end of the welfare state. Keep in mind that it's not the Bible, but Karl Marx who teaches, "to each according to his need, from each according to his ability". The Bible simply says, "you shall not steal. You shall not covet what is not yours."

The Socialist/Communist/Marxist View

These worldviews teach that to be fair to all people, the government must be enabled to take ownership of another's property as they see fit. Now, if it was your property they confiscated, and you had worked hard to purchase it or create it would you consider that fair? Would you call it stealing?

How Communism Nearly Wiped-out the Pilgrim Colony

One of the earliest and arguably most historically significant North American colonies was Plymouth Colony, founded in 1620 in what is now known as Plymouth, Massachusetts. The original colony had written into its charter a system of communal property and labor. As William Bradford recorded in his *Of Plymouth Plantation*, a people who had formerly been known for their virtue and hard work became lazy and unproductive. Resources were squandered, vegetables were allowed to rot on the ground and mass starvation was the result. And where there is starvation, there is plague. After 2 1/2 years, the leaders of the colony decided to abandon their socialist mandate and create a system which honored private property. The colony survived and thrived and the abundance which resulted was what was celebrated at that iconic Thanksgiving feast.

https://www.forbes.com/sites/jerrybowyer/2012/11/21/how-a-failed-commune-gave-us-what-is-now-thanksgiving/#7f4f0c1167e5

These economic systems reward those who don't work and contribute, and penalize those who do. The biblical system encourages everyone who is able to contribute, and it discourages laziness, selfishness, and covetousness. The question is *which idea is better and works to the benefit of the people?*

The Dangers of Empowering Government to Dispense Charity

As an example of the danger of giving government control over charity, let's look at a story from Congressman Davy Crockett. From his biography "The Life of Colonel David Crockett" we read,

"Crockett, as a member of the House of Representatives, once voted to give $20,000 to the homeless victims of a fire in Georgetown. Now one of Crockett's constituents, Horatio Bunce, told Crockett that he would not be voting for him in the coming election because of that vote, and of course Crockett objected," he said, "Certainly nobody will complain that a great and rich country like ours should give the insignificant sum of $20,000 to relieve its suffering women and children, particularly with a full and overflowing treasury.

"But Mister Bunce explained "Mister Crockett, first of all, the government ought to have in the treasury no more than enough for its purposes because the power of collecting and dispersing money at pleasure is the most dangerous power that can be entrusted to any man. While you are voting to relieve one, you are drawing money from thousands. And if you had the right to give anything, the amount was simply a matter of discretion to you. And you had as much ability to give 20 million dollars as $20,000. And if you have the right to give to one, then you have the right to give to all. And as the Constitution neither defines charity nor stipulates the amount, you are then at liberty to give to anything and everything which you may believe or professed to believe is a charity, and then to any amount that you may think proper. You will easily perceive what a wide door this would open for fraud and corruption and favoritism, on the one hand, and for robbing the people on the other.

No, Mr. Crockett, Congress has no right to give charity. Individual members may give as much of their own money as they please, but they have no right to touch even a dollar of the public money for that purpose because when Congress once begins to stretch its power beyond the limits of the Constitution, there is no limit to it, and then no security for the people."[27]

The Cost of Entitlement Programs Designed to Care for the Poor and the Sick

This is one of the most personally impacting economic matters of our day because it affects everyone's income and taxes; thus, it is worth everyone's consideration.

A Real-World Example

The budget for the US government in the year 2019, as an example, was projected to be 4.11 trillion dollars. If we counted off $1 every second of every day for a year, it would take *over one hundred thirty thousand* years to reach 4.11 trillion dollars. That means that our government spent *nearly 8 million dollars every minute in 2019 – and nearly 1.6 million dollars of that was borrowed every minute!!* This wild spending brings us to the most critical question of today: *how can we pay for this debt?* How can we stop from going broke, each and every one of us? One side says *raise taxes on the rich. They're not paying their fair share,* even though the top 20% of wage earners in America pay about 70% of all the taxes in the nation. But the other side says, *cut government spending, cut taxes, cut regulations. Simply reduce the size of government and give freedom back to the people. Let the people keep their money and let them decide how best to invest it.*

How the U.S. Government Pays the Bills

Let's look at these two ideas in reality by first asking how is the federal government paying for this debt? Using 2019 as an example (**see the chart on the right**), we see that the U.S. required $4.11 trillion to cover its bills. $3.3 trillion is all the money the government planned to collect

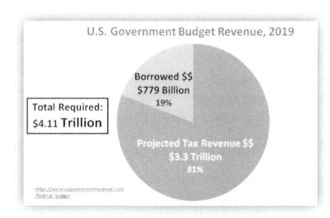

U.S. Government Budget Revenue, 2019

Total Required: $4.11 **Trillion**

Borrowed $$ $779 Billion 19%

Projected Tax Revenue $$ $3.3 Trillion 81%

https://www.usgovernmentrevenue.com /federal_budget

in taxes. Keep in mind that *the government doesn't make any money*. It collects all of its revenue by taxation. So, where does the lighter section of money come from as shown in the chart? That remaining area represents nearly 20% of the money needed, but it is *borrowed*. How would that work for you if you tried that at home?

Where does the Money go? How is it spent?

1.25 trillion pays for the entire cost of the government. This means that it pays the salary of every senator, every congressman, all their staff, their offices, their desks, their pencils and paper, all their cars and the gas to fuel those cars, and all of their insurance programs. And it pays for the entire cost of the US military. According to the Constitution, that was mostly all that the federal government was supposed be responsible for prior to the Great Depression. Before that time, the remaining areas never existed. So, where is that money spent? The answer:

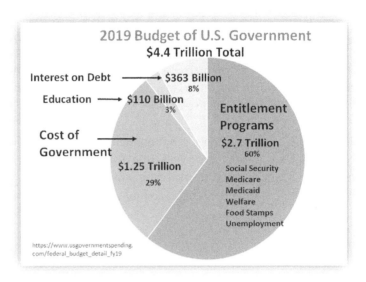

2.7 trillion dollars goes to entitlement programs. That means programs like Medicare, Medicaid, Social Security, and miscellaneous programs like food stamps and unemployment and so on. Now even though our Constitution doesn't give Congress the right to control programs like this, let's just presume for a moment that it does. Where, again, do we get the money to pay for it all?

Let's Tax the Rich (more)! …An Example of How that Might Work (or not)

Let's think through the idea that taxing the rich is the answer to taking care of all the sick and poor people in the country. We'll use as our example the budget of the U.S. in 2010 which was 3.2 trillion dollars. Let's start on January 1st by taking every dime of profit from every Fortune 500 corporation in America. But it's Super Bowl time, so let's impose a retroactive tax that allows us to collect every dollar spent for every Super Bowl ad run ever since the very first Super Bowl was played back in 1967. But as you can see by the chart below, that pays our debt only up to February 8th. So, we'll confiscate all of the earnings from every sports athlete in America. That's not nearly enough, though. That pays our bills for another two days.

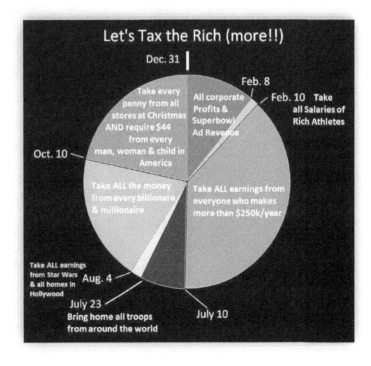

Next, we'll take all of the personal earnings from everyone who makes over $250,000 a year. Now we're paid up only to July 10th! So, how about ending all of the wars we're involved in? Let's bring everybody back home from Iraq, Afghanistan, Germany and everywhere. That ought to save some serious money! But that pays our bills for only another two weeks! What now? Well, everyone knows that Hollywood has tons of money, so, let's take all of the money from the Star Wars businesses that has been made from all of the movies and the sale of all the merchandise since the '80s. Then, we'll confiscate every home in the Hollywood Hills, sell them all and apply that all to the debt. That pays our debt for another 3 weeks. It seems we'll need to get a lot more serious.

America has over 500 billionaires and a whole lot of millionaires. Let's just take *all* of their money! That ought to do it! Now we're paid up to October 10th - - but we're still short! So, even though it's the holiday season, let's take every penny from the sale of every holiday item from every store in America until Christmas. However, we still need more money. Okay, we'll take all the money that we usually give to foreign aid and apply that to the debt. But the bad news is we're still short. So, we'll just have to collect a check for $44 from every living, breathing person in the United States.

Congratulations! We finally paid our debts! We made it to December 31st!!!!

But the bad news is, tomorrow is January 1, 2011, and our debt has increased to 3.8 trillion dollars. What do we do now? There's no one left to tax. All the corporations and all the people with the money to give us the jobs that we need are all broke, and so are we.

The bottom line is that there is not enough money or resources in all the world to provide all the free services and outrageous retirement programs that the government has been promising many people in America, unless everyone is working and contributing, creating products and providing services for the benefit of all the others. But that won't happen as long as so many people are getting paid not to work.

Lesson 6 Study Questions

1. Regarding the sidebar titled *"How Communism Nearly Wiped-out the Pilgrim Colony"* explain in your own words why Communism failed among the Pilgrims: _____

    _____

    _____

2. How would you explain "Economic" or "Social" Justice? _____

    _____

3. What effect could this economic system have on your ability to succeed based on your own hard work or creativity? _____

    _____

4. Regarding the account of Crockett/Bunce, why did the Founders NOT make government responsible for taking care of the poor, sick, and needy; **and** whose responsibility is this and why? _____

    _____

    _____

5. After reading the "Let's Tax the Rich More" section, what are your thoughts about the idea of raising taxes specifically on the rich in America to pay for our debts? Give specific reasons for your answers.

    _____

    _____

    _____

6. Why do you think most employees aren't paid more than the owner/creator of the company they work for? _____

    _____

7. What happens to a company's ability to hire workers or give raises to their workers if its taxes are raised or if the company is forced to pay a minimum wage by the government? _____

    _____

    _____

8. If businesses are taxed more because of their degree of success, what effect might that have on the future productivity of that company and why? _____

    _____

    _____

9. What are your thoughts about entitlement programs in light of today's study?

    _____

    _____

    _____

Lesson 7 – The Biblical View Charity

Now that we've seen what the world's answer to charity and health care is. Let's see what the Bible says.

3 Biblical Tests for Determining Who is Worthy of Charity [118]

The Apostle Paul gives detailed instructions on how churches are to dispense charity in First Timothy, Chapter 5:3-16. In this section Paul imposes three tests to guide and govern charitable giving. (NOTE: in these examples, the Church is defined as all individuals who profess Christianity and the local church organizations they are affiliated with)

1. The Means test. Do you have the *means* to work? In other words, are you strong enough and healthy enough to perform a job? In that case, you don't need to receive charity from the church or from the government. Also, if your family can help, they should be the first to assist.
2. The Age test. If you're too old to work and not able to work to earn the money needed to take care of yourself, then the church should help out. That only makes sense.

3. The Morals test. This is probably the most important of all. Paul clearly says that we're not to support young widows unless they meet certain qualifications, the foremost of which is a lifestyle test. Why? Because sometimes we do more harm than good by helping or enabling someone whom God is disciplining for the bad moral choices that he or she might have made. All charity, then, is to be governed by the moral lifestyle of the recipient. Therefore, anyone who advocates for legal or moral entitlements using unaccountable political giving, or anyone who says that some people deserve help simply because they're human beings is going against the laws of God.

Charity as Defined in Colonial Days

In 1821 two men from New Hampshire by the name of Woodbury and Whipple reflected the thinking of that day when they wrote, "The poverty which proceeds from improvidence or rebellion and vice or immorality ought to feel the consequences and the penalties which God has laid out for them".[119] In 19th century America, charity organizations and societies considered those worthy of relief to be those who were poor through no fault of their own and unable to change their situation quickly. The Founding Fathers distinguished - just as Paul did - between the deserving and the undeserving poor. James 1:27 says, "Pure and undefiled religion before God and the Father is this, to visit orphans and widows in their trouble, and to keep oneself unspotted from the world." In other words, don't do the things the way that the world does them. This is a call for individuals to care for those in need, not a detached third party.

The Bible says that we're made in God's image. God loves to take care of His people. He defined the greatest love as when a man would lay down his life for his friend. And since we're made in God's image, it's a blessing from God to help each other. We say it's better to give than receive, isn't that true? Isn't that a big part of what makes our lives meaningful? Therefore, charity is designed by God to come from each of us personally, not from an impersonal government handout.

These are valid reasons why the biblical model brought such prosperity to America and blessed the world. When we cooperate with the Laws designed by the Creator of the universe, we are promised success!

---

[118] John W. Robbins, *The Ethics and Economics of Health Care* http://www.trinityfoundation.org/journal.php?id=266
[119] IBID

Charitable Giving

What's the result of America's original Christian worldview of charity? Americans give more to charity per capital and as a percentage of their gross income than the citizens of any other nation. Now as of the most recent year the data that are available, Americans gave per capita or per person 3 1/2 times as much to causes and charities as the French, seven times as much as the Germans, and 14 times as much as the Italians. You see it was the foundational Christian principles of hard work and personal responsibility that produce the

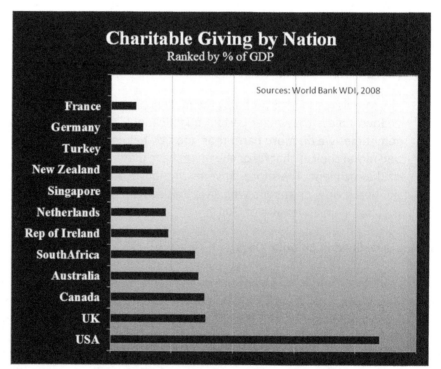

amazing prosperity of Americans who give so generously and out of thankfulness and out of compassion to others.

Lesson 7 Study Questions

1. What are your thoughts about the 3 tests (Means, Age, Morals) the Apostle Paul lists for determining whether or not someone is to receive charity from the church? _____

    _____

    _____

2. We say that it is better to give than to R_____. Can you give an example of an instance in your life when you experienced this first-hand? _____

    _____

3. Why do you think Americans give more to charitable causes than any other nation?

    _____

    _____

4. From what you've learned in today's class, what do you think are the consequences *to the Church* when the government is given the responsibility to provide free healthcare, free food, and free disaster relief?

    _____

    _____

Remembering Woodbury and Whipple – the Early American View of Charity

5. They wrote: "The poverty which proceeds from improvidence (rebellion) and vice (immorality) ought to feel the consequences and penalties which God has laid out for them." Read Ezekiel 23:36-39, 46-49; Joshua 7:19-25. What were God's instructions for dealing with open rebellion against God's law?

    _____

    _____

    _____

6. Why do you think the punishment was so severe in those examples?

    _____

    _____

    _____

7. Read Deut. 8:3-5. What are some of the purposes God has for us when we are hit with hard times?

    _____

    _____

8. Read Job 5:17-27. Name some of the blessings missed out on when someone is "bailed-out" of the troubles caused by their own rebellion and foolishness: _____

    _____

    _____

Lesson 8 – Man's Way vs. God's Way

Summary of the Proper Roles of Christians and Government

No study on the Christian view of Economics would be complete without asking the question, 'What would Jesus do? To answer, we'll turn once more to Mr. Robbins[120], who said, *"Jesus Christ had power to end all types of sickness and illness while He was on the earth. Yet He did not do so because the Father was unwilling for Him to do so. Not because He was unable. He restricted His healing ministry to those in a tiny corner of the world, …and not even all of them were healed."*

We may draw 3 conclusions from this observation:
1. Since Christ never sinned, it was not a sin for Him to fail to heal everyone, even when He had the power to do so.
2. Christ had one instrument for healing: Belief. If a person lacked belief, he did not heal him.
3. Christ did not want any disciples who were interested only in His ability to feed and heal them.

He considered belief in the truth and having faith in God as our provider to be more important than physical well-being.

The Problems of Runaway Power

Big government policies of redistribution including state "welfare" programs only multiply problems of the poor. Statistics, history, and common observation prove this to be true. These programs create needless bureaucracy, waste the citizen's money, and concentrate far too much power into the hand of government bureaucrats - feeding their sinful nature.

On the other side, capitalism – or free market economics – encourages freedom for the individual to create his own wealth. This removes the danger of excessive dependence on the state instead of on God. And it leaves each individual with more money personally to give to charitable causes as God puts on his heart.

Five basic principles of God's economics:

1. Remember that God is our provider – It's not the state, not our job, not even the strength or abilities we have. God is our provider.
2. All our gifts and talents are gifts from Him, including the upbringing and education we received. Even the people we met at just the right place and right time who gave us our jobs - all of this has been orchestrated by God.
3. Thankfulness is a critical priority. Every good and perfect gift comes from above, from the Father of lights.[121]
4. We are personally responsible for bringing fruit from our lives. We have a mission – a job to do. We've each been given these gifts and talents immeasurable, and a lifetime to develop them. God expects us to the best we can with what we have.
5. This responsibility is for our blessing – and for the blessing of others.

But it not for us to take on this duty in our own strength. God simply calls us to step out in faith and try.

For the eyes of the Lord run to and fro throughout the whole earth, to show Himself strong on behalf of those whose heart is trusting in Him. – 2 Chronicles 16:9

---

[120] J.D. Robbins, The Trinity Review, *The Ethics and Economics of Health Care (Sept-Nov 2009) Pg 8*
[121] James 1:17

Conclusion

We have presented these contrasting worldviews to make all aware of what happens when the government is allowed to claim responsibility in areas it has not been given according to God. Thus, when be grant more power to the state to do things that, according to the biblical worldview, are meant for the people to do - such as taking care of the poor, the sick, and the elderly - we are robbed of the blessings which God had in mind for us. We are not saved by our works, but doing good works is our biblical responsibility individually and collectively. As stated in Ephesians 2:10: *"For we are His workmanship, created in Christ Jesus for good works, which God prepared beforehand that we should walk in them."*

When we insist on taking care of others' needs rather than giving that responsibility to the state,

1) We have the privilege of loving our neighbor and enjoying the virtuous benefits that come from giving freely to others, serving them as Christ served us by laying down His life for others
2) By loving our neighbor, we are loving God and showing our gratefulness for what He has done for us
3) We are working alongside God to model, guide, and teach others the lessons of good stewardship of our time, talents, and resources.

None of the above can be found in Scripture to be the responsibility of the secular government.

We must not lose sight of the fact that those of us who have been blessed to be citizens of America live in the only nation in the history of man that is built upon fundamental principles taken from the Bible, and those principles govern by the codified law of the land – the U.S. Constitution and Bill of Rights. That is a deep and profound statement because as citizens of this nation *of the people, by the people, and for the people*, we are the governors; thus, we bear the responsibility for loving and serving the society we live in. Let us remember the line from the Horatio Bunce in Chapter six.

> "When Congress (the government) once begins to stretch its power beyond the limits of the Constitution, there is no limit to it, and then no security for the people."

The Greatest of all Biblical Economic Principles

Trust in God and Keep His Commands

Hebrews 11:6 says, *"But without faith, it is impossible to please Him, for he who comes to God must believe that He is [God], and that He is a rewarder of those who diligently seek him."*

Matthew 6:24-32 says, *"No one can serve two masters, for either you will hate the one and love the other, or else he will be loyal to the one and despise the other. You cannot serve God and mammon [money]. Therefore, I say to you, don't worry about your life, what you will eat or what you'll drink, nor about your body, what you will put on. Is not life more than food and the body more than clothing?*

Look at the birds of the air for they neither sow nor reap nor gather into barns, yet your heavenly Father feeds them. Are you not more valuable than they? Which of you by worrying can add one cubit to his stature? Now if God so clothes the grass of the field which today is, and tomorrow is thrown into the oven, will he not much more clothe you, oh you of little faith? Therefore, don't worry, saying, 'what shall we eat? What shall we drink? Or what shall we wear?' For after all these things the Gentiles seek. For your heavenly Father knows that you need all these things."

> *"But seek first the kingdom of God and His righteousness, and all of these things will be added to you. Therefore, don't worry about tomorrow for tomorrow will worry about its own things. Sufficient for the day is its own trouble."* Matthew 6:33-34

What other worldview presents such a magnificent hope for us than that spoken by the God of the Bible?

Economics and Morality

Economics is a moral issue; therefore, Christians have a responsibility - especially in America - to know what the Bible says on the subject. In line with this, it is wise for us to understand why a socialist or a communist system is immoral according to Scripture.

Lastly, we were created above all to honor, respect, and obey God voluntarily and out of gratefulness and appreciation for all that he has done for us. When we trust his laws and his ideas in all the areas of our life, when we work hard and apply ourselves to the best of our abilities, He promises to provide for us.

When we seek after Him above all other things in life, He promises *abundant* life, …not only in this life but in the life to come as well!

> *For I know the thoughts that I think toward you, says the Lord, thoughts of peace and not of evil, to give you a future and a hope.* - *Jeremiah 29:11 (NKJV)*

Lesson 8 Study Questions
5 Basic Principles to God's Economics

1. God is our provider. Read Matt. 6:26,30,33; Psalm 65:9-13. Why should we trust God over anyone or anything   else? _____

_____

_____

2. Acknowledge and remember that all your natural gifts, talents, and abilities are a gift from God. Read I Peter 4:11; Eph. 2:10; John 17:7; Rom. 12:6-8; 1 Cor. 2:12. Therefore, why is it unwise to be prideful over our talents or giftings? _____

_____

_____

3. Thankfulness. Read Heb. 2:12 (note: in this passage, who is speaking, and to whom is he speaking?); Luke 17:11-19; Psalm 100:4; Rom. 1:20-21. Why is thankfulness so important in a Christian's life?

_____

_____

_____

4. We are personally responsible for bringing fruit from our lives. Read Luke 12:16-21; Luke 12:48; Luke 19:26. (a) Why is this principle so critical in Christianity, and (b) why do you think it is so lacking in our world today?

_____

_____

_____

5. This responsibility is for our blessing and for blessing others. Read Matt. 6:2-4; Matt. 14:15-21; Psalm 128:1- (esp. vs. 2). What happens when we are diligent in applying our gifts, talents, and energy wisely, – even when we think we have little to give? _____

_____

_____

Conclusion

6. Read Matt. 6:19-31; Phil. 4:11-13. What is more important, a person's economic condition with no assurance of Heaven, OR his/her spiritual condition including peace with God? Or, put another way, which matters more? Riches in this life without contentment, or riches and contentment in this life and the next, and why? _____

_____

_____

_____

Subject Six: The Christian Worldview of Science

Lesson 1- Intro to the Christian Worldview

From the time the Bible became available to the common people, Scripture was considered the inerrant Word of God, the source of all Truth. But today, instead of quoting Scripture as Truth, we quote the latest scientific research. We have come to believe that what scientists say is more reliable – more true - than what the God of the Bible has to say. We are told – and many outside (and inside) the church believe – that the Bible has nothing to say about the complex issues we deal with in the 21st century; thus, we should turn to the modern scientist to guide us in our evolution as a species. But just a glimpse at the condition of our world today begs the question: *How's that working out for us?*

In the last few decades, the intelligent design arguments have begun to affect the evolution/creation debate in quite a profound manner. And in order for the average Christian to be even somewhat effective in debating a skeptic in this area, we often must be extremely familiar with the arguments on both sides. Usually, we are forced to follow the skeptic into rabbit-trail-after-rabbit-trail in order to "catch" him in a flaw in logic.

We believe that an even more powerful (and simple) tool of persuasion is the tool of Truth. Absolute truth is truth that never changes regardless of where you are in space or time. Yet we are told in this "scientific" world we live in today that there is no such thing as absolute truth. Truth, they say, is always relative to where you are in time and space. In other words, truth is always changing, and science will keep us informed as it does.

Therefore, we believe that the best argument is the one *that can be supported in the real world.*

If a proposition is true, we should see it verified repeatedly in the real world. If we cannot verify it, we must be very cautious in depending upon it as true.

In our study of the world of modern science, we must begin by asking a few simple questions: Can science give us absolute Truth? If it cannot, should science be relied upon to teach us about "changing morals" and proper behaviors? On the other side we should ask: Are Science and Christianity compatible? Can a Christian be a scientist? Why do we need Christians in the fields of science?

The bottom line of this issue is that science has positioned itself as the god of this age. White-robed scientists are the priests, and the latest scientific research is their "book of truth". All the while, our world is becoming more venomous, vicious, and volatile. Is there a connection?

Let's put a microscope to it.

Our Purpose in this Chapter

Before we begin digging into the Christian worldview of science, it would be helpful to clearly state the intention or the ultimate goal of these lessons. First, let us state what is *not* our intention. While we will look at the many limitations of science, it is not our intention to criticize science just for the sake of criticizing it, nor do we wish to discourage anyone from studying science or from pursuing a career in the sciences. In fact, it's quite the opposite. The author of this text has conducted extensive scientific research, taught science courses at the university level, and is currently practicing as a health professional in the medical field. Christianity and Science are most certainly compatible with one another, *but science must never be held in higher esteem than God.* Unfortunately, though, we live in a day and age where many people look to science to give them truth rather than to God. And this is where Christians must take issue. Is there any source of truth other than God? That is a question everyone must wrestle with.

In this chapter, we will see that scientific methodology does not and indeed *cannot* provide a logical basis for knowing *absolute truth*. And knowing absolute truth - truth that is true for everyone, everywhere, and at all times - is our goal. We will often refer to this as **Capital T Truth** (as opposed to **Little T Truth** which we will define later). Absolute truth, or **Capital T Truth**, is defined as *all of the propositions of the Bible - the word of God - and their logical implications.* Truth is <u>always</u> propositional (see the last chapter)!

Logical Implications from Biblical Truths

As stated before, a proposition is *the meaning of a declarative sentence that expresses something that can be true or false.* For example, in John 14:6, Jesus says "I am the way, the truth, and the life. No one comes to the Father except through Me." Here we have four propositions, the first one is "I am the way". In other words, this passage states clearly that faith in Christ is the only route, the only path that leads to eternal communion with God in heaven. The second proposition is "I am the truth", which is to say the teachings of Jesus were the actual words of God. According to this biblical proposition, everything that Jesus taught is absolutely true because He is simply God clothed in the human body. God is the source of all truth. When Jesus was speaking, God was speaking, for Jesus is God. As Jesus himself says elsewhere, "I and the father are one". The third proposition, "I am the life", emphatically states that only through the imputed righteousness of Christ is one safe from the wages of their sin, which is eternal death. And the fourth proposition is, "no one comes to the Father except through Me".

Consequently, *a logical implication* is that not all roads lead to heaven, for Christ alone is the way. No one comes to God through the teachings of Buddhism or the Quran or the Book of Mormon, or by reading science textbooks, for only the teachings of Christ are wholly true. No one is declared righteous by placing their faith in Buddha or Mohammed or Joseph Smith or Charles Darwin, or anyone else. Though the Bible doesn't explicitly make these statements, they're logically implied. This is what is meant by Capital T Absolute Truth. All of the propositions of the Bible, the word of God, and their logical implications are true, absolutely.

> **Absolute Truth** (Capital T Truth):
> All of the propositions of the Bible
> (the Word of God)
> and their logical implications.

The Correspondence Theory of Truth

Little T Truth is any proposition or statement that accurately describes or corresponds with the world. And this is known as the *correspondence theory of truth*. It is temporal truth, ...true only as long as there is a world that it can correspond with; and it is how most people understand truth. However, this is not biblical truth. Biblical truth is eternal because its source is God, and God is eternal.

Those who hold to the correspondence theory of truth believe that *truth is only found through man's sensory experiences, by observing the material world.* In other words, the secular scientist considers truth to be only those propositions or statements that accurately describe or correspond with the world as obtained through the scientific method. Truth is therefore independent of God's word. It is divorced from the Bible. According to the correspondence theory of truth, biblical truth is only true insofar as it can be scientifically verified. Thus, the Bible is to be interpreted through man's eyes and ears, nose, touch, and tastes. Truth is dependent upon sinful man's senses, rather than on God's holy words. *These views are clearly in opposition with one another*. They can't both be true. Our purpose is to equip the reader with the knowledge necessary to decide which view of truth is both rational and reasonable.

Four Goals of this Chapter

In this chapter, we will be discussing the biblical worldview of science and answering the following questions:

- Does science give us truth?
- Does science disprove the existence of God?
- Are religion and science at odds with each other?
- Can a Christian be a scientist?

Who Cares? Why a Christian Worldview of Science is Critical in Today's World

Before we scrutinize science under the microscope, we might first ask the question, "is it worth it?" Why is it important to have a biblical worldview of science? A brief illustration from today's education system will explain.

The Suppression of Opposing Ideas

Nearly everyone who receives scientific training in public colleges or universities will be dogmatically taught that the theory of evolution is no longer a theory, but it is fact. Most often, the professors will look down on religion and demean Christianity, ridiculing and intimidating anyone who would even consider an opposing view. As the student experiences this strong anti-Christian bias, he may find his faith being challenged and questioned. We trust that the information we are providing in this chapter will allow each student to consider and weigh both arguments and reach a reasonable conclusion in this vital issue. For the Christian student, our goal is to present such a persuasive case for the biblical worldview that it will result in giving him courage, strength and peace of mind knowing, in fact, that the word of God alone is the only source of truth, and that science cannot provide any absolute truth.

A Christian worldview of science is important because much of today's culture
believes that science is the sole gateway to all of knowledge. But is it?

Science is paraded as being omniscient (all-knowing) and God is not. For many, the phrase "thus says the Lord" has been replaced by "it has been scientifically proven". Many believe that Christianity is to be rejected because - while Christians have *subjective, blind faith* - the scientist has *objective facts and needs no faith*. Christians have *superstitious religion*, a religious crutch that they like to go through life hobbling around on; whereas the scientist *employs reason*. But are these statements true?

Is There Such a Thing as Absolute Truth?

A Christian worldview of science is important because the Bible and modern science represent conflicting *authorities*. Our goal is to arrive at *absolute* truth; that is, truth that never changes - it's true for every man, woman, and child in every place and at every time, whether a person is rich or poor, male or female, whether they lived in the 1300s, the 1800s, or 2020 and beyond. Christianity claims that absolute truth is true for everyone, absolutely; and the Bible alone (our authority) reveals true knowledge, which is to say *absolute truth*. However, many today believe that science alone (their authority) reveals true knowledge (while at the same time agreeing with the educators and philosophers that say there is no such thing as absolute truth - as if truth and knowledge can be separated). Thus, secular science and Christianity disagree on this most critical principle. These are incompatible worldviews. They can't both be true. And if science is the only way to know truth, why would anyone put his trust in what the Bible says?

In this chapter, our desire is for you to know what the biblical view of science is. We will look at what the Bible has to say about faith and truth, and we will contrast this with what science has to say about faith and truth. As we contrast these two opposing worldviews - Christianity and naturalism (or empiricism) - we see to prove that Christianity provides the only basis for objective, absolute truth, and that science cannot give us any truth, ...not certain truth.

Lesson 1 Study Questions

1. Why is a Christian Worldview of Science important?

_____

_____

2. Words mean something. What happens when Christians are unable to define the key terms of our beliefs (like *faith*, *religion*, or *tolerance*, etc.)?

_____

_____

_____

3. Explain your understanding of what is meant by the phrase *absolute truth consists of all of the propositions of the Bible - the Word of God - and their logical implications; then give 2 examples from the 10 Commandments (remember that for every negative command there is a positive implication (i.e., if lying is wrong, then telling the truth is right)*

_____

_____

_____

_____

4. What happens when we allow non-Christians to define the key terms of our beliefs for us?

_____

_____

5. In your own words, what is *Absolute Truth*?

_____

_____

6. What would you think of those who claimed to speak the truth, but you could find no evidence to support their statements?

_____

_____

_____

7. What would be the result if scientists were not allowed to present an alternate or contrary theory to one that had been previously deemed to be correct?

_____

_____

8. Explain in 150 words or less why it is important to understand the Christian worldview of science.

_____

_____

_____

_____

_____

_____

Lesson 2 - The Christian Worldview of Science

Let us begin by looking at a passage in Romans chapter one that is probably familiar to most of us, and that is particularly relevant to our topic. In Romans 1:18-25, we read, *"for the wrath of God is revealed from heaven against all ungodliness and unrighteousness of men, who suppress the truth in unrighteousness, because what may be known of God is manifest in them, for God has shown it to them. For since the creation of the world his invisible attributes are clearly seen, being understood by the things that are made, even his eternal power and Godhead, so that they are without excuse, because, although they knew God, they didn't glorify him as God, nor were thankful, but became futile in their thoughts, and their foolish hearts were darkened. Professing to be wise, they became fools, and changed the glory of the incorruptible God into an image made like corruptible man, and birds and four-footed animals and creeping things. Therefore, God also gave them up to uncleanness, in the lusts of their hearts, to dishonor their bodies among themselves, who exchanged the truth of God for the lie, and worshiped and served the creature rather than the creator, and who is blessed forever, amen"*.

According to this passage, we can make several observations.

- Knowledge of God is innate to all men. God has put a knowledge of Himself into every single human being so that we are all without excuse. All men are therefore responsible to God for that knowledge.
- Creation, which is the visible world around us (it's the physical reality that we see), reveals the invisible *attributes* of God. For example:
  a. God is a lawgiver
  b. He is majestic
  c. He is powerful
  d. He is wise, et cetera.
- These *invisible* attributes of God are *displayed* through his visible creation to all of mankind.

However, if we keep reading, Romans chapter 3 tells us that because of man's sinful heart, not a single person in all of mankind is searching for God, not even one (Romans 3:10-18). Therefore, if man is not searching or looking for God, he certainly will not see (know, or understand) God as he looks at His creation. Man does not see God as he is revealed in creation because he is blinded by sin. And he suppresses the innate truth of God's existence, wanting to be accountable to himself rather than to God.

It is the word of God - and we refer to this as *special revelation* - that *reveals* (defines and makes clear) the invisible attributes of God to man. And if a man is regenerated by the Holy Spirit and believes the word of God, he will be given spiritual eyes to see the invisible attributes of God as they are reflected to him in creation, which as we pointed out earlier, is referred to as *general revelation*. So, *special revelation* is the Word of God that tells us specifically that God is a lawgiver, that He's majestic and wise and so on. And then when we look at His visible creation, if we believe the Word and we have the Holy Spirit in us, we see all of these invisible attributes visibly on display. Without the Word of God, the Bible (special revelation), and His Holy Spirit, the sinful man could never know the *invisible* attributes of God as revealed through creation or general revelation, for he would never be looking for them.

Blinded by the Sight

By way of analogy, in Greek mythology, there is a character named Narcissus who was celebrated for his beauty. He was exceptionally proud, however, in that he disdained those who loved him. Now, there's another character in this story named Nemesis. Nemesis was the spirit of divine retribution against those who were arrogant before the gods. Those, Nemesis had to teach a lesson. Nemesis, seeing the pride of Narcissus, attracted him to a pool where Narcissus saw his own reflection in the water and fell in love with it, not realizing it was merely an image. Narcissus, unable to leave the beauty of his own reflection, couldn't pull himself away from the pool, and eventually died there. *He was so in love with himself, so fixated on what pleased his own eyes that it cost him his life.* His vanity destroyed him. Now, like Narcissus, natural man is utterly self-absorbed, admiring himself, gazing at his own reflection rather than admiring the God who is reflected in creation. Like Narcissus, death is the divine retribution for such arrogance before the one true living God.

The Great Lie

The natural, simple man wants nothing to do with spiritual things, and is therefore blinded to the spiritual truths that are revealed in physical reality; thus, the natural, sinful man is living in a false reality of his own creation because in his spirit he has not only suppressed the innate truth of God's existence but has exchanged that truth for *the lie*. Note that in the original Greek texts it actually says *the* lie, not *a* lie, as many of today's Bibles translate it. So, what is *the lie* that Paul is referring to?

The *great lie* is that *the all-powerful God of the universe* who is sovereign over all creation, time, space, matter and physical reality, *does not exist*!

That's the great lie. And this greatest of all lies divorces the one true God - the creator - from reality, or all of creation. According to this great lie, which deceives every single man unless he comes to Christ, the only reality that exists is creation, time, space, and matter; therefore, sinful man chooses to worship the things of this world, that which is physical and temporal, rather than the God who created this world who is spiritual and eternal. This is foolish because Heaven and Earth - this physical reality - is passing away, but the Word of God - the Truth - will never pass away and is eternal.

Living Like the Animals

Those deceived by this great lie, become *professors of wisdom.* They profess to be wise, placing their trust in only what can be known by the power of observation or science, and have become fools because the spiritual reality that they scorn and neglect is the very reality that has a monopoly on all absolute truth.

Consequently, God gives these foolish professors of knowledge over to the sinful desires of their heart. If they choose to believe that man is just the product of evolution - that he evolved from monkeys and is just an animal that wears shoes rather than a being made in the image of God - why should we be surprised when we see people living like animals? How could we expect otherwise?

What You See is Not Always What You Get

Having looked at what happens when man's eyes are fixated on himself and the things of this world rather than the truths contained in God's word, let us now see why it is absolute folly to place one's faith in his own eyes.

As we said earlier, many advertise that science is the sole gateway to all knowledge. However, this is simply a case of false advertisement. We'll look at three reasons why science can never give us certain truth (there are more reasons than just these three, but we think these three alone will be sufficient):

1. Personal experience and scientific observation cannot provide absolute truth.
2. Science employs inductive reasoning and can therefore never provide absolute certain truth.
3. Scientific equations are always selected, they're never discovered.

Defining Terms

One may ask *why bother defining terms*? Because strict definitions and strict adherence to these definitions are essential to intelligible discussion. Many arguments could be avoided, or at least be much less contentious, if the key terms in the argument were properly defined from the start. Oftentimes, it just turns into "he said - she said" battle. We often use the phrase *we're not on the same page*. So, how do we get on the same page? Well, one way is by literally opening up our dictionaries to the same page and defining our terms. Properly defining terms provides clarity and Christians should always seek to present their worldview - their religion - with clarity, because only the Christian worldview provides absolute truth (this is the Christian worldview), and the truth should always be made clear.

Science, the Scientific Method and Empirical Knowledge Defined

We all have a basic understanding of what science is, but we should still be careful to define our terms. Science comes from the Latin *Scientia*, meaning *knowledge.* Science is systematic knowledge concerning the physical world and its phenomena as obtained through the scientific method. But this then begs the question *what is the scientific method?* Let's define that term.

The scientific method is *the principles and procedures for the systematic pursuit of knowledge involving the recognition and formulation of a problem, the collection of data through observation and experiment, and the formulation and testing of hypotheses.*

That may seem like a long, scary definition, so let's break it down into its simple parts. Basically, the scientist finds a problem and comes up with a *hypothesis* - a way of testing a likely solution to the problem. He then tests his hypothesis through experimentation, observation, and the collection of data. Once he's collected all of his data, he analyzes the data and draws conclusions. As he reflects upon those conclusions, he either accepts or rejects his hypothesis.

That's basically the scientific method, and this process leads scientists to what can be described as *empirical knowledge*. Let's define that term.

Empirical knowledge is *knowledge that is derived solely from sensory experience or observation.*

To be clear, the Christian and the secular scientist do not disagree upon what we both find in the naturalistic/materialistic world. The differences come in *how we interpret what we see*; and what we consider to be *knowledge* is always *influenced* by our individual worldviews – our basic presumptions and underlying beliefs.

Lesson 2 Study Questions

1. From the Romans 1:18-25 passage it was noted that mankind has been given innate knowledge of God. The visible creation is meant to stimulate man's mind to recollect the God-given ideas (e.g., God's invisible attributes) that man possesses intuitively. In other words, when man interacts with God's creation, which demonstrates God's glory, power, and wisdom, man (as God's image) is forced in some sense, to "think God."

   With this in mind, read the following verses that reveal specific attributes of God. Consider the examples given of how creation reflects these attributes, then add a few observations of your own. If you are not familiar with a particular example (for instance, if you don't know what the laws of thermodynamics are) we encourage you to look it up.

Verses	Attribute	Reflected in creation
Psalm 104 (the whole Psalm) and vs 24 in particular; Romans 11:33	Wisdom	The unique properties of water, photosynthesis, the womb
James 4:12; Isaiah 33:22	Lawgiver	Laws of gravitation and relativity, electromagnetism, laws of thermodynamics
Psalm 36:5; Lamentations 3:22-23; Genesis 8:22	Faithfulness, Mercy	Sunrise, sunset, the seasons, harvests, rainbows, breathing, heart beating
Psalm 33:5; Ps 136; Ps 145:15-16; Acts 14:16-17	Goodness, Mercy	Rain, rest from our labors, abundant food/clothing/shelter, sensory pleasures
Psalm 62:11; Ps 29; 89:6-13; Jeremiah 10:12; Job 26 (especially verse 14)	Power	The sun, nuclear energy, hurricanes, tornadoes, earthquakes
Psalm 8 ("majestic" is also translated as "excellent"); Ps 68:34; Exodus 15:11	Majestic	The Grand Canyon, the ocean, the Milky Way Galaxy

2. One of God's attributes is holiness, which is exhibited in His wrath against sin (Psalm 7:11). Looking to the Scriptures below, <u>how has God used His creation to exhibit His holy wrath against sin?</u> Read the following passages: Genesis 6:1-8 and 13-20; Exodus 7:14 to the end of chapter 10; Exodus 14 (especially verses 26-28); Numbers 16 (especially verses 31-35); Numbers 21:4-8; Jonah chapter 1 (especially verses 4 and 17).

_____

_____

_____

_____

3. If you are a Christian, how did God pour out His wrath against your sins? Read Romans 5:6-11 (especially verse 9) and John 3:36.

_____

_____

4. Though general revelation (man's God-given innate knowledge) is sufficient to reveal God's existence to all men, leaving mankind without excuse (personally responsible), it is insufficient to give sinful man a saving knowledge of God. What are the two requirements for sinful man to have saving knowledge of God? Read the following passages: John 17:17; John 14:6 and 15-17; Hebrews 4:12-13; 1 Corinthians 2:6-16.

_____

_____

_____

5. Define *Science*

_____

_____

6. Reread 1 Corinthians 2:6-16. Note in verse 9 that those who love God (i.e., Christians) do not come to know the things of God through their senses (eyes and ears) or through their own reasoning (the heart of man, which is biblically defined in this case as *the mind*). The Holy Spirit must reveal the things of God to man. From these verses, how can we know the truth of God?

_____

_____

7. Why is defining scientific terms so critical? _____

_____

8. Define the Scientific Method:

_____

_____

Lesson 3 – First Questions

Now that we've defined some terms, let's start asking some questions.

1. If scientific, empirical knowledge is based on experience, can it provide us with objective truth?

    Can *personal experiences* provide objective truth? Does the scientist ever say *"okay guys, let's stop all experiments, hang up our lab coats, because when it comes to this problem, we've got it licked! We don't need to do any more experiments because we've finally arrived at the absolute certain truth that will never change"*. No, scientists never do this.

2. Can a scientist ever be certain that every single variable has been accounted for and controlled for in his experiment? (see the Pause and Consider titled "All Crows Are Black??" below)

3. Can science give us objective truth about the future, since scientists cannot test or experience the future?

    If all of knowledge comes to us through our experiences, can we say anything with certainty about tomorrow, or even five minutes from now, if we have not yet experienced it? There haven't been any scientists yet to test what's going to happen five minutes from now or tomorrow; so how can we say anything with certainty based solely off of tomorrow's experiences?

4. Can science give us any objective truth about the past?

    If we can't say anything with certainty about the future, what about the past? Are there any scientific observations that have been made in the past that all scientists agree upon that will never change in the future? Again, the answer to this question should be obviously no. Is today's scientific knowledge the same as our scientific knowledge 10 years ago, or even 10 minutes ago?

    As we continue to make observations, as we continue to be innovative, science is forever changing. Who knows what the future might hold tomorrow when it comes to music or video for example. If truth is derived from experience alone, then nothing can be said with certainty about the future since no one has yet experienced it, and neither can anything be said about the past because often two people can observe the exact same event at the exact same time and yet walk away with contradictory truths.

> # Pause and Consider
>
> ## *Can We Always Rely on our Observations to Give Us Truth?*
>
> If the scientist is studying crows, he might observe 999 crows and they are all black. But is he ever able to assert that <u>all crows are black</u>?
>
> No. The next crow he observes might be an albino! One can never observe all crows - past, present, and future. *Instead of being valid or invalid, inductive arguments are either strong or weak*, which describes how <u>probable</u> it is that the conclusion is true but cannot conclude with certainty.

Why Must the Scientist Conduct Multiple Experiments?

Experiments are always repeated, and the results almost always differ in some way. Why? Because observation is unreliable. The senses tend to deceive us, they're not to be trusted. In an experiment, numerous readings are taken in an attempt to guard against the inaccurate observations we may make. So much is this the case in science that tests with unrepeatable results are never taken seriously.

If a scientist was to try to publish a scientific finding having performed only one experiment, he would never find a publisher.

Inductive Reasoning Defined

If observation is so unreliable, if the senses are so easily deceived, if the results frequently differ, why should one ever believe that he has discovered truth through observation?

The Limitations of Finite Observations

One of the primary reasons our observations are so unreliable is that every observation we make is finite, which is to say it's limited. Our eyes, our observations, cannot account for all variables; therefore, any conscientious scientist knows that no matter how many finite, limited, subjective experiences that he may pile up - we'll call these Little T Truths - they'll never amount to an infinite, non-limited, absolute, Capital T Truth. So, when the scientist begins with Little T Truths - or specific instances - the best he can hope for is to come to a generalized principle or conclusion. This process is known as inductive reasoning, or bottom-up logic. Although this method can produce high probabilities that the conclusion is reliable, it cannot conclude that it is absolutely true. However, it does allow the scientists to come up with workable conclusions that often produce wonderful results.

Which Story is True?

Two people are on two opposite corners, and they witness a car accident involving car A and car B. When the police arrive and make a report of what happened, they ask these eyewitnesses what they saw. One witness says, "from my vantage point, car A was clearly at fault", whereas the other eyewitness on the opposite corner who witnessed the exact same event (they both had the same experience) says, "no, it was clearly car B that was at fault". These are contradictory truths.

How can that be if they both observed the exact same thing at the exact same time? Here we see that even though two people can share identical experiences in space and time, they can walk away with contradictory truths. *Can our experiences always provide truth?*

All the natural sciences - physics, chemistry, biology, et cetera - are *inductive*. The scientist first collects evidence by applying the scientific method. The scientist then takes specific instances, specific results, and tries to guess (hypothesize) from those the general principles to create general rules, or laws. It is impossible to justify inductive reasoning because one can ever be sure that what is true in a specific case or instance will always be true in general. This is because *inductive reasoning allows for the possibility that the conclusion, the general principle, is false*, even if all the specific instances or the premises are true.

Sherlock Holmes and His "Uncanny Powers of Deduction"

Sir Arthur Conan Doyle's character of Sherlock Holmes is perhaps the most iconic detective in literature. His character continues to enthrall us. In fact, in 2009, and again in 2011, Robert Downey, Jr. played Sherlock Holmes on the big screen, and more recently the BBC created a series featuring a modern day Holmes. One of the things that makes Sherlock Holmes so captivating is his seemingly supernatural ability to deduce specific facts about people and situations based upon his careful observation and "deductive reasoning". In fact, in the BBC series where Sherlock Holmes is a detective in modern day London, the program created a website titled

The Science of Deduction. However, we just saw that all of science employs *inductive* reasoning, not *deductive* reasoning.

For example, suppose Sherlock Holmes comes to your house, and seeing that you're wearing your wristwatch on the right wrist, he *induces*, not *deduces*, that you're left-handed. He went from a specific instance to a general principle.

Note that his conclusion is not necessarily true. Perhaps you just like wearing your watch on the right wrist. Now, suppose Sherlock Holmes also notices that you have a notebook that is specifically made for left handers on your coffee table, and next to it on the coffee table is a coffee mug with the handle turned out to the left, and the coffee mug reads *everyone is born right handed, but only the gifted overcome*. Perhaps you're even wearing a shirt that says *kiss me I'm left handed*.

Sir Arthur Conan Doyle was himself a physician, a man of science, so it should come to no surprise that the character of Sherlock Holmes uses inductive reasoning - not deductive reasoning - to draw his conclusions. After all, Sir Arthur wrote the story. He knew the end from the beginning!

Now, although these several specific instances may present a much stronger argument, the conclusion that you are left-handed is *not* a deduction and his generalization is not necessarily true. Maybe you just have a really obnoxious left handed roommate and you didn't have any clean laundry and you wore his shirt and used his coffee mug, et cetera. Maybe you recently visited a specialty store for left-handers where everything was on sale and you just can't resist a good bargain; or maybe you just desperately want to be left-handed because you know that only left handed people are in their right minds (only left-handed people may appreciate this humor!).

Some logicians have referred to what Sherlock Holmes does as *Holmesian deduction* in order to distinguish it from deduction itself. Holmes is postulating through well-informed inference, or inductive reasoning. Holmes goes from the specifics to the general, which is what most all modern scientific investigation involves (note that in previous chapters we pointed out that most of the prominent early innovators in the sciences began their research by employing deductive reasoning based upon truths as discovered in the Bible).

But from the examples above, we see that science can never give us Capital T Truths - infinite truths, or absolute truth - because infinite, universal, absolute, Capitol T truth can never be validly obtained by making inductions from finite, limited, or subjective observations.

Now, Sherlock Holmes seems to have a supernatural ability to always come to the right conclusions, but that's because the author - whether it's Sir Arthur Conan Doyle or someone writing for the movies or television show about Sherlock Holmes - is always omniscient. The writer knows everything. He knows the end from the beginning and thus he can write into his story that any time Sherlock Holmes makes an inference, it's always correct. However, in the real world, Sherlock Holmes does not exist, and science is often wrong, and never produces certain truth – as we will see in the coming chapters.

The Christian View

In contrast to logical induction from scientific methodology, Christian methodology is logical deduction from Scripture. Deductive reasoning or "top-down" logic is the process of reasoning from one or more Capital T Truth statements (premises) to reach a logically certain conclusion. Deductive reasoning links premises with conclusions. If all premises are true, the terms are clear, and the rules of deductive logic are followed, then the conclusion reached is necessarily true.

Here is an example of deductive reasoning or "top-down" logic:

- First premise: *God is infinite truth*
- Second premise: *God has revealed Himself through the Bible*
- Logical, certain conclusion: *Therefore, the Bible reveals infinite truth*

Another example:

- First premise: *God is a God of order*
- Second premise: *God established spiritual laws to govern man and keep order in society*
- Generalization from material observation*: The physical universe reveals order*
- Logical, certain conclusion: *Therefore, God established physical (natural) laws to govern and keep order in in the universe*

Isaac Newton on the Importance of Order and Law in the Universe

From Isaac Newton's writings, we see that his worldview was clearly formed upon the foundations of the Eternal God of Scripture, who created the universe with order and governed it by laws.

He stated, "Now by the help of these principles, all material things seem to have been composed of the hard and solid particles, above-mentioned, variously associated in the first creation by the counsel of an Intelligent Agent. For it became Him who created them to set them in order. And if He did so, it's unphilosophical to seek for any other origin of the world, or to pretend that it might arise out of a chaos by the mere laws of nature; though being once formed, it may continue by those laws for many ages." [122]

"From His true dominion it follows that the true God is a living, intelligent and powerful Being; and from His other perfections, that He is supreme, or most perfect. He is eternal and infinite, omnipotent and omniscient; that is, His duration reaches from eternity to eternity; His presence from infinity to infinity; He governs all things and knows all things that are or can be done." [123]

Who Makes the Rules?

When secular scientists are asked by what authority they can make certain claims about the universe, they appeal to *finite* (not eternal) primary sources in the scientific literature. But Christians seeking objective truth that never changes, we appeal to an infinite primary source:

- Malachi 3:6 - For I am the Lord, I do not change

- Hebrews 13:8 - Jesus Christ is the same yesterday and today and forever.

- Psalm 100:5 - For the Lord is good; His mercy is everlasting, and His truth endures to all generations.

> ## Pause and Consider
>
> **Infinite, objective Truth must come from an infinite objective source.**
>
> **The Christian's primary source for truth is *infinite*, whereas the scientist's primary source for truth is *finite*.**
>
> **Infinite Truth never changes or fades. Thus, infinite truth is absolutely reliable as the foundation for scientific discovery.**

---

[122] The last query of Optics, or, a Treatise of the Reflections, Refractions, Inflexions and Colours of Light (1704, London, 1730, 4th edition, quoted in Sullivan, p.125-126
[123] Principea, Isaac Newton, Published July 7, 1687

Lesson 3 Study Questions

1. Why should one ever believe that he has discovered absolute truth through observation? _____

   _____

2. Why are our observations or experiences unable to provide absolute truth? Give 3 reasons from the text.

   1) _____

   _____

   2) _____

   _____

   3) _____

   _____

3. What are your thoughts regarding the statement "if truth is derived from experience alone, then nothing

   can be said about the future, since no one has yet experienced it."

   _____

   _____

4. Holmes could have come to various incorrect assumptions in the segment about the "left-handed"

   perpetrator of a crime. Can you state an instance where you came to a conclusion based upon an

   observation you made that later turned out to be untrue?

   _____

   _____

5. Why are multiple tests on the same experiment so important in the scientific method?

   _____

   _____

6. Define inductive reasoning and give one example

   _____

   _____

_____

_____

7. Reflect on the three scriptures stated at the end of this lesson. What is God saying about the reliability of

    the Words of Scripture, and how can a foundation of absolute truth guard us against "bad science"?

    _____

    _____

    _____

    _____

8. Can you think of some examples of "bad science" that resulted from inductions built upon a faulty

    foundation?

    _____

    _____

    _____

    _____

Lesson 4 – Faith vs Facts, Religion vs Reason

If you remember, we said that many object to Christianity because they claim that Christians have blind faith whereas the scientist has objective facts. Or they claim that Christians have superstitious religion whereas the scientist employs reason. Are such objections merited, faith versus facts, or religion versus reason? Let's define our terms and see.

Faith - is synonymous with *belief* or *trust* and is defined as *intelligent assent to understood propositions*. And for additional clarity, *assent* in this context means *to agree with, believe and place trust in, to the point of submission.*

What does the word *proposition* mean? Let's define this term.

A Proposition - is an idea or a plan that has been put forward for a consideration or a discussion. It is a declarative statement, and we weigh that declarative statement in our mind, determining whether or not it's true or false. If we think about the idea in our mind and we decide it's true, we assent to it. We agree. We have now exercised *faith*, or *belief.*

Everyone exercises faith! Everyone must intellectually process the myriad of ideas that are proposed in a lifetime, which will lead them to come up with a belief system, a religion, or a worldview that they will refer to when making important decisions.

Fact - A fact is anything that is done or that comes to pass. It is an act, a deed, or an event, which is fixed and unalterable in reality. It is always true.

Religion - Religion can sometimes be a difficult term to define. *Religion* and *worldview* are synonymous. When we talk about a religion or a worldview, it is a belief system; and when we talk about beliefs, we just defined what a belief is. Belief or faith is assenting to a proposition; so, a belief system is then comprised of many propositions that we have either accepted or rejected from which we then derive our values and our moral standards. The collective propositions that we have agreed to or disagreed with make up our worldview, our religion. Thus, as we think about *faith* and *belief* or when we speak about *religion* and *worldview*, we can see that everybody has a religion or a worldview and everyone exercises faith. This is true because everyone has to weigh ideas in the mind and either agree with them or disagree with them.

Therefore, the atheist has a religion just as much as the Christian does, and the scientist exercises faith just as the Christian does!

Key Principle:

What it Means to "Assent"

As an analogy, whenever we have state or federal elections, there are usually many propositions that are put on the ballet for state elections. Several years back, many states placed on their ballets a proposition stating that marriage should be defined between a man and a woman. Now, this is an idea was being proposed, and we were being asked to take this idea and weigh it in our mind.

If we agreed with it, we would assent to that proposition by voting yes. We were affirming that we believed it to be true. If we didn't, then we dissented, or we disagreed, and we voted no. This is the basic concept of faith or belief. Taking in ideas, weighing them in the mind, and either agreeing or disagreeing, either assenting or dissenting.

The question really becomes *which religion is more reasonable and rational to believe?* Which one takes *more* faith? The worldview of an atheist or a evolutionary scientist, or the Christian? Which one is actually practicing *blind faith* (a faith that has very little or no supporting evidence)?

Reason - Reason is the power of comprehending, inferring, or thinking, especially in an orderly, rational way. It's the proper exercise of the mind. Now, when some say that Christians have religion, but the scientist has reason, think about what's being said. We might infer from that statement that religion is unreasonable, particularly the Christian religion. That should be offensive to a Christian. Is it sensible to think that Christians don't employ reasoning? Do Christians not properly exercise the mind, yet the scientists do? Let's critically think this through.

Contrary Foundations

Secular scientists - or non-Christian, evolutionary scientists - tell us that life evolved from non-life, that all of life came from non-living material. This is their starting point, their foundational premise, their **axiom** (see Chapter 3, Day 2). Christianity, however, teaches that life was created from life, that the eternal, living God created all living things. This is our starting point or **axiom**. Thus, once again we can see that these are two different ideas which are contradictory propositions. They can't both be true.

Which Foundation is Solid?

Let's look at these two opposing propositions. Which proposition is consistent with reality, is more reasonable, and provides a sufficient ground of explanation or of logical defense?

Life from Non-life

Where is the time-lapse photography showing a rock giving birth?

Has any scientist ever observed life being produced from non-life? No, of course not. We *always* see that life comes from life. No one has ever once made the observation of non-life, non-living material, somehow spontaneously generating into life. Thus, how much evidence is there for that proposition? Zero. There is zero evidence for this foundational premise of the evolutionary scientist!

Is it a fact that non-life produces life? Or is it a fact that life always comes from life? Which axiom is more reasonable? Which one has more evidence? Of course, 100 percent of the evidence reveals that life *always* comes from life. No one has ever observed otherwise.

Is it reasonable to assent to a proposition - to agree with and believe in an idea - that denies all of reality? Is this the proper exercise of the mind? Is this reasonable? Are we to agree with the idea that non-life produces life, even though every time we look at reality it is consistently denying that supposed "fact"?

Which religion, worldview, or belief system is more reasonable? The one whose foundational premise is entirely inconsistent with reality, or the one whose foundational premise is always affirmed by reality?

Life from Life

Time lapse photography of life coming from life

Which religion requires blind faith? Christians do not assent to - they don't agree with nor put faith in - the idea or the proposition that life comes from non-life because we simply don't have that kind of blind faith!

> # Pause and Consider
> ## *Who Has Faith?*
>
> Does it require faith to get on an airplane the first time? Is that faith blind or does it require trust in the knowledge that thousands of people get on and off airplanes daily without incident? Even a young child places trust in a parent who has proven trustworthy in the past to lead them onto an airplane. *Everyone practices faith on a daily basis!*

It is in fact the evolutionary scientist who has the blind faith - who is denying all of reality by saying that non-life produces life. Therefore, Christians can state with all confidence when in discussions with others who believe those things that we don't have their faith. Their faith is too great for us because they're denying what is consistently proved to be true every single day -

---

Key Principle: *Life always comes from life!*
Life begets life!

Pause and Consider

Faith vs. Facts?

The secular scientist pits faith against facts, thereby insinuating that faith is irrational. However, the secular scientist is not without faith. For example, the secular scientist intellectually assents to the proposition that life arose from non-life. Thus, by definition he is exercising faith. The difference between the secular scientist and the Christian is in the propositions assented to. The secular scientist intellectually assents to the proposition that life originated from non-life, whereas the Christian intellectually assents to the proposition that life originated from life (God). These are incompatible propositions, they cannot both be true. Either the secular scientist or the Christian is dead wrong about the origin of life.

The secular scientist is all about empirical facts, but the fact of the matter is that there is *zero* empirical evidence supporting the proposition that non-life produces life. No one has <u>ever</u> observed non-life generate life. Life <u>always</u> begets life. Thus, Christians don't assent to the proposition that life came from non-life because Christians don't have that kind of blind faith!

Lesson 4 Study Questions

1. Define the following terms:
   a. Faith/Belief-

   _____

   b. Fact –

   _____

   _____

   c. Religion/Worldview –

   _____

   _____

   d. Reason –

   _____

   _____

2. What is the difference between faith and blind faith?

   _____

   _____

3. Why is it considered blind faith to believe the proposition that all of life came from non-life?

   _____

   _____

4. As we've stated before, it's foolish to trust our eyes (sensation) to give us truth rather than what the Bible says is true and real. Read Genesis 3:16-19. What are the consequences of man trusting his own eyes rather than God's Word?

   _____

   _____

5. Summarize the two opposing axioms of the evolutionist theory and the biblical creation theory.

   _____

   _____

6. Which theory of the beginning of life makes logical sense, Darwinian Evolution or Biblical Creationism, and why?

   _____

   _____

   _____

Lesson 5 - Is Matter All That Matters?

At this point, we have discussed some of the reasons why science cannot give us absolute or certain truth. This is of vital importance because when evolutionary scientists begin their research with fundamental assumptions that have no basis in reality - for example, that non-life can produce life; that random chaotic matter can become increasingly complex over time, going from disorder to order; that information can arise on its own without an intelligent informer - their conclusions often will be not only foolish and irrational, but dangerous. This type of "blind faith" or worldview suppresses truth, ignores reality, and exchanges truth for lies – accepting propositions as fact that are never seen in reality.

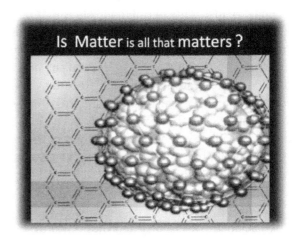

In today's study it will be further shown why personal experience and scientific observation, as well as inductive reasoning, cannot provide absolute truth; and we'll also look at a third reason why science can never give absolute truth: because scientific equations are always *selected*, they're never *discovered*.

Let's look at the Matter

In this class we'll be looking at *matter*, because many claim that *matter is all that matters*. That only in studying the material universe can man have any real knowledge or truth. We'll also examine how scientists discover truth by analyzing the process of scientific experimentation, which ultimately boils down to measuring lines. We will see that while all of science is preoccupied with the measurement of lines, one cannot accurately measure a straight line, …straight lines must be *constructed*.

A Matter of Morality

Now, some of you may be asking, "What does it matter if someone thinks that matter is all that matters? Who cares if some people want to put their trust in the lines or the equations of science?" It matters because, while science may not be able to measure a straight line, it can be used to *cross the line*. Those who place their faith solely in science -- naturalists or materialists -- far too often cross the line that they have no business even trying to measure: the line of morality.

Those who believe in naturalism or materialism frequently use science to argue issues of morality. Now, there is a definite relationship between science and morality, but science doesn't define that relationship, morality does.

Science can be used to *cure* disease just as easily as it can be used to *cause* disease. It can cause *biological welfare* just as easily as it can cause *biological warfare*. Nuclear power can be used to generate heat and electricity for millions of people and can just as easily be used to build bombs that can kill millions of people. Science instructs us on *how to do*, not on *what we ought to do*. Studying the nature of matter cannot tell us what's right and what's wrong, or how we should live our lives. Ideas concerning what's right and wrong are just that, they're ideas; and ideas are not made of matter. Ideas may find their expression in the material world, but ideas are not themselves made of material. Yet often we're told what's right and what's wrong in the name of science.

For example, euthanasia, eugenics, stem cell research, human cloning, are just some of the many ideas that people try to advance in the name of science, but these are all moral issues. What about global warming? They say man has sinned against Mother Nature. Worse than a cardinal sin, it's a carbon sin, and he must repent by cleaning up his carbon footprint. Regarding abortion, they say a woman should have the choice to destroy an unwanted human life, because according to science it's just a fetus. It's unwanted tissue, a tumor. And since science supposedly sets the rules, then surely a woman should have the right to remove a tumor from her body if she so desires. Right?
Wrong!

When Science Tries to Dictate What is Moral

How can science tell us what is sinful, immoral, what we must repent of, what we should or should be allowed to do? Isn't this completely backwards?

Should science be guiding our moral practices?
Or, should morality be guiding our scientific practices?

How about homosexuality? Science is often used to promote the homosexual agenda. Some claim that we shouldn't judge homosexuals because they're born that way. They've said it's in their genes, ...the so-called gay gene (which, by the way, has never been proven to exist). But even for the atheistic, evolutionary biologist it doesn't make any sense to promote the gay agenda. The whole point of evolution, if there is any point at all, is to evolve; but how can we evolve, how can the gene pool increase, if homosexuality increases? Natural selection selects against homosexuality, because homosexuality doesn't allow for procreation, which is the only way that life can evolve.

What about racism and genocide? Now, let it be unequivocally stated that we are not implying that naturalists and materialists are by nature racist. Nevertheless, evolutionary biology separates man according to various races, and many wicked, evil men have regrettably used evolutionary science to promote racism and execute genocide.

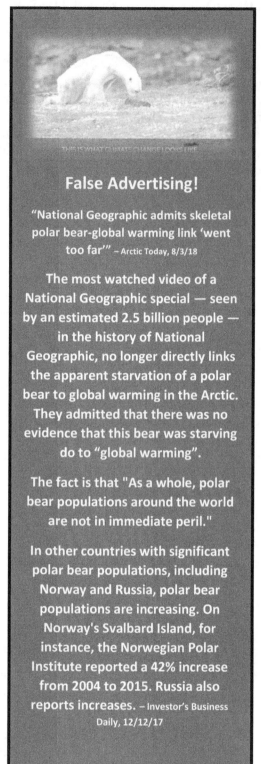

False Advertising!

"National Geographic admits skeletal polar bear-global warming link 'went too far'" – Arctic Today, 8/3/18

The most watched video of a National Geographic special — seen by an estimated 2.5 billion people — in the history of National Geographic, no longer directly links the apparent starvation of a polar bear to global warming in the Arctic. They admitted that there was no evidence that this bear was starving do to "global warming".

The fact is that "As a whole, polar bear populations around the world are not in immediate peril."

In other countries with significant polar bear populations, including Norway and Russia, polar bear populations are increasing. On Norway's Svalbard Island, for instance, the Norwegian Polar Institute reported a 42% increase from 2004 to 2015. Russia also reports increases. – Investor's Business Daily, 12/12/17

The underlying belief of racism, which can then lead to genocide, is that some races of man are superior to others. They say that not all races are created equal, because they're not created, they evolved, and some more than others. Hitler and the Nazis are a good example of this type of thinking. Hitler was an evolutionary naturalist who believed that the Aryan race was superior to all other races, particularly the Jewish race. In Hitler's mind, he was simply helping Mother Nature out by speeding up what evolution would eventually do anyway, ...exterminate the weaker races of man.

In stark contrast to this, Christianity does not look at man according to race. Galatians 3:28 says, *"There is neither Jew nor Greek"* - that is, racism. *"There is neither slave nor free man"* – there is no classism. And *"There is neither male nor female"* – there is no sexism. The verse concludes by saying, *"For you are all one in Christ Jesus"*. God is no respecter of persons, He doesn't look on the outward appearance of man. Man judges according to outward appearances which causes division; but God looks at the inward man, the heart of man, which unifies rather than divides, because the heart of every man is sinful. Romans 3:23 says,

---

"All men have sinned and fall short of the glory of God"

What Really Matters?

Hopefully now we can see why it's necessary to show that science can't give us truth. Many today have elevated science to a godlike status, and unfortunately many base their moral compass on what science says, rather than what the Bible says. Therefore, as far as absolute truth is concerned, it must be shown that it doesn't matter what science tells us.

One of the primary assumptions for those who put their trust in science is that matter is all that matters. They say that only that which can be experienced through the senses - that which can be seen or heard, smelled, tasted, or touched - can give man any real knowledge or truth. The idea of materialism - that matter or that which is physical is the only thing that exists - isn't a new idea. For example, the Greek philosopher Democritus, who lived from 460 BC to 370 BC and is considered the founder of atomism, said this: "The first principles of the universe are atoms and empty space, everything else is merely thought to exist". And an often quoted variant of this saying is, "nothing exists except atoms and empty space, everything else is opinion". It should come as no surprise that many consider Democritus to be the father of modern science; but as popular as this idea continues to be - that matter is all that matters - is there perhaps more to this *matter* than meets the

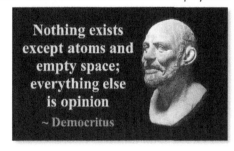

Nothing exists except atoms and empty space; everything else is opinion
~ Democritus

eye? If we accept the proposition that *matter is all that matters* is true, then what can science tell us about matter? What kind of knowledge or truth can the study of matter give us?

In tomorrow's study we'll define our terms so that we can more fully appreciate *the matter*.

Lesson 5 Study Questions

1. What is the relationship between science and morality?

    _____

    _____

2. Why is it irrational to base ideas of morality on our observations of matter?

    _____

    _____

3. Thinking back to the examples given in this day's study, what potential dangers are there in arguing moral issues based on the truth claims of science? What can it lead to?

    _____

    _____

4. Read Psalm 8. According to this Psalm, how does God look at man in relation to the rest of creation?

    _____

    _____

    _____

5. Why does this view of man make more sense logically than the Darwinian view that man is no better than an animal?

    _____

    _____

    _____

6. Read 1 Corinthians 1:25, 1:27, 2:14. What does the God say about the foolishness of man in relation to the wisdom of God, and why do you think He says this?

    _____

    _____

    _____

    _____

Lesson 6 - What's the Matter?

Defining matter can be difficult; but at the most basic level, the universe is made up of two types of matter,
1. Baryonic matter (which includes atomic matter) and
2. Non-baryonic matter (which includes dark matter).

I. Baryonic matter - sometimes called ordinary matter, can be defined as *material substance that occupies space, has mass, and is composed predominantly of atoms.* Nearly all of the matter that is encountered or experienced in everyday life is made up of atoms or is ordinary atomic matter. So then, what does science tell us about ordinary atomic matter?

Science estimates that only 4 to 5% of the entire universe is actually made up of atoms, or visible matter. Every atom of visible matter is divided into two parts: the nucleus, which contains protons and neutrons, and the electron cloud. But what about the distance between the electron cloud and the

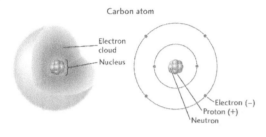

Carbon atom

nucleus? This distance is huge! For example, if a nucleus were the size of a golf ball, it's been estimated that the electron cloud would be located about 1.5 miles away. What is the empty space between the nucleus and the electron cloud of an atom filled with? Science can't tell us because it's not observable. Over 99% of an atom is empty, immaterial space, which means only less than 1% of an atom is actually observable matter. Think of how much empty, immaterial space that is, and all of it's unaccounted for. What is it?

No matter (pun intended).

What Do We Know About the Atom?

Now, if over 99% of an atom is unobservable empty space, this leaves only the electron cloud and the nucleus of an atom for us to actually observe, so let's move on to the moving electron.

Electrons travel in specific orbits and move at incredibly high velocities around the nucleus of an atom. However, it's impossible to ever know with certainty where an electron is or where it's going next. This is referred to as the

Heisenberg Uncertainty Principle, which basically states that *in order to know the velocity of an electron we must measure it, but to measure it, we're forced to affect it; therefore we cannot know with certainty both where an electron is and where it's going next, because the moment we try to observe an electron we change the electron's velocity.* This is called the Heisenberg Uncertainty Principle for a reason, for how can we have certain knowledge about something that changes the moment we observe it?

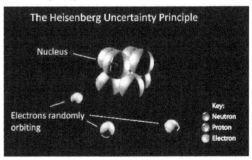

The Nucleus

Thus far it doesn't seem like we know an atom from Adam. Therefore, since true knowledge about the electron is so elusive, let's turn to the nucleus of an atom to see if we can get this *matter* cleared up.

The nucleus of an atom is made up of protons that are positively charged, along with neutrons that have no net electrical charge. If opposite charges attract and like charges repel, what keeps the protons within the nucleus from flying apart? In other words, what explains the nuclear force that holds every nucleus of every atom together? Well, the scientist's answer is to put a *quark* in it. Quarks are meant to explain the nuclear force that keeps protons and neutrons together.

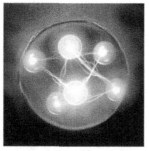

Quark

There are six types of quarks, known as *flavors*. There's an up quark, down quark, strange quark, a charm quark, a bottom quark, and a top quark. It should be noted, however, that no one has ever seen a quark by itself. Quarks have never been directly observed or found in isolation.

Let's review. What are we actually looking at here?
Science can't account for the empty, immaterial space between the nucleus and the electron cloud of an atom, which, by the way, makes up over 99% of an atom, and of the remaining less than 1% of an atom that can be measured, science can't tell us with certainty the exact position and velocity of an electron at any given point in time, and science's answer to what keeps the nucleus of an atom from exploding, the nuclear force, is quarks, even though no one's ever actually seen or isolated a quark.

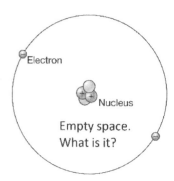

II. Non-baryonic Matter

Dark Matter

Now, to make matter worse, here is a different matter altogether. Dark Matter. Science estimates that roughly 23 to 25% of the universe consists of non-baryonic cold dark matter. This cold dark matter is a hypothetical form of matter that is invisible; it doesn't absorb or emit light; and it doesn't collide with atomic particles but exerts gravitational force. To repeat, dark matter is hypothetical. It's not made of atoms. Like the empty space between the nucleus and electron cloud of every single atom, dark matter is unobservable.

Dark Energy

So, if only 4 or 5% of the universe is made up of visible baryonic matter – atoms - and another 23 to 25% of the universe is made up of non-baryonic matter (which is this hypothetical dark matter), what makes up the rest of the over 70% of the universe? Answer: Dark energy.

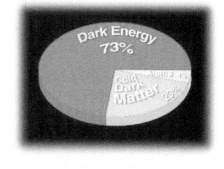

The universe is expanding at an accelerating rate which scientists attribute to *dark energy*, so-called because its exact nature remains a mystery. But something must fill the vast reaches of space to account for the accelerating expansion. Dark energy is the name given to the anti-gravitating influence that's accelerating the rate of expansion of the universe. It's not composed of known particles like protons, neutrons, or electrons, nor of the particles of dark matter, because these all gravitate. We simply don't know what it is.

Conclusion

With so much scientific speculation and uncertainty about atomic matter and dark matter, how trustworthy is the proposition that matter is all that matters - that truth can only come from knowledge of matter? Especially since observable matter is only the tip of the iceberg of our universe.

Since 70% or more of the universe doesn't even consist of any matter at all. It would appear that our knowledge of the matter leaves much to be desired.

Lesson 6 Study Questions

1. Baryonic matter (which includes atomic matter), otherwise called _____ matter, is defined as:

    _____

    _____

2. According to scientific estimates, how much of the universe is made up of atoms? _____% Of this atomic matter, how much is actually visible? _____%

3. Describe Dark Matter:

    _____

    _____

4. What percentage of the universe is made up of Dark Matter: _____%

5. Describe Dark Energy:

    _____

    _____

6. What percentage of the universe is made up of Dark Energy: _____%

7. Therefore, according to scientific estimates, how much of the universe is not made up of physical, observable matter at all? _____%

8. Why then, is it foolish to believe the statement – *matter is all that matters*?

    _____

    _____

9. Knowing that all the material universe relies upon the nucleus of atoms as the foundation of all matter in the cosmos, and that science has no answers for why the positively-charged protons in an atom do not repel each other as they should and fly away into oblivion (which would result in no life), read Hebrew 1:3 and Colossians 1:16-17. How do these verses provide a reasonable answer to this mystery?

    _____

    _____

    _____

10. Read and consider 2 Corinthians 4:18 in the context of today's focus. What does this say to you about the prescient (prophetic, predictive, visionary) truth of the Bible?

    _____

    _____

    _____

Lesson 7 - Measuring a Straight Line

What's the Bottom Line?

What can science tell us with certainty? Well, let's ask the question in a different way. How is scientific truth obtained?

All scientific truth is obtained from experimentation. If scientific experimentation is to be understood, careful thought must be given to the measurement of a line. Regardless of how intricate an experiment may be, its basic process is the measurement of a line, ...measuring the distance of change from one point of a line to another. Even though most scientific data is numerical, it still involves measuring lines, or the distance of change between two points. For example, the distance of the line that could be drawn between the number one and the number three is shorter than the distance or the line that could be drawn between the numbers one and six.

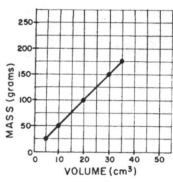

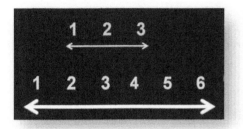

This is why graphs are often used to present scientific data. Graphs are used to show lines of measurement between various points of numerical data. Therefore, an analysis of the process of measuring a line is instructive for determining what science can and cannot tell us with certainty.

Example: *At What Exact Point Does Water Boil?*

Can science measure a straight line? Let's find out.

Suppose we want to measure the boiling point of water in degrees Celsius at standard pressure. We slowly bring a pot of water to a boil and measure the temperature with a thermometer labeled in degrees Celsius. We repeat this experiment several times and obtain the following data, arranged from lowest to highest. Here's our data (see the chart on the right).

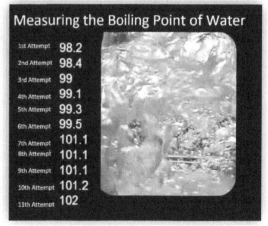

Measuring the Boiling Point of Water

1st Attempt	98.2
2nd Attempt	98.4
3rd Attempt	99
4th Attempt	99.1
5th Attempt	99.3
6th Attempt	99.5
7th Attempt	101.1
8th Attempt	101.1
9th Attempt	101.1
10th Attempt	101.2
11th Attempt	102

If we take these numbers and calculate the average, we get 100 degrees Celsius. Is this, then, a scientific fact or truth that water always boils at 100 degrees Celsius? How did we induce a generalization of 100 degrees Celsius when none of our specific instances were 100 degrees Celsius? And why did we average the numbers? There are other ways to statistically analyze data that are just as valid. What experiment or sensory experience compels us to average the numbers? Remember, we should only operate according to what science tells us, so when did science tell us that we should average numbers? Is that the only way to look at data?

For example, we could have chosen the *median*, which is the middle number in our list: 99.5; or we could have chosen the *mode*, which is the number that occurred the most often in our list: 101.1. Note that we get entirely

Which is the Correct (true) Number?

98.2
98.4   Average (mean) = 100
99
99.1   Median (middle #) = 99.5
99.3
99.5   Mode (most # of times) = 101.1
101.1
101.1   Note that we get entirely
101.1   different "truths" depending
101.2   on the way we choose
102   to analyze our data

different "truths" depending on the way we choose to analyze our data. Which number is right – or true? Wouldn't the mode, 101.1, be the closest thing to reality, since at least this is the fact that we observed the greatest number of times? Yet we chose as our fact or truth a number that we never once saw in all of our observations: 100 degrees Celsius. Why in this essential step of scientific procedures would science just throw all the facts from our observations out the window and stick to what is not a fact, the unobserved average?

Adding Variable Error into the Equation

To further confound things, science requires that we calculate the variable error of our data set. We can do this by determining the standard deviation above and below, which is plus or minus the average of our data. In our example, the standard deviation (the degree of uncertainty) above and below, or plus or minus, our average of 100 degrees Celsius is 1.31985.

But why do scientists have to calculate the error that is inherently built into an experiment? How can truth have error built into it? Truth, by definition, is not erroneous. In fact, why do scientists have to repeat their experiments at all? If their observations provide *certain, unvarying* truth, shouldn't their observations always be the same and never deviate from the truth? Shouldn't the scientist be able to observe something once and simply record the truth that he has seen and move on?

How can the truth change every time the scientist takes another look?

Let's Get This Straight

Maybe scientific data isn't exactly 100% true and certain knowledge, statistically speaking, but surely the lines in the scientific equations that we construct from the data are true, right? Let's see how this works...

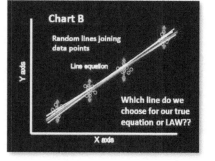

Once a scientist has conducted a series of experiments and has accounted for the variable error, the scientist may wish to construct an equation, a line, that may become a scientific law. The equation or the line that will be called the law can be made by plotting the several averages of the data with their variable errors, the standard deviation above and below, plus or minus each average, onto a graph (Chart A).

After the scientist plots all the data points with their variable error onto the graph, the scientist will then pass a line through these areas, and this line

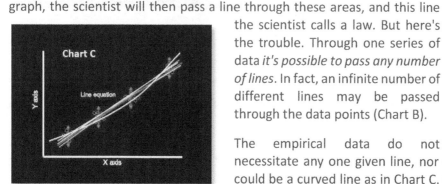

the scientist calls a law. But here's the trouble. Through one series of data *it's possible to pass any number of lines*. In fact, an infinite number of different lines may be passed through the data points (Chart B).

The empirical data do not necessitate any one given line, nor does it necessitate a straight line. It could be a curved line as in Chart C. In other words, as far as observation is concerned, the scientist could have chosen a law - an equation - other than the one that was actually selected.

than the one that was actually selected.

238

The point is this, the graph allows the possibility of an infinite number of lines. Or to put it another way, *measurements with variable errors allow an infinite number of natural laws*. The particular law or equation that the scientist announces to the world is not a discovery forced on him by so-called facts, it's rather a choice from among an infinity of laws or equations all of which enjoy the same experimental basis.

Key Principle

Scientific Laws are Chosen, NOT Discovered!

The data does not force upon the scientist an equation, a scientific law; rather, the scientist forces an equation - a scientific law - upon the data!

The scientist wants mathematical accuracy. The universe doesn't provide mathematical accuracy. Therefore, what the scientist cannot discover, he creates. Since the scientist chooses his law from among an infinite number of equally possible laws, the probability that he has chosen the true law, or the true equation, is one over infinity, which is zero. In plain English, the scientist has no chance of hitting upon the absolute, invariably true laws of nature. The scientist can only provide an approximation of the true laws of nature. Therefore, even the laws of physics cannot give us certain, unvarying truth.

Why does the scientist do this? Science makes equations and laws because by these equations scientists can *do things*. Equations are extremely useful. The equations can be of invaluable use within reality, even if they're not an absolutely perfect representation of reality. But let's get back to our original question...

Can science perfectly measure a straight line?

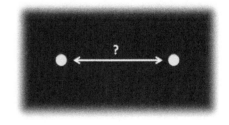

We've seen that science can create straight lines, or equations, but can a scientist measure an observable straight line within nature, ...even one? In order to measure a straight line it will first require two fixed points in space and time. But we must not forget that everything in the universe is in motion. Nothing in the universe is fixed. Every electron of every atom is constantly in motion, changing its position, so much so that we never know exactly where it is at any given point in time, or where it's going. If everything is constantly changing, if there are no fixed points, how can we measure a straight line? If we used a ruler, we would quickly realize the impossibility

of attempting to draw a straight line because we would see that atomic matter is never fixed. In fact, the atoms that make up the ruler are themselves constantly changing. So is the hand that's holding the ruler, because the hand is, too, made up of atoms. The only way to measure a straight line in an every-changing universe would be to freeze-frame a moment of time so that one could measure between two fixed points. Obviously, this is only possible with science fiction.

Real-world science cannot perfectly measure a straight line and provide us with an absolute law that never varies anytime, anywhere, and under any circumstances.

Key Principle
Observing physical matter that is always changing cannot provide truth that is unchanging.

The Bottom Line

Therefore, what should we place our faith in, the false lines of science or the true lines of scripture? What holds atomic matter together, the power of Christ or the power of quarks? Which is a sure foundation for explaining the universe -- dark matter, dark energy, or the light of the world, Jesus Christ? Colossians 1:15-17 says,

"He, [that is, Jesus Christ], is the image of the invisible God, the firstborn over all creation. For by Him all things were created that are in heaven and that are on earth, visible, or material, and invisible, immaterial, whether thrones or dominions or principalities or powers. All things were created through Him and for Him. And He is before all things, and in Him all things consist."

Again and again we see (pun intended) that our eyes and our power of observation deceive us and cannot give us absolute truth. Only God can reveal absolute, unwavering, eternal, "Capitol T" Truth to man.

Lesson 7 Study Questions

1. What is meant by the phrase *the basic process of scientific experimentation is the measurement of a line*?

    _____

    _____

2. Can science measure a straight line perfectly? _____ Why is this important to consider?

    _____

    _____

3. How does the example of measuring the boiling point of water support the statement: "Scientific equations are never discovered - they are selected"?

    _____

    _____

4. Why do scientists come up with scientific equations and laws if these equations and laws cannot provide certain truth? _____

    _____

5. Modern atheistic science claims to be the highest authority when it comes to measuring matter. Read

    Genesis 1:1 along with Job 28:24-26 and Isaiah 40:12. Which authority do you consider more trustworthy,

    and why?

    _____

    _____

6. Recalling the example of using a ruler to measure a straight line between electrons, what is the only way this can be accomplished perfectly? _____

    _____

7. Read Job 38:5. When it comes to measuring a line, what does God say about man's abilities to do so with absolute accuracy?

    _____

    _____

8. Finish this sentence: "Observing physical matter that is always changing cannot provide Truth that is

    _____".

9. In your words, what has been the main point of this entire segment?

    _____

    _____

Lesson 8 - A Naturalist Scientist Meets God

"I bet you can't guess how old I am"

Suppose God challenged an evolutionary scientist to estimate how old things were at the end of the six days of creation.

God tells the scientist that any and all scientifically advanced technology can be used. The scientist agrees, and God first asks the question how old is the universe? After some experimentation and calculation, the scientist responds 12 to 14 billion years old, give or take. God says "hmm, how did you get that number?" "Well," the scientist says, "I can use either the Traditional Method or the White-dwarf Cooling Method, and they're kind of complicated, God, so allow me to explain them both to you."

"If I want to use the Traditional Method, I can measure the universe's expansion rate to calculate the age of the cosmos. I determine the expansion rate by measuring the distance of Earth to nearby galaxies. I then compare those measurements with the speed at which those galaxies are receding from Earth. This in turn gives me the age of the universe.

On the other hand, I can just as easily use the white-dwarf cooling method. With this method, I study the faintest white-dwarfs in a globular cluster. You see God, globular clusters are among the oldest clusters of stars in the universe, and the faintest and coolest white-dwarfs within globular clusters represent the oldest stars in the clusters. And so, using my handy dandy Hubble telescope, I can observe that the first stars formed less than one billion years after the universe's birth in the Big Bang. And so, finding the oldest stars within the oldest cluster of stars enables me to calculate the universe's age."

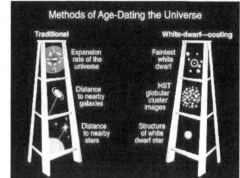

God says, "Okay, how old is the Earth'?" The scientist does some experimentation and calculations, perhaps using carbon dating methods, and says to God, "It's about 4.6 billion years old". God replies, "Are you certain about that?" And the scientist smugly retorts, "Of course. It's science". God follows up with another question, "How old is this man"? And God shows Adam to the scientist. The scientist yawns and says, "Uou know, God, this has been fun and all, but I'm starting to get a little bit bored. He's a strapping young lad, and if my eyes don't deceive me, I would say he's probably somewhere in his early to mid-20s". God replies, "Are you sure there isn't more than meets your eye?"

Not Everything is as It Appears

God then asks one last question, "How old is this lady"? (see the image on the left) You see, depending on how you view the image, you will either see a young lady wearing a thin necklace with her face turning away, or you will see the profile of an old lady with a rather large nose and thin lips. Things are not always as they might appear. God concludes, "Actually, those stars you were using in your calculations, I made two days ago. By the way, I know every one of them by name, because I named them myself. You know the dry earth that you were using in your calculations? I made that about three days ago. And that man that you thought was at least 20 years old based on his appearance alone? I made him 30 minutes ago".

"The universe", God says, "is only six days old! It just has the appearance of being much older because in order for it to function, it had to be formed complete, with every part in place and capable of performing its designed purpose. Your calculations are so completely off because I made everything from nothing, yet complete and operable; therefore, everything has the appearance of being older than it actually is. You could cut down any tree you see here, count the rings, and tell me how old you think it is. You would be wrong, because you can't judge the age of the universe by its cover. You have to judge it by its author, and that would be Me".

Looking at the Age of the Universe Debate in Another Way

"As I've said in my Word, I stretched the heavens out like a curtain", God says. "For example, I had my prophet Isaiah write this in Isaiah 40:21-22:

'Do you not know? Have you not heard? Has it not been declared to you from the beginning? Have you not understood from the foundations of the earth? It is he who sits about the circle of the earth, and its inhabitants are like grasshoppers, who stretches out the heavens like a curtain and spreads them out like a tent to dwell in'."

From this verse alone, we can see that the Earth is circular, and we can also see that if God is stretching the heavens out like a curtain, it shows that the universe is expanding - something that we've only known scientifically for a very short while. Now, if God stretches out the universe - time and space - like a curtain, can we assume that He has always been stretching the curtain of the universe at the exact same rate? Could He not initially stretch the fabric of time and space at an accelerated rate so that what appears to us to be billions of years old was in fact a mere wrinkle in time? Time is on God's side, because whether our scientific calculations point to a young Earth and universe, or to an older Earth and universe, or both simultaneously, it makes no difference to Him because He made everything having an appearance of being older than it actually is. To the naturalist scientist, God says, "You, however, have backed your theory into a 12 to 14 billion year old corner. Because if any of your scientific evidence suggests that My Earth and/or the cosmos are young, then your entire evolutionary model is false."

What is the Truth made of?

Real truth, absolute truth - truth that is always true for every single human being that has ever lived or will ever live - isn't made of material stuff. It's not made of matter. It consists of ideas - propositions that can be weighed in the mind. Christians are called to walk by faith in *propositions that we know are true; and all true propositions have their basis in Scripture.* If it proves true in reality it can always be traced back to a principle in the Bible. We don't walk by sight or our sensory experience of physical matter. 2 Corinthians 4:16-18 reads, *"Therefore we don't lose heart, but though our outer man is decaying, yet our inner man is being renewed day by day. For momentary, light affliction is producing for us an eternal weight of glory far beyond all comparison, while we look not at the things which are seen, but at the things which are not seen, for the things which are seen are temporal, but the things which are not seen are eternal".*

The Christian's eyes are to be on heavenly things, not things that are material and corruptible. Matthew 6:19-21 reads:

"Do not lay up for yourselves treasures on earth, where moth and rust" [and if we wanted to be more technical, we could equate that to the law of entropy] *"destroy and where thieves break in and steal; but lay up for yourselves treasures in heaven, where neither moth nor rust destroys and where thieves do not break in and steal. For where your treasure is, there your heart will be also".*

Conclusions

How Do We Know What is True?

Truth can't be observed under a microscope or shoved into a test tube. Real truth - absolute truth - is revealed by God who is spirit, not physical. God has put some of His truth within the heart of every man and has more fully revealed His truth through the Bible. The Bible is the revealed truth of God as He communicated it directly by way of the Holy Spirit to various men. The Holy Spirit revealed and is still revealing God's truth to the spirit of man. Spirit to spirit, immaterial to immaterial.

TRUTH can't be shoved into a test tube!

In addition to this, real truth will always be in harmony with reality. Since it will never contradict reality, reality can be used to test whether or not a certain proposition is true. However, absolute truth is true even if there is no material universe in which to test it in, because truth is not made of physical material. This is why Jesus said, *"Heaven and earth* [which is to say the material universe]*, will pass away, but my words* [my truth which is immaterial]*, will never pass away."* Immaterial truth is not dependent upon the material universe. It doesn't rely on the material universe in order to be shown to be true. The material universe is dependent upon immaterial truth.

The secular scientist has it all backwards. He believes that truth, which is immaterial, can only be known - or is dependent upon - that which is material, ...by studying the material world. The Bible says the opposite. The material universe is entirely dependent upon the immaterial Word of God. God's Word not only created the material universe, but is also actively sustaining the material universe, holding all things together.

In short, the Christian view is this:

The material universe is entirely reliant upon the immaterial absolute truth of God, for God made matter by the power of His immaterial Word.

So, how old is the earth? How old is the universe? A scientist working within the framework of absolute Truth (the words of the Bible) and verified in the material world of reality would conclude six to seven thousand years. God states in Genesis, chapter one, that our material reality was formed in six specific days, not over millions of years

The Principle of Irreducible Complexity

American biochemist Michael Behe provides support for the claims of a young earth in his argument titled "Irreducible Complexity". In simple terms, this idea applies to any system of interacting parts in which the removal of any one part destroys the function of the entire system. An irreducibly complex system, then, requires each and every component to be in place before it will function. As a basic example of irreducible complexity, Behe presents the common mousetrap. If any one of the 5 components was removed, the device would be useless and have no purpose. It had to be fully assembled in order to work. This is what Behe found as he studied the cell. Behe asserts that the complicated biological structures in a cell exhibit the exact same irreducible complexity seen in the mousetrap example. In other words, they are all-or-nothing: either everything is present and it works, or something is missing and it doesn't work. All creation consists of billions of irreducibly complex systems that could not have evolved, they had to be created fully complete – just as the Bible says in Genesis One.

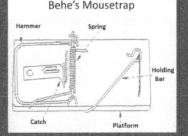
Behe's Mousetrap

Lesson 8 Study Questions

1. We believe it is impossible for all life to have evolved- from a "single cell", or an explosion, or millions of mutations. We see no evidence in all of creation to support such statements. However, we stated that there is evidence that everything had to be created with the *appearance of age*. How does this provide an intelligent argument for a young earth?

   _____

   _____

   _____

2. Read Matthew 24:35, Psalm 119:89, Isaiah 40:8. What is more important, the physical, material things of the earth, or the invisible, spiritual things? Why?

   _____

   _____

3. Discuss the statement that was made: "Truth cannot be analyzed in a scientific lab, observed under a microscope, or shoved into a test tube". Why not?

   _____

   _____

4. Which is more important – the age of the earth/universe, or how it came to be? Explain.

   _____

   _____

   _____

5. Watch the YouTube video titled "Irreducible Complexity" at https://www.youtube.com/watch?v=NaVoGfSSSV8. In your own words, explain the proposition that is presented here, using the example of the mousetrap.

   _____

   _____

   _____

6. From a Christian perspective, does it matter what science thinks about the age of the earth and the age of the universe? _____ Why or why not? _____

   _____

   _____

7. If there is **any** trustworthy evidence for a young earth or a young universe, then the Darwinian theory of evolution is completely falsified (according to Darwin himself), since life has to have enough time to evolve. Is there any physical evidence to suggest a young earth and/or universe? Do some research on the internet and record what you find (we would suggest AnswersinGenesis.org.) Don't forget to cite your sources!

_____

_____

_____

8. Read Isaiah 40:21-22. Does the Bible teach that the earth is flat? _____
9. Verse 22 says that God stretches out the heavens like a curtain (causing the universe to expand). When was

the book of Isaiah written (do an internet search)? Why is this an important fact?

_____

_____

10. When did science first discover that the universe is expanding (do an internet search)?

_____

_____

11. Should the Bible conform to science, or should science conform to the Bible, and why? What do you think

would happen if scientists accepted the Bible as the only source of truth and knowledge?

_____

_____

_____

Lesson 9 - Four Main Conclusions

Having seen the limitations of science, how are we as Christians to view the sciences?

Unfortunately, many continue to place their faith only in what their eyes can see, and they do this so that they may feel justified in doing whatever is right in their own eyes. For them, seeing is believing, which is to say *only science is trustworthy*. Thus, in this chapter we've been obliged to humble science back to its proper place. But what is science's proper place?

From our study, it's easily seen that science isn't capable of giving us any absolute or certain truth. We've seen that science can't even measure an absolutely perfect straight line.

So, what is the Christian worldview of science?

1. <u>Science enables us to fulfill the mandate given in Genesis 1:26-28.</u>

   This reads, "Then God said, let us make man in our image, according to our likeness, and let them have dominion over the fish of the sea, over the birds of the air, and over the cattle, over all the earth and over every creeping thing that creeps on the earth. And so, God created man in His own image, in the image of God he created him, male and female he created them. And then God blessed them, and God said to them, be fruitful and multiply, fill the earth and subdue it, have dominion over the fish of the sea, over the birds of the air, and over every living thing that moves on the earth."

   Science gives us directions for doing things, for operating in this world, but it can't discover Truth. It is a method for dominating and utilizing nature. It's merely a practical discipline that helps us live in God's universe and subdue it. To this end, science is useful in accomplishing its purpose of subduing the earth. But that's all it's useful for, nothing more.

2. <u>Then, how can science be so successful?</u>

   If science cannot provide truth, how can it be so successful? It depends on what is meant by success (see the sidebar).

   Science makes space exploration possible. It helps us to treat and sometimes cure disease. It allows us to travel from one side of the planet to the other in a matter of hours, and to communicate with others around the world at the speed of light, the touch of a button. These are all examples of scientific success.

What is **Success** in Science?

Success in science is when a desired objective or goal is attained by means of manipulating the natural order of things. As an example, coronary artery bypass surgery is a procedure that's used to treat blocked or narrowed coronary arteries which are the blood vessels that supply oxygen and nutrients to the muscle of the heart. Traditionally, to perform this procedure, the chest is opened in the operating room and the heart is stopped for a time so that the surgeon can perform the bypass. A bypass machine, also known as a heart-lung machine, is necessary to pump blood while the heart is stopped and kept still so that the surgeon can perform the bypass operation. Now, from this example, it can clearly be seen that the natural order of things is being manipulated to accomplish a goal. Obviously, a man can't live if his heart stops, unless a machine is pumping his blood for him. Neither can a man survive on his own in outer space without a space suit; or even get to outer space, or fly in the air from one side of the planet to the other, or communicate with others around the world at the speed of light at the touch of a button without the assistance of science. Science enables man to do amazing things that the natural world would not otherwise permit!

3. <u>Though science is extremely useful, it has limitations!</u>

Every time a scientific objective is met, it is considered a success. We've seen, however, that the scientific knowledge that allows us to do things is always incomplete. It's imperfect and constantly changing. But this is irrelevant to scientific success. The ends justify the means (except when moral laws are violated). Even with such incomplete, imperfect, and constantly changing scientific knowledge, we're still able to achieve extraordinary scientific and technological advancements. But truth, Capital T, absolute, infinite, eternal Truth is something that by definition never changes. It is something that science can't successfully provide for us.

4. <u>Science is successful when one understands its purpose</u>

Although flawed equations can sometimes be very useful, we find that science can be quite successful – when operating according to the eternal rules that govern it. To put it another way, science *rules* when we understand the *rules* that govern science. Science allows a very special glimpse into the mind of our creator and inspires a sense of awe and wonder at the brilliance and creativity of His mind. But we must never worship the creation, the material universe, nor place our trust in the methods that allow us to investigate it, ...science.

The End Result

Hopefully now we see the importance of defining our terms and thinking things through. And hopefully your faith has been bolstered, as you are better able to distinguish between what is fact and what is fiction with regard to science. We need not be intimidated by the false claims of those who worship at the altar of science.
While science is useful, it is limited, and cannot offer any absolute, certain truth.

Summary

- Biblical truth is not to be examined under the microscope of science; rather, science is to be viewed through the lens of a Biblical worldview.
- Science has its place in the Christian philosophy. A very important place. But science is never to be seen as a means of learning Truth.
- Put another way, the Word of God does not bend the knee to science; science bends the knee to the Word of God.
- The Christian must understand the limitations of modern science and argue the sovereignty of God.
- Truth is found in the scriptures alone.
- It is the Word of God that we must believe, not our own experience.
- Belief in God and His Word provides the correct framework for scientific observation.

<u>Key Principle</u>

The Bible has a monopoly on all truth. It is God's Word that must be believed, not the experiential knowledge of simple men.

The fear of the Lord is the beginning of knowledge (science), but fools despise wisdom and instruction.

Lesson 9 Study Questions

1. What is the mandate that God gives to man in Genesis 1:26-28, and how does this relate to the uses of science?

    _____

    _____

2. Name at least 4 technical advances that have assisted us in improving the lives of mankind through science.
    1)_____
    2)_____
    3)_____
    4)_____

3. Name at least 4 risky or deadly technical "advances" that have harmed the lives of mankind through science.
    1) _____
    2) _____
    3) _____
    4) _____

4. Discuss the proposition: "Success in science is when a desired objective or goal is attained by means of manipulating the natural order of things." What do you think this means?

    _____

    _____

    _____

    Give a few examples
    1)_____
    2)_____
    3)_____

5. Read Isaiah 40:12-14 (New King James version) and note the words measured, calculated, weighed, scales, and balance in verse 12.
    1) What does God think about man's abilities to measure, calculate, and weigh with scales and balances the things of heaven and earth? _____

        _____

        _____

    2) If this is what God thinks, should we as Christians be placing our faith in the measurements and calculations of men? Have you been guilty of this? How so? _____

        _____

        _____

3) Note the words directed, counsel, instructed, taught, knowledge, and understanding in verses 13 and 14. Man thinks that his direction, counsel, instruction, teaching, knowledge, and understanding is trustworthy because of his abilities to measure, calculate, and weigh with scales and balances. Does this sound familiar? Is God impressed with man's scientific knowledge and understanding? What are your thoughts on this subject?

_____

_____

_____

6. Read 2 Corinthians 4:16-18. The passage begins by stating that we do not lose heart (we as Christians do not get discouraged). Why can we get discouraged if we focus too much on the things that we see?

_____

_____

7. Read Hebrews 11:1-6. How are we encouraged by taking our focus off of the things that we see or feel?

_____

_____

8. What is the Christian Worldview of Science (how are we to view the sciences)?

_____

_____

_____

_____

_____

Also available from GTI Ministries
Catalog

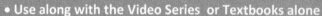

Made in the USA
Middletown, DE
19 September 2024

60714683R00150